Advance praise for *Dialogue*

This book will sustain you. It is a hand outstretched offering guidance in the permanent whitewater of organizational change, a raft of skills for individual and collective practice in the art of developing authentic conversation. . . . It can make a significant difference in the way we think and act together.

If you are seeking to bring the spirit of inquiry and learning into your organization this book is important to your success. It will provoke your thinking and inspire you with questions, strategies, and specific suggestions. A must read.

Traditional ideas of leadership and what it takes to fully develop an organization's potential will never be the same after reading this book. Ellinor and Gerard spell out how taking the time for reflection, inquiry, and deep listening can lead to renewal of the spirit and of collective vision. I highly recommend this book.

This book is rich not only in its practical applications of dialogue, but also [because] of the heart from which it emanates. . . . In an era of e-mail and voice-mail, where the 60-minute meeting is sacred, it's great to see a book advocating that we all take a moment to truly reflect on our day-to-day activities to make sense of the whole. . . . This book will be a valuable resource from which present and future leaders can learn.

Linda Ellinor and Glenna Gerard are cofounders of The Dialogue Group, a consulting firm specializing in interpersonal communications, collaborative work processes, community building, and leadership. Linda Ellinor is on the adjunct faculty of the Center for Creative Leadership and has over 20 years' experience in consulting, corporate planning, and organizational work. She has held management and staff positions with Mnemos, Exxon Office Systems, AT&T, and International Paper Corporation. She holds an M.B.A. from Columbia University.

Glenna Gerard is on the affiliate staff of Interaction Associates and has 20 years' experience in business and education, devoting the last 7 years to working with dialogue in a variety of organizational settings. Prior to consulting, she had management positions with Kaiser Aluminum and Chemical, Castrol USA, Corning Medical, and the National Science Foundation. She holds a B.S. in Chemical Engineering from Columbia University and is a certified instructor for Tom Gordon communication skills program.

DIALOGUE: REDISCOVER THE TRANSFORMING POWER OF CONVERSATION

LINDA ELLINOR AND GLENNA GERARD

John Wiley & Sons, Inc.

New York • Chichester • Weinheim • Brisbane • Singapore • Toronto

This publication is designed to provide accurate and authoritative information in regard to the subject matter covered. It is sold with the understanding that the publisher is not engaged in rendering legal, accounting, or other professional services. If legal advice or other expert assistance is required, the services of a competent professional person should be sought.

Lyrics from *The 59th Street Bridge Song* copyright 1966 Paul Simon. Used by permission of the Publisher: Paul Simon Music.

Rilke poetry reprinted by permission of Riverhead Books, a division of The Putnam Publishing Group, from *Rilke's Book of Hours* by Anita Barrows and Joanna Macy. Copyright 1996 by Anita Barrows and Joanna Macy.

Selection from T. S. Eliot's "Four Quartets," East Coker. V., from *Collected Poems 1906–1962* by T. S. Eliot, reprinted by permission, Faber and Faber Limited, London.

"The Opening of Eyes" copyright by David Whyte, reprinted by permission, Many Rivers Press.

Library of Congress Cataloging-in-Publication Data:
Ellinor, Linda.
        Dialogue: rediscover the transforming power of conversation /
    Linda Ellinor and Glenna Gerard.
            p.   cm.
        Includes bibliographical references and index.
        ISBN 0–471–17466–1 (cloth : alk. paper)
        1. Dialogue analysis.   2. Conversation analysis.   I. Gerard, Glenna.
    II. Title.
        P95.455.E44 1998
        302.3'46 — dc21   97–35606
                                                                            CIP

Printed in the United States of America.

10 9 8 7 6 5 4 3 2 1

Dedications

To David Bohm for the inspiration he has been in our lives and work and to all those before him who have recognized the profound value and power of dialogue in human affairs.

To our children's children and all the generations to come.

Acknowledgments

We are deeply grateful to our friends, families, and colleagues for the unwavering support they have given us; the pages read, the honest and sometimes difficult feedback, for understanding when we chose not to participate with them because we were "in the book." Special thanks to Sarita Chawla, Judy and George Gerard, Robert A. Harrison, Jr., Gary Jackson, Fred Korn, Dawna Markova, Kenneth Moncrief, Sally Nissen, Cathy Rooney, Teresa Ruelas, and Larry and Carol Spencer. Most of all we thank them for their love and their belief that the writing of this book was work worth doing and in service to a larger community. We thank our editors Janet Coleman, who initially sought us out, and Renana Meyers who stuck with us, asking tough questions, working always to redirect us toward our readers, all the while listening to our concerns.

We also especially want to acknowledge all those men and women past and present who have poured their passion, energy, and time into the exploration of dialogue in many and diverse contexts. It is beyond the intention and the scope of the book to review all the contributions that have been and continue to be made to the field. Please accept these words as an acknowledgment of the debt that we and many others owe you. We thank you.

CONTENTS

Part III   Bringing Dialogue to Work   163

A look at the predominant conversational patterns in our work environment and strategies for bringing the principles and skills of dialogue into day-to-day work to help foster collaboration, partnership, and shared leadership.

Part IV The Transformational Power of Dialogue   239

Descriptions of shifts that occur in the thinking of those who commit
to an ongoing practice of dialogue.

Part V A Dialogue on Partnership   305

An edited transcript of a dialogue with margin notes that help identify
different skills (inquiry, self-reflection, assumption identification,
etc.), followed by participant reflections and a short epilogue about
how three people have used what they learned in the months since.

FOREWORD

Early this year I (Glenna) was sitting with a good friend, Sarita Chawla, talking about who we might ask to write a foreword for the book. Sarita asked me a question that resulted in the pages you are about to read. She asked "Why does it have to be only one person?" That single question opened up a doorway of possibility. Further conversation with Dawna Markova encouraged me and sprouted a beginning list of people, all of whom have extensive experience with dialogue and bring diverse perspectives. The list grew to include the eight people listed below who graciously gave of their time and attention to help create what we think is a conversation you will enjoy reading and one that will set you thinking. We extend our gratitude to them for creating such a valuable addition to this book.

Juanita Brown — Juanita is the founder of Whole Systems Associates and collaborates as a strategist and thinking partner with senior leaders in developing knowledge-based organizations and large-scale change initiatives based on living systems principles. She has served as a Senior Affiliate at the MIT Center for Organizational Learning and is currently a Research Fellow with the Institute for the Future.

Sarita Chawla — Sarita is majority owner and president of MetaLens Consulting, Inc., which focuses on learning organizations, dialogue, diversity, and coaching individuals and organizations in the art and practice of sustainable excellence. After over 20 years of working within a large corporation, Sarita is now focusing on her own areas of passion about learning, dialogue, diversity, and generative coaching. She has played a role in initiating, participating, and designing the International Women's dialogues, global Women's Initiative, and other local women's dialogues. She is coeditor of Productivity Press's 1995 anthology, *Learning Organizations: Creating Cultures for Tomorrow's Workplace.*

Joe Jaworski — Joe is chairman of the Centre for Generative Leadership, a consulting firm that works collaboratively with clients to effect large organizational change and develop values-based leadership.

Joe was a practicing attorney for 20 years. In 1980 he founded the American Leadership forum. In 1990 he joined The Royal Dutch/Shell Group of Companies in London to lead a multinational team of experts in creating global scenarios. He is author of *Synchronicity: The Inner Path of Leadership.*

Dawna Markova—Dawna tells stories, writes, teaches, and facilitates groups of people who are learning to think together about the same old things in new ways. The books that have come through her are *The Art of the Possible, The Open Mind, Random Acts of Kindness, How Every Child Is Smart,* and *Unused Intelligence.* Dawna cocreated Partnering the Possible, Inc., an alliance that seeks to evoke creative vision and humane action in organizations.

Daniel Martin—Daniel works as an independent consultant in the area of personal and organizational change and development. Clients range from public health to the religious world. He is the founder and director of International Communities for the Renewal of the Earth (ICRE).

Ron Patrick—Ron is a psychologist working with schools and mental-health systems around the country. Over the last 25 years he has specialized in systems theory, cooperative learning, community building, dialogue, and the creation of safe environments that foster learning, wonder, and growth for children of all ages. He is currently working with the Mentor Exempted School District in Mentor, Ohio, as Director of Psychological and Student Services. He is also a consultant and master trainer for Center Source Systems and owner of the consulting firm, The Circle Project. He is currently exploring the development and use of the dialogic process within school environments with staff, students and parents.

Peter Senge, Ph.D.—Peter is a Senior Lecturer at the Massachusetts Institute of Technology where he is part of the Organization Learning and Change group. His areas of special interest focus on decentralizing the role of leadership in an organization to enhance the capacity of all people to work productively toward common goals. His work articulates a cornerstone position of human values in the workplace, namely, that vision, purpose, alignment, and systems thinking are essential if organizations are to realize their potentials. He is author of the widely acclaimed book *The Fifth Discipline: The Art and Practice of The Learning Organization,* and coauthor with Art Kleiner, Richard Ross,

Bryan Smith, and Charlotte Roberts of *The Fifth Discipline Fieldbook: Strategies and Tools for Building a Learning Organization.*

Margaret Wheatley, Ph.D. — Meg is a writer, public speaker, educator, and organizational consultant. She is president of Berkana Institute and a partner in the firm of Kellner-Rogers & Wheatley, Inc. She is eagerly engaged in helping a very diverse group of people from many countries and types of organizations realize that there is a simpler way to organize human endeavor. She has been intrigued by how life "self-organizes" and spends her time describing the possibilities of human organizations where freedom, creativity, and self-determination prevail. Her two books are *Leadership and the New Science* and *A Simpler Way* co-authored with Myron Kellner-Rogers.

The intention of the conversation you are about to read was to create a larger framework for this book by engaging these eight people in an inquiry using the questions below as a starting point.

○ What is the importance of dialogue, and why is it emerging in the world today?

○ What is it about dialogue that is worthy of a businessperson's attention, and why?

○ What role do organizations and dialogue have to play in shaping new ways of living and working on this earth?

In the beginning each person speaks about their intention for the conversation and any particular quality that they wish to bring forward to support the inquiry. Because the intention with which we come to any endeavor has an essential influence on the nature of the experience, we have included these initial remarks and then continued with the conversation itself.

Transcript of a Dialogue on July 24, 1997

Glenna: First of all, I'd just like to say welcome and thank you for being here, for participating and giving of your time. One of the intentions that we held in inviting you was for you to be in conversation with others you would be interested in speaking with. We hope this inquiry will create a greater context for the readers. We also intend that you have fun and explore new territory with each other. To create the container for the conversation, perhaps each of you could offer a brief statement of the intention that you hold for the conversation and any particular quality that you would like to bring into the conversation to support the inquiry for this morning.

(a somewhat lengthy pause)

Meg: Oh, aren't we a good group? Okay, this is Meg, and I'm just going to take this role (laughter). I think this is a wonderful opportunity to spark new ideas and insights, and I would like to be in this group with a quality of openness and be less opinionated than I usually am because I do believe this is an incredibly important arena for us to be thinking in together. This whole question of dialogue and conversation, and how it moves into our organizational lives together, feels more and more essential to me as the path of inquiry.

Joe: This is Joe. You ask about our intent. I think that is a wonderful way to begin because my experience, and deep belief, is that the way to set the field in an organization or an institution for dialogue depends very deeply on one's intent. So, for you to put your finger on that at the outset, here, I think is really important. My intent is one of great reverence for what we are doing here and for the people in this group, and I'm here to learn. I want to participate and add something to it, but I'm really here with an open heart right now, and I think that we can collectively gain new insights. I think we all know how incredibly important this is.

Danny: My intention for the group has something to do with serious play. My sense of ritual is a strong sense of coming together like this, as people who are serious about what we are doing, but at the same time realizing that we don't really have as much control as we would like to think. (laughter) This would suggest the juxtaposition of serious play. And the quality that I would like to offer would be a sense of the mystery, a sense of the sacred that lives in us and empowers whatever dialogue that takes place. So, I will try and keep that in my heart as we work and play together.

Sarita: Danny, you really resonated with what was coming up for me. I was thinking about the quality first, and there were two. One is respect and the other uncertainty, and that really spoke to the mystery that you were speaking to. The more I live in this world, the less certain

I am of anything. The intention that was coming up for me was almost the quality of a sacred responsibility to support, with a great deal of sincerity, any kind of effort to bring this different type of listening and speaking into the world that we sometimes call dialogue. I choose the word sincerity with great reverence. I think that we are losing the meaning of that word. That is the intention that I am bringing in.

Juanita: I think the intention that I would hold for this conversation is to listen for the threads, the diverse threads, of life and being that we each bring into this conversation, the wonderful richness of different and complimentary life experiences. And I want to listen for that deeply, to the current that runs even beneath that complimentarity and that diversity. And, I think the quality I want to bring is wholeness: the wholeness of my own self and the wholeness of what we may be able to touch into together as part of this conversation.

Dawna: We just came back from a trip to California where we did a two-week retreat on improvisation, spontaneity, and being in the present moment. On the way back, there were thunderstorms over Chicago. As we ran to make our connection through that infamous terminal in O'Hare airport, there was a woman in a wheelchair who was really upset, saying she wasn't going to make the flight from Chicago to Burlington. I said "I'm on that flight. I'll hold the plane for you." I ran like crazy, which is not easy for me at my age, my weight, and my present physical condition. I got there and they had closed the door, but the plane was still at the gate. I proceeded to use everything I knew, but mostly this sense of fun and wonder, to convince the agents to open the jet way . . . which they did. I stood with one foot on the plane and one foot on the jet way explaining to everybody why they couldn't move that plane until this woman in the wheelchair made it there. While I was waiting, I realized this was such a perfect statement for where I am in my life and for how I want to be in my life. As long as nothing moves too quickly so it pulls me apart, here I am as this kind of bridge and this broker. Both my intention and the quality that I bring to the conversation are contained in that story. (laughter)

Ron: The quality I bring, I hope, is one of a great sense of joy. The longer I work, the richer my life gets. Joy is something I am aware of all the time as I walk in the world and try to make sure that I focus on those possibilities of how we, and I, and each of us, can live a joyful experience in the moment. My intent is to bring a sense of wonder. I hold dialogue in great reverence in the sense of the possibility of how it can be helpful to us, both as individual and as community. I have a deep commitment to be honest about it, about where it works and where it doesn't work; not to fall in love with dialogue, but to stay in love with the wonder of what we are doing together, to hold those very gently together and try to keep both of those juggled at the same time.

Glenna: Linda, did you want to say anything about your intention for this conversation?

Linda: I am extremely honored and thankful to be with everyone, and I know that whatever we are discovering together through this conversation will be very helpful to people who will choose to pick up the book. So, welcome everyone.

Glenna: Someone said to me yesterday, when I was describing this conversation that was going to take place, "Have you ever done one of these calls before with this many people?" I said "No, but these people know each other and they've been in dialogue, and I simply trust that this is going to be an absolutely incredible conversation." So, that is an intention and a way in which I wish to participate. I will not be participating directly in the conversation with you, but I do want you to know that I am here with you and I am holding that trust and faith.

Danny: The ever-present listener.

Glenna: We had sent you some questions that we thought could be an initial focus. I'll read those questions now and then just open the floor. The first one was, "What is the importance of dialogue, and why is it emerging in the world today?" I want to thank you, Meg, for inspiring that question. The second is "What is it about dialogue that is worthy of a businessperson's attention, and why?" And the last one, "What role do organizations and dialogue have to play in shaping new ways of living and working on this earth?"

Joe: I'll say a word or two. I actually feel that dialogue is emerging as one of the most important elements of transformational change in the world today. And, I am spending almost all of my time and 110 percent of my energy in the direction of organizational change, trying to find one or two highly respected organizations, global in nature, who, if they transformed, others could really not ignore: they would provide a model for others. One thing that I have come to deeply believe and am practicing in the transformation work in this one particular company, is that dialogue is a way to establish a foundation for profound institutional change; that through dialogue we can set organizational fields that reflect the quality of our relationships, the depth of our commitment, and the qualities mentioned just a few minutes ago—openness, listening, etc.—to me, that is the importance of dialogue. I think it is also a statement of why it is worthy of a businessperson's attention.

Danny: Let me begin with something that came as I glanced at the questions this morning. The first thought was that dialogue does offer a way of being in the world that is more present, more conscious, and, by implication, more skillful. You know my love of poetry. I do believe the poets are perhaps the bridge that Dawna was talking about in a particular kind of a way. Rilke has a couple of lines where he says: "To work with things in the indescribable relationship is not too hard for us. The pattern grows more intricate and subtle and being swept along is not enough." And that offers me a sense of a larger context within which I think we are all working. We are working in the service of *logos*, in the service of unfolding meaning. Let me just reflect a little bit on something I was saying earlier, that we are a whole lot less in control than we realize, and dialogue enables us, therefore, to be able to be in that relationship. It offers a way of working with things without either having to feel that the responsibility is ours alone or to live out of the illusion that we are controlling things. There is a relationship involved here that dialogue taps into in a very profound way. Conversation of this nature, it seems to me, from my sense of history, is the way human beings have always invented and reinvented themselves. In more recent times, I'm reminded of some of the work of social systems design. I was rereading *The New State* by Mary Parker Follet. It is probably a classic on democracy. She defines democracy as "self-creating coherence."

Meg: That is wonderful.

Danny: It is a wonderful statement. Self-creating coherence. The essence of democracy seems to be participation in that mystery that is unfolding and that we are part of. So, my basic comment at the outset is that dialogue is so important because it enables us, with very basic, obvious, but forgotten skills, to participate in the world, with life, in the service of life, to "work with things in the indescribable relationship." Maybe I'll stop there.

Ron: The majority of my work has been with mental-health systems and schools. In education, we are in such a crisis of understanding of what our purpose and mission is, that I think dialogue is very critical to slow down the conversation enough to really understand at a deeper level what we're doing together. I think we are starting to attune to that as a great need. Tying into what Danny said, I wonder if dialogue may be an evolutionary step, a learning step in terms of taking democracy to a different level. In the past, our model of leadership has been about how we give people answers, as opposed to wondering at a much deeper level collectively, about what are we doing together and how are we being in relationship with one another. I wonder how we can take our young, our children, the people who are going to be leaders and help them, teach them skills around listening and dialogue that will allow them to make better decisions than we've made, to make better commitments of relationships and resources and all the things that go along with that. In the educational field our product takes so long to develop; it's 13 or more years, if you talk about post-secondary kinds of things. It really amazes me that we spend very little time with our children teaching them to listen at a very deep level. And I think that has tremendous impact on businesses as they look at how we transform and change and reidentify the importance of what they are doing together. Our relationships with business in educational communities are critical, coming together and saying "What skills do we need to learn together?" To use the analogy of trying to change a tire at 70 miles an hour, how do you slow down to do this well enough at a time when we can't stop? And I think that is the problem. We fragment when schools do their part and the business community does its part and governmental agencies do their part. If we don't all wonder together and support that learning together, I think we are going to experience some very difficult times together.

Juanita: I really appreciate, Danny, both what you said, and Ron, how you built on that. I'm still really reverberating with the phrase you shared, Danny, about democracy as self-creating coherence. Part of why I think of dialogue as being important in the world today, not so much because it is emerging, but because perhaps we are remembering what we have long known, deeply, as a collective, that somehow, that quality of conversation is the heart of coevolution. And, Ron, you talked about learning together. I think about it as "knowing together," at that deeper level, with conversation enabling that uniquely human capacity to know together, to invent together, to learn together, and to make and remake ourselves as collectives. For me, at a time when the complex issues we are facing are so crucial to our survival, both of our organizations, and of the planet, somehow remembering that it is in conversation together that we coevolve our common futures and that we create ourselves collectively. This is what makes this arena of dialogue and conversation so important. It is at the heart of our capacity to create our common future and to recreate and to create ourselves again in ways that will be life-sustaining. And I think that is worthy of a businessperson's attention because it is true at every level of a system, whether it be at the family level, the organizational level, the community level, or much larger systems in terms of a global question.

Sarita: Juanita, you took me back to an image that I haven't thought of for years. I was just remembering sitting outside my grandfather's house, in the courtyard, where the beds were brought out in the summer and after dinner everyone sat until it was dark and then actually slept out under the stars because it was too hot inside. In those evenings what I remembered was the quality of listening and conversation that, as a child, introduced me to what meaning was. Sometimes I refer to dialogue as the language of listening. At the most basic, simple level, I think it is emerging in the world because we are more aware of the complexity and of our inability as individuals to be creative or coherent about sensing what is emerging and making meaning of it. Each of us, individually, are born into cultures and organizations and ways of seeing and thinking about the world that are very particular to the life experience that we've had. I'm blind and unable to listen into what I don't know that I don't know. But, as a collective, where we are thinking and listening and speaking together, it gives me much more access into a wider metalens far bigger than my own two eyes and ears and others' senses can perceive. A larger part of the system becomes available to us. And the very nature, in some way, of change is changing in terms of the complexity and our ability to even understand and comprehend the current problems. We don't know how to listen to each other or to listen to the whole, or as Ron was mentioning, how to listen into the future of unborn generations. And, yet there is such a deep yearning for that.

Meg: Well, Sarita, you just said something that is helping me deal with what I have been struggling with. Dialogue, conversation, people being able to talk and thereby create the world, feels to me now as absolutely true, and it feels like it is validated everywhere I go except when I go into organizations. When you described learning about meaning and meaning-making in those conversations, I flashed to the realization that the way we are in organizations, the way we've been trained and conditioned to look for meaning is making it almost impossible for many of us in organizations to think that something as simple as people talking about their future, their present, their lives, their concerns, their passions, that anything meaningful would come out of that. We've been enculturated to believe that in organizations meaning is found through all these systems and measurement and numbers. And I'm feeling a deep level of frustration in how to communicate how simple and straightforward it is to engage people in conversation, and that that is all we need to do to resolve any issue. And my frustration, I realize, it is a crisis in meaning and how we are conditioned to construct the world. I think there is one more thing I want to say . . . but I can't think of it now . . . so I'll wrap this and say that, for me, it is a different issue right now. It's not describing or recognizing the value of dialogue or conversation. It is how do we break through this technocratic society of ours so that business leaders of the kind, Joe, that you are seeking, could really believe that something as straightforward and basically human as wanting to talk to another human being about what is important to you right now, that that is really the path to the future and to resolving organizational crises and dilemmas? That is such a different vision that it becomes a very deep communication problem. We are not operating in the same world of shared meaning.

Dawna: Meg, when I hear you, I flash back to an experience I had with a group of 75 people from a large automotive company. We were brought in to help them discover what it means to learn in an organization. Late at night I played pool with a lot of them. I'm a really lousy pool player and that became obvious to them very quickly. So, it also became obvious that I was pretending I was playing pool so that I could listen to them. They were almost all men. They considered themselves at the top of the hourly workers. They were the people that were the bosses of the hourly workers. I don't know what their title was. Playing pool was a place that I could listen and find out what was really going on. They called us the "vision pimps for the company." And that was really stunning for me, so I wanted to really know more about what that meant for them. Some of these guys had been working for this company for 30 years, and as the pool game went on one of them said, "You know, we're supposed to be here to do this thing called dialogue," and when he said it his lip curled. He said, "They don't want us to talk because when we talk they tell us we are being victims. They don't want to really hear about how hard things are for us." And, I was stunned. He says, "My boss came back from this dialogue thing, this dialogue workshop, you know. And so, we had this dialogue thing, and I began to tell him how hard it was for me with all the downsizing and everything else and boy did he shut me up quick, and then he used what I said in my evaluation meeting." Somehow that flashed back to me when you were talking, Meg, and also it wove in with this poem that started writing itself in my head this morning when I was walking. All I have is the first line and it is "in the darkest of times, in the whitest of thinking." And I think it comes from a line from James Hillman [a Jungian psychologist and author] about white thinking and what is white thinking. And for me, right now, this is somewhat of a dark time and somewhat of a time of being in the unknown. And, in a dark time all I can do is find the edge of things. I can't find the whole space, so I feel for the edge. And it seems that, whatever organizations I'm working in, I keep coming to these edges and then this abyss between one side and the other and not knowing how to cross. Sometimes inside me there is this silent scream, like there was in this company, and I just wanted everybody to stand up and scream, "We don't know how to do this!" And then sit down and be silent together and to wait in the silence for what would come out. So, it is a dark time, and in the places that I travel and these edges that I stand on, this white thinking doesn't allow some real serious lessons that could emerge from pain and suffering, that we label as victim thinking, to emerge and teach us.

Danny: Dawna, I find that really moving, what you said. The experience in the poolroom sounds to me from my experience, too, to be a common one within organizations for those who don't have power and who feel that even this dialogue is yet another gimmick on the part of those who have the power to continue the manipulation process. An image was coming to my mind, too, about how white thinking is sort of like the light that breaks through the cracks. Perhaps dialogue allows a space for the cracks to be exposed, like the people in the poolroom and it is through those cracks that something new is born. My friend Rilke again says something comparable talking about the old ways and how they are gone. He is really saying how the gods used to be around and they are not around anymore but he calls on them and he says, "Your dawn gleams on every crack and crevice of our failure." An old friend that I had long ago in graduate school would talk about a definition of faith, not as a personal little clump of beliefs but as a powerful Dionysian life force that hides in the interstices of things and the cracks and that it is only in being present to the cracks that something new is really born. There is a certain honesty in it.

Ron: One of the great concerns I have is that the simplicity is so overwhelming to us that we look for greater complexity in something that may be right in front of us. Can we trust that process at a deep enough level to allow the work to come forward? It ties back to whether we really believe in a democracy. I mean, do we really believe that together we create our future? The great fear I have is that dialogue will become stylized, the next new thing to do in organizations and, again, we will run right past it. We will run right past the magic that can be created with it and the potential of it if we don't really, again, slow down to look at our thinking and how we are listening together. That is one of the fears I have, that it will be the next wave and that we will wave right past it and miss it, again.

Meg: I think that has already happened, hasn't it? This conversation at the poolroom and what you just said, Danny—I think it is our great fear of each other, even in schools or communities where we are not under this great technocratic influence. I don't think a lot of people do trust democracy, and that is a scary thought . . . that we are claiming the beauty of a process that exposes our beliefs about one another and a lot of those beliefs about one another are very fear based right now. And I certainly see dialogue in organizations right now being used as another technique by which we do coerce and fool people except that they can no longer be fooled. It is not about encountering another human being as the source of possibility for this organization. Until that shifts, until we really recognize that we are together in this work and we need each other and I need to be talking to you, whoever I am in this organization, I need you. Until we are at that place of recognition, I think this may only be another technique that I do because somebody told me that I have to do it. And I'm sorry to be so depressed. I just want to apologize for that. I'm not going to give it up, but I'm sorry to be so depressed.

Joe: You know, Meg, I think what you are saying and what Dawna is saying is so important. I guess one of my problems is that I'm sort of an eternal optimist. But, one of the things that I have begun to believe is that the way to try to address some of the issues that you all have been raising is to begin at the very top of an organization or an institution and so begin with the top 200 people so that you create a transformation. You allow those people to transform themselves and create a space for everybody else, to give permission to everybody else to do the kind of work that you are talking about. And I'm wondering what you feel? We've had lots of failures at that, but we have had some real successes with realizing that these people at the very top are just as afraid, just as vulnerable as all the people down below, and if we find a way to engage them in deep dialogue, that is when some of these changes begin to take place.

Dawna: Joe, as I listen to you, where my mind goes is an image of being on the ground in my garden yesterday with my partner of 20 years. I found myself totally incapable of even noticing that I had a single assumption, assessment, or judgment. All I was was right! (laughter) I am amazed. I really think that I am the most beginner of anybody in the entire field of learning organizations because I just don't get it sometimes. I really don't get it. It's hard. And then when I do get it, like I hear you talk about the top of an organization, I don't know what the top of an organization or the bottom of an organization is. How do you find a top and a bottom and what shape does that imply an organization has to be? And lately all I've been able to do is think in terms of webs, you know like spider webs, and I keep getting caught in them myself, or finding myself catching other people in them. I've heard people talk about how simple this is. For me, it is really challenging and that is the truth. And my other truth is that I don't know about the top of an organization. I think that in the last five years some of the most powerful conversations that have moved me and have influenced me the most deeply have been like those at the pool table. And it is scary for me to say that to you. Something in me says I'm not supposed to say that.

Joe: No. No.

Meg: Well, Dawna, I have a question. Have those poolroom conversations influenced the organization?

Dawna: No.

Meg: See, I think that is the question that I want to be in. You raise a constant question. If any of us look at organizations, Dawna, I would say, I don't know what an organization looks like. If I really tried to understand how work gets done, it is a spider web and it is messy. But, there is the other reality that these organizations as described with tops and bottoms actually do work that way in the minds of the leaders and they still exert enormous control over people's lives. I don't know the answer to working with the top, bottom, middle, the whole thing at all, but I was struck by a colleague's comment when she said "if the senior executive hasn't found out that he has a spirit, then to ask him to talk about the spiritual dimension of a worker's life is just a technique or it is just a ruse." And that made a lot of sense to me, that I can only describe the world through myself and that maybe there is enormous work to be done at the top level so that there is an embodiment of what needs to be seen differently.

Joe: See, this is what I've come to believe. I mean, you've expressed it beautifully, Meg. And Dawna, I really understand what you are saying about this top, bottom, middle thing, and what I'm talking about is the traditional way things are organized right now and so I can only describe some experiences I've had over the last three years or so, where this transformation has taken place in these people. This spirit that Meg is talking about has emerged. In a given organization out of 12 people at the very top, the people on the leadership council, maybe 6 out of the 12 have clearly undergone that kind of transformation. Out of 200, maybe there is 20 or 30 percent now. But the relevance to this conversation is that the genesis of that transformation actually was in deep dialogue, listening, and modeling a different way of being and doing that over a year, year and a half.

Danny: Joe, may I share something with you?

Joe: Yes, please.

Danny: I am hearing you say that the way an organization might change is whenever the top leadership sort of gets it. I heard a little bit the same thing in Meg, that if the top leader is grasped by the spirit, whatever that is, that this essentially is how change happens in the organization, and this has implications for strategy. Is that what I'm hearing?

Joe: Yes, I think that is it. Part of what I'm saying also is that there is a symbolic power of hierarchy and if it is in place, that is one possibility, of starting there.

Danny: A second part of the question. Because I'm thinking of, Dawna, the poolroom people, the sort of derisive curl of the lip whenever they think of what the top leadership is doing. Is there not something in that? Without some kind of a shift there, too, the best intentions of the top really don't go anywhere either. So, is more illusion being created? And does that not have implications for strategy? That's maybe what I'm trying to say.

Joe: Yes.

Juanita: I'm wondering if there is not also sort of a complimentary doorway into this that may not either be the question of top or bottom, in terms of where the entry point is, but in thinking about what might be the doorway into the importance of building collective intelligence in the organization, as its key to survival. Now, I'm thinking from a strategy point of view. Think about that kind of innovative learning, whether it be at a personal level or about a new product, coming from that deep level when people are in conversations with each other about whatever is real to them. Think of the kind of spirit and excitement and insight and innovation that come when that happens. That is something that can involve everyone, at all levels of an organization, particularly when its survival depends on it. And, I'm wondering if one doorway into thinking about involving larger numbers of people, not as an either/or, but as an additional doorway in, might be thinking about how we create the conditions where larger and larger numbers of people can participate in those simple initiating conditions that would allow learning conversations to expand throughout the organization as a whole, becoming a transformative force.

Sarita: What you are causing me to wonder about is how does one connect the poolroom conversation with the boardroom conversation? As I've been listening for the last few minutes, I have watched this tiny baby spider walk in and out of my keyboard and it has been weaving and jumping off of the hard drive and jumping onto the keyboard, and I've just been watching and wondering what we can learn from this little baby spider. How can we connect those conversations if we are only working at the highest levels? How will we simultaneously work on furthering democracy? Those two models are not coherent. Maybe that's one reason why people may not remember the value of democracy in their day-to-day lives. They don't live it in organizations.

Joe: One of the things that I'm a little worried about is perhaps what I said might have been taken to mean that you wouldn't work in the middle and in the larger context. I was just pointing out one way of beginning somewhere, but then work in parallel everywhere.

Meg: I want to try to see if this piques anyone's interest besides mine. Where we started on this present path right now and, Joe, when you came in with the top 200, was for me the question of how can dialogue or conversation move into traditional organizations in a way that it won't be bastardized or abused? For me, that is a huge question and it has a lot of fear around it because the history of large hierarchical organizations is a history of great concepts like learning organizations or dialogue or self-organization getting misunderstood, unconsciously applied, and ending up with no value whatsoever, and then we have to wait for it to recycle another 15 years or so. And, we can't wait anymore, and so for me it is a question, and I know Juanita is in this all the time with me, is "What is the work?" It is not just proposing dialogue, or teaching it. There is this whole dimension of what is going to happen to this truly humane and humanizing process when it gets into this great machinery.

Danny: I'm thinking of a parallel from an earlier experience of mine, liberation theology and the small-base communities. There is nothing more hierarchical than the Catholic church. And nothing more controlling from the top down. Let me preface this by saying, this is not necessarily a success story, at least in normal terms. But when I look back on the base-community movement, it really was a great liberation for people. They were within the organization, but something enabled them to take a hold of this methodology, something comparable to dialogue, and run with it. And perhaps one of the things that it did was create a local, immediate, concrete focus that allowed them to address something that was relevant to them at that level without trying to think about how it was changing the larger organization. But in doing so, and then beginning to find links with other comparable little cells, there was the beginning of a swell that did begin to impact the larger organization. One might add that the larger organization as yet has really not paid that much attention to that, but I feel that when movements like this start they really do change a consciousness and awareness; that may not have its effects immediately, but certainly will have its effects. So, is there something in that parallel that speaks to you who have more experience in business organizations? Is there any way in which little cells like that can be engaged that can keep the freshness?

Dawna: I'm thinking about a friend named Parker Palmer, who talks about change through movement. And then, Juanita and Danny, about what you said. Juanita, what I've heard you talk about the living-room conversations about things that really matter. Parker offers a wonderful question, "How can we live divided no more?" He says that we reach a point within ourselves where the division and the fragmentation that exists within us, the lack of coherence, and therefore the lack of democracy, becomes such that we begin to seek conditions where we can share that with other people and have that pain or that suffering received. Not fixed or ignored, but just received so that someone can learn something from it. And I think what I was reminded of in the garden was how difficult it is to receive someone else's pain. And I think the organizations I've been working with are ripe for that. Someone's fired, and within four minutes they have to leave the building and there are guards standing at their desk . . . so no one should see their pain. And that doesn't mean to me the absence of joy. In my experience with organizations in the midst of this tumult, when people are standing around the coffee machines or sitting in living rooms really beginning to talk about what matters to them, a lot of pain comes out. And one of the powers of dialogue is that it can teach us to develop a membrane or a muscle so that we can be big enough to receive someone else's pain deeply enough to learn from it.

Meg: And realize that is the source of healing and going forward. I just returned from South Africa. My partner, Myron Kellner-Rogers, and I went to sit in on the Truth and Reconciliation Commission that Mandela founded three years ago, by which anyone who suffered under apartheid can tell their pain, their story. It is covered in the press, it's on the news, it's on the radio. People are finally visible for their suffering and grief. We were stunned by what a healing process that was. The second part of it is that one can request amnesty if you have committed a crime. You can come forward and confess and ask forgiveness. You may or may not get amnesty, but you can ask for forgiveness. We asked to see this process and were blessed with the opportunity. We were there at a time when the three young black killers of an American Fullbright scholar, three years ago, a woman named Amy Beale, were confessing and describing how they murdered her in front of her parents. And the mothers of these black youths were there also. It was an overwhelming experience. The boys asked for the parents' forgiveness and the parents forgave them. And I thought, if we could just talk with each other about these things.

Juanita: Meg, as you speak, I was just reminded of conversations in New Zealand that we have been a part of in this last year of two in which Maori indigenous leaders and senior people from the government and businesspeople, in very intimate and, in this instance, unpublicized settings are beginning to sit down to raise questions that are at the heart of their common future. And in the midst of the pain of the land having been taken away and all of those struggles, to begin to really talk together, beyond the labels of their roles, and calling on the wisdom of their ancestors, and of the land itself, to hold them together into what is the common conversation that will sustain their future. It also reminds me of the conversations at the home of the Norwegian ambassador, between Arafat and Rabin, where they came with their wives and their children and were able to walk on the grounds of his summer house and stay there in a quality of conversation that allowed both the pain and the healing to begin to emerge. Creating contexts where that can happen is so important.

Meg: The principle behind the Truth and Reconciliation Process is so simple. The truth is the path to reconciliation. And if I take that into an organization or back to the poolroom conversation, Dawna, I just feel the fear; and Joe, I'd like your reaction to this, the fear that comes up in leaders. My sense is that I, as a leader, often feel that if I just give people a little opening to tell me the truth of their lives with me, as workers in this organization, that they would devastate me. And they would also want to kill me in some ways. They certainly wouldn't want to stick around. So why would I ever think that reconciliation and truth telling is our path to the future? It is just holding the lid on something that I'm scared to death of knowing, for fear it will destroy me and the organization. And, yet, I think we've all had the experience as colleagues, as employees, that we just need to be able to speak the truth, and we still want to be there.

Joe: Meg, I felt like I was right there as you were saying this. I don't know the answer to all this, but one part of it is the fact that every one of those people, most of them, let's say, who are symbolic leaders at the present time or in leadership positions, have all those same feelings themselves. These people have been treated that way themselves on the way up, and they can't speak of it, and so if we give them an opportunity to begin getting in touch with the pain that they all hold, then they can actually do the same thing for others in the organization. This is one pathway. You follow me? I mean, these people, as you were describing this, I'm saying that these people who are the leaders right now have all had most of those experiences, been treated that way, and it is a total undiscussable among themselves.

Ron: Joe, it seems from my observations and experience with leadership, that people seem caught in the issue of control. You can be ugly, immoral, mean, or whatever—anything—but if you are not in control of what is going on in your organization, that is like the kiss of death. And it creates the paradox of "How do I be more human, how do I listen, how do I really talk about who I am and what I'm about, move outside of a role that demands me to be in control in some way?" It really challenges us, for both the leaders and the people in all levels of the organization, to come to some agreement together to say "This doesn't work. Is there a possibility of us being together in a different way?" And that is the linkage and the webbing and the others things I think are so powerful. We were saying earlier, we need each other so badly that if we don't recognize that and start to create environments that are at least initially, as Bill Isaacs[1] talks about it, "dangerously safe," we may lose the opportunity. And that is the great challenge I see in organizations I'm involved in is "How do we create those opportunities together for people to talk?" I think control is an illusion. I think a much more powerful dynamic, confluent with dialogue, may be to be "in influence" as opposed to being "in control."

Danny: There is a question, Ron, as you speak, that comes once again of strategy. Where would you begin, what would that look like, and how would you begin to draw people in a gradual way into this process? Because I'm reminded of the deep roots of not only personal assumption but the experience of history. You can hear from my voice that I come from Ireland. I come from Belfast, where the peace talks once again were postponed yesterday over the issue of the decommissioning of arms. And I've seen the pain for years, and I've heard exactly what we have described this morning. But there is another kind of experience that tells people "look, those that have power will only give up power when they are forced to" and history seems to suggest it. So, how do we draw each other in a gradual way into a process of weaning, for example. The example is very valid here in terms of arms, the decommissioning of arms. Here are people, the IRA, who've managed to get their way to the table through arms and now they are being asked to lay them down before talks can happen. And of course their logic is "Are you kidding me? This is the only card we've ever had. Why would we lay them down now before anything has happened?" And so, the tension of finding a way to gradually move step-by-step towards something raises its head for me. Does anyone have any feelings about that? Because I hear what we are saying, but I'm thinking about what are some of the practical kinds of steps that would move us in that direction.

Dawna: Well, one of them, Danny, you have been using this whole conversation. Which is a sacred question. You offer questions and, in my education, that was not an option. You were asked a question, you offered answers. In my work in organizations, that still is the predominant form of communication. But sometimes, an exquisitely crafted question can create just enough space in the collective mind that it stops and there is a gasp, where maybe God can enter. At least a sense of wonder. I think this happened in South Africa. I don't think what happened there has ever happened in the history of humankind, and yet, many people that I talk to don't even know that it is happening. When I begin to ask people what they think about it, many of them respond with "Well, what about justice?" The question opens a whole range of questions. What is justice for you? What are your experiences of justice? This kind of inquiry, this capacity to be fully present in a question and just not know, may be one of the more sacred gifts of dialogue. It is very, very difficult and very powerful.

Ron: That has been my experience, too. It's like asking questions to get people to stop long enough to consider where they are and what they are doing in relation to everyone else. Those questions inside systems like schools and mental-health centers are things that are truly so critical because you can't make statements; if you make statements you get a debate going. It is like a gift. When you tell the truth or ask a question that makes people pause, it is like inserting a knife without it hurting. It allows people to be present with the truth but not make them fearful of it, yet cause them to stop and think and wonder.

Sarita: There is another piece in that, especially in the South Africa model. I, too, was there last year for an international women's dialogue. There was one young woman in the dialogue who lived in the township. She was in her early twenties and, as part of the introduction, as people were beginning to bring themselves into the group, she shared a story. She brought with her a little aloe plant. The story she had with the plant was that she went into the village where her grandparents lived. She and her family went there because there had been a massacre. And they found her grandparents hacked to death and their limbs strewn all over the place on trees and there was blood dripping onto an aloe plant. As people began to move towards her in sympathy, wanting to do something about it, she, very composed and very aloof, said "I want you to just listen." And there is that quality of listening without action that is so difficult for us.

Peter Senge joins us.

Sarita: I'm done with the story. We talked about questions. But there was also this particular quality that I think that dialogue does bring of listening without necessarily taking action that can lead to the kind of healing that we are talking about.

Meg: I was in the presence of a wonderful man, Bernie Glassman, who is a Zen roshi, working out of Yonkers, New York. He described what happens to us when we don't hear the stories; how people actually go crazy when they don't hear the stories of their past or their ancestors or their parents. Someone asked him a question and said, "But we have to be telling the right stories. These can't be self-serving stories or myths we are weaving about ourselves or any of that. These have to be stories about bearing witness." And he looked at her and he said "No. No. When people are telling their stories, it doesn't matter what the story is, they are talking together." And I just loved that moment.

Danny: I'm thinking of Ireland. The stories don't even have to be true. (laughter)

Dawna: Well. They have to be real.

Danny: Well. What is real?

Dawna: All right!

Danny: Just because they are not true doesn't mean to say they are not real.

Meg: Danny, you did raise the other question about how can you ask someone to lay down their arms when it has been their only wedge, their only power. And I often wonder if what we are asking of corporate leaders is that they conduct the revolution and give up their power. That is completely unusual and maybe now it is possible. I think that is a lesson from South Africa so far. But if it is not possible that the leaders are going to willingly lead this revolution, then for me where I go, is "Okay, we're still talking about revolution" and what does that mean for the individuals I've been speaking to? I know I certainly talk a lot more about courage now than I did in the past because, if this is a revolution, then it does require acts of courage and acts of self-sacrifice.

Danny: A number of us have been saying that it is in the revealing of our own fears or in the vulnerability that the change happens that this is the most powerful revolutionary weapon, so to speak. Your statement that if the leaders are not able to do it, it is still revolution. What does that mean? Can you take that a little further?

Meg: I'm saying that it still has to happen. To define it as revolution. I'm finding that when people really get a glimpse of what this new world is in which conversation and dialogue are the heart of our creative process, when people suddenly know that, they know it inside them. Then I don't think we really have a choice any longer but to work on behalf of that. And one of the places I think a lot of us get stuck, and I felt very stuck until about a year ago, was that I was trying to work for this new vision but within the old rules and within the old logic, trying to justify this in traditional business terms. And I think that is a real dead end. To declare it as a revolution in thought, in consciousness, in ways of being together, means that in as nonviolent a way as any of us are capable of expressing this, it is not about conforming, being co-opted or even honoring the old logic. It is about stepping out with what we know to be true in our bodies and in our spirits as the way we want to be together and then trying to make that happen wherever we can.

Joe: I'm really tracking you. I think you have hit upon this thing that I was trying to express. My feeling is that if you can help people know it inside of them and give them this experience, then, in your words, they have no choice but to begin working this way. It is this path of personal transformation which, to me, is the only way that this revolution can operate. It is the only way that it will lead to profound institutional change.

Juanita: As I'm listening to this, I'm wondering, I'm trying to think about it in the frame of remembering, remembering that kind of future. In other words, we think about it as a remembering in our body, that conversation and dialogue, Meg, as you said, are at the heart of the creative process. Somewhere we already know that as a species. We know there is not a "them" there in the leaders, for example. There is only us. And it is in creating the context at whatever level we work, whether with senior leaders or with schools where people can experience that fundamental remembrance; it is in those conversations that the new will arise, that what is life affirming will arise. To me, that is the revolutionary potential of this work, at all levels of system, so that everybody can participate, wherever they find themselves, whether in a local community or working with very senior leaders at a global level or working with the folks on the line in a manufacturing plant. The simple act of creating the context where people remember would be a revolution.

Joe: I love that, Juanita.

Danny: I'm thinking that a very powerful religious need has always been the essence of ritual, which is so lost in our society, that is, the need for people to remember who they are and where they come from. Everything from the Jewish remembrance of their history to a Christian Eucharist with the essential theme of "do this in memory of me," in memory of who you are. When we talk about creating the context or the conditions, it's like offering people back a sort of forgotten dimension of ritual in simple ways in their everyday life.

Meg: What would happen if we thought of dialogue as ritual, rather than as technique?

Ron: Certainly in my cultural background of indigenous peoples it was very much ritualized; the deep connection between the collective conversation and leadership shared among everyone in the tribal community. It was the westernized or Hollywood edition of American Indian cultures that they had one leader, which was not the case at all. There were many leaders, in many ways, and I think that one of the things that we've got to look at is "How do we give away the issue of leadership to everyone?" Going back to the question of evolving in terms of democracy and what role dialogue has to play in this, "How do we celebrate the importance of every person in organizations having a part to add to the greater whole and recognize that if we don't do this we cannot even begin to transform ourselves into a different pattern of relationship?"

Sarita: I was struck by your metaphor, Meg, of ritual versus technique. Then, my mind went to what may be ritual for one may be perceived as technique for another.

Meg: I would love to play with this for a minute. When we go in and we present dialogue and we give whatever simple rules or complex rules, we are just feeding right into the orientation of our present-day culture. What if we went in and offered it as a ritual in which everyone participates from the realization that they know how to do this because this is a remembering? I wonder how it could create an entree for people; that this is a ritual space that they are familiar with and already know everything that they need to know. And this, of course, would introduce where we started, with the mystery and the sacred. I would be intrigued by anyone's thoughts on this.

Juanita: We might ask them, Meg, to simply remember common sense. (laughter) Looking at common sense in its deeper meaning.

Joe: I think there is real value in what you are saying about this way of being without instructing, as if it is remembering the way that we deeply are, before all of this was socialized out of us. I think it is absolutely right on target. I mean, I feel like these conversations can take place one-on-one or three-on-one or in larger situations, and that it is probably a lot more productive to do it that way rather than to talk about the rules of the game. I'm feeling that the heart of this is the intent that we go in with. If we are helping to bring the people together, the way we enter is foundational.

Danny: If we look at the kinds of things that are bringing people together, again, today. They certainly are not confined to our head, or to words, so there might be an entry point somewhere there. I'm thinking of the sort of groundswell in things like dancing—tap dancing, square dancing, Irish dancing. There are groups all over the country. I'm thinking of the need that people have to get into their bodies and sort of balance the overemphasis on the abstract with something earthy. There is a wonderful little book that came out recently by David Abram called *The Spell of the Sensuous.* He talks about how our words have increasingly become abstractions and are not related anymore to the actual experience. In the beginning, they were more pictorial and, over time, they became increasingly abstract. What kinds of things could we do in a group, depending on the setting, of course, without becoming completely ridiculous, that would be ways of tapping into that other deeper memory in our bodies?

Joe: I know it is sort of old hat, but I feel like I have to mention it, and that is being out in the wilderness, as a way to bring this memory back. I've had a lot of experience in a ten-year time frame, up in the mountains with people, and all of the things that occur when you are getting into the deep place in dialogue. I don't know how to describe it, but it's palpable; you feel it. I wish we had words. But, anyway, this was before anybody even knew anything about calling it dialogue. The experiences that occurred up in the mountains around a campfire were indescribably beautiful. The open hearts and the healing, everything that we are talking about here.

Dawna: Joe, one thing that comes up for me as you speak is a line from Van Morrison: "the inarticulate speech of the heart." One of my concerns about dialogue is that, in ritual and in ceremony, symbolic language is used, whether it be dance or music or art or representation. It is the brain's natural way of thinking connectively. Every symbolism and symbolic gesture reveals relationship. That's how the brain does it. To broaden the sense of dialogue for those who are not verbally articulate but who sense wholeness and connection in the woods, in nature, in music; to have that be an acknowledged, accepted, respected weaving, as you put it, Juanita, of the tapestry, is important. There are experiences I think everybody here has had that cannot be articulated in linear verbal terminology and yet need to be included in our collective wisdom.

Ron: I wonder, too, about the significance of play in all of this. This is such serious work and such serious things we are dealing with. But I wonder if play is a way of creating more opportunities that would open up more possibilities for conversation together. It seems we get so tied into roles and predictable ways of being. I notice that four-year-olds have this capacity to be open and respond without evaluation. Play is a form of listening and learning for them. As adults, we get so regimented or stuck or so cognitive that I wonder about the relationship of play and if that would offer a medium for us to expand the possibilities of exploring together.

Juanita: What that raises for me, Ron, is the whole arena of conversation where people are playing together, with new ideas, with insights, with innovation. Where it is not so much about personal healing, but where, in conversation, people are actually experiencing that depth of creative spirit together, where they are cocreating in very profound and important ways that are transformative for them. It need not be personally focused. It could be a new product or something that children are creating together in their classroom. It could be in whatever domain, whether political organizing or a board meeting. Wherever that quality of conversation exists that sparks the cocreative process, there is something transformative at the personal level through what happens in the collective. And that is a thread that would be kind of intriguing to play with.

Danny: There is a friend of mine who talks about music, about singing, as a conspiracy. Conspiracy comes from the Latin root "to breathe together." In Ireland, we use a lot of singing. When my family gets together, we always sing. It was the most natural thing in the world. When I came to this country, people would be much shier around singing and would see it as "Well, you had to be able to sing in order to sing . . . you had to be a good singer . . . you had to perform." And, while that might not go down so well in the boardroom, it may fit in a lot more places where dialogue is equally important. What would that look like? What would that sound like?

Sarita: Like a bridge from the poolroom to the boardroom. (laughter)

Joe: I think it is a marvelous bridge. I've seen Ben Zander do unbelievable stuff with people who are principally boardroom types and senior leaders. Once, in Belgium, he had all these people, very conservative types, and they were singing together in the most unbelievable way. It was actually a miracle.

Meg: So, what are we doing to your dialogue book, Glenna?

Glenna: You are definitely creating a much larger context, just as we hoped for, and I am delighted.

Danny: Maybe you could put a few songs in the Appendix.

Juanita: It does relate to your third question, though: "What role do organizations and dialogue have to play in shaping new ways of working and living on this earth?"

Joe: One of the most profound things that everyone has been talking about here is the healing power of listening. I don't want to rehash anything, but I'm just sitting here with the knowledge that that is a key piece to this whole thing. It seems so simple, but to be able to deeply listen to another without trying to fix, but to just be there with them, it is transformational in itself.

Meg: I just want to underline that ten times, Joe. For me, more and more in organizations, I have just seen, if people have the chance to feel really seen, which is partly really listened to, that is all they need. It doesn't lead to more demands. It doesn't lead to anything negative. It just leads to being more present with one another in a way that, as you said, is transformational.

Dawna: I think I want to speak for the difficulty of listening. In my own experience, both with myself and others, it is so rare and becoming more so, that we take the time to deeply listen to ourselves. It is so hard to hold silence. I've been counting how long any collected group of individuals can hold silence and be present while holding the silence. In the group I was with in California, people were stunned when they were asked, "When was the last time you were just alone with yourself, not doing something, not being useful or productive, but just listening to yourself deeply?" And there were people that said, "Oh, I don't know, four or five years ago. I don't remember when it was." We can't give to someone else what we don't give to ourselves.

Meg: What did you just say?

Dawna: I said we can't give . . .

Meg: I was joking! I was pulling your ear, there . . .(laughter).

Peter: I would like to raise a question, since I've now opened my mouth and said something. I've long felt that there are deep parallels between dialogue and meditation, that dialogue seems to me often a kind of collective meditation. And, the last few comments about listening and the difficulty of listening really got me thinking about that again. There are a million ways to define meditation and a million forms of meditation. But it seems to me one thread, at least, of many meditative practices has to do with cessation. Cessation in the flow of thought, which for most of us is an incomprehensible notion. Cessation in breath because, at least in Buddhist meditation, you actually can get to the point where you stop breathing. In advanced practice it is actually said that the heart stops as well, which is mindboggling to me. All of which, of course, has to do with achieving deeper and deeper levels of silence. I kept thinking about that, when you were talking about listening and the difficulty of listening. It reminds me of the statement of Krishnamurti's that all listening starts in silence. (long pause) Many of you have seen the quote where he talks about the extraordinary difficulty in suspending the background of our minds, the continual movement of our minds, which for most of us is how we define reality. So I am definitely with Dawna on the difficulty of listening, which at some level is the difficulty of cessation. And, if there is anything parallel between dialogue and a collective meditation, it is that it orients us more to the discipline rather than just merely the practice of it—the rigor of it, the consistency, the patience, the perseverance, and ultimately, I think, deep down, the almost unbelievable aspiration of it. Because I think that what lies at the heart of any real discipline is nothing but profound aspiration. Without profound aspiration, discipline is a type of self-punishment. It is the love and the imagining of something that is so far beyond anything that you can otherwise imagine that actually is the wellspring of any real discipline. Those are the things I find myself wondering about.

Danny: Peter. I find that intriguing. I was reminded of the first dialogue session or training that I was part of and someone said to me at the end of it, "You know this is unbelievably hard and only the few can ever attain this." And I was reminded of the challenge of every religious tradition; that in every one there are very few who reach enlightenment, or *satori*, or conversion, or whatever it is, and yet there seems to have been a value in offering this to everyone. I don't want to sound elitist. I think you know what I'm saying. Is there something in there that is worth teasing out a little bit? Because there is a certain purist, idealistic approach and yet is there some way in which dialogue could be generally useful to people, that could foster a process of more consciousness or more creative participation in our lives or our organizations?

Meg: For me, it goes back to this notion of dialogue as about being together in ways that are creative and opening, and as something we are remembering. And I, personally, do want to pull it back from the ultimate discipline, even though it requires a lot of discipline on our part, given how we have been socialized to not listen and to move quickly through things. But, I do want to hold onto this quality of dialogue as basically human and that what we are remembering is how to be in conversation. And I particularly want to hold onto it as sort of a "race memory skill," because I don't want it to become so complicated that it gets—I guess it already has—that it gets into such serious technique that it just becomes something else for people to learn. And there is a real tension here, because discipline requires a certain intention, a constant attending to and yet, at the same time, in our culture, people hear this as simply another skill set and that takes it off in the wrong direction.

Juanita: Maybe, Meg, this takes us back almost to where we began the conversation with the whole question of holding intention and placing attention on certain things that are important in contrast to learning something new. I'm thinking, for example, Danny, when you were asking the question of how could this become large scale, knowing that there will be always people who have real mastery. But when I think about Paulo Freide, the Brazilian educator, or the study circles in Scandinavia or workers circles; they are trying to do ordinary things but they are trying to do them with a quality of attention and intention, to, in a sense, really listen for the deep creativity and new learning that is present among them. When I think of how transforming that is for people at all levels when they participate in this way, it takes me back to the democratic question we were raising earlier, how by placing intention and attention we can help the deeper experience of democracy become possible for larger numbers of people. And maybe it is those who have really been deeply touched with the remembering, Peter, who are able to go forth, not as teachers so much, but as hosts or conveners of the same kinds of conditions that would enable this quality of remembering to spread.

Peter: I was thinking about something Alan Kay said. When you were talking about remembering. I think comments could be easily misheard as saying this is only for a small number who are really serious, and actually I don't see that as an implication at all really. Alan used to say that "we have a nation of musically illiterate adults because people are taught scales before they have developed an impulse to music." And, it really gets right at the heart of the concerns we all have about technique. And, so, to me the remembering you were talking about is, "What is the impulse here?" What is the impulse in all of us as human beings, perhaps sentient beings, who knows, that is at work in dialogue? Because it is clearly universal. One of the things that has struck me again and again in our experiences in the last six years or so is the people who shock the hell out of you by their absolute love of the opportunity for conversation. It seems to be so basic that there is clearly a profound impulse, quite analogous and maybe even in some ways the same, as the impulse to music. I have never forgotten that phrase. For anyone interested in teaching anything, I think it is one of the most useful of guides: to never waste your time teaching without the presence of genuine impulse. What is the impulse to music, the impulse to dialogue? That's what the remembering is, and I think it is universal.

Ron: And that is what draws me to this work in terms of the schools. How can we create environments for children to do that? Because kids come to learning naturally. Four-year-olds come to the world with all kinds of questions and we educate that out of ourselves. Listening becomes a metaphor for "Shut up, sit down, and be quiet." What we are finding as we work with more and more school systems is that the issue is not even with kids. The question is "How do we help the adults who have been afflicted? How do we help ourselves transform, to give ourselves the opportunity to learn from children?" How do we re-attune ourselves to that natural impulse we have for being together in conversation and playfulness that we've learned to ignore?

Sarita: Linda and Glenna, I'm wondering how you are feeling about the conversation about dialogue as a technique given the book that you have put together.

Glenna: I feel fine about it. I don't believe the impulse and skills are inherently at odds, rather they interweave, reinforce, support each other. I believe that there are specific ways we can focus our attention and increase our capacity to remember our natural impulse towards dialogue. So, for me it's about reminding ourselves that skills are not recipes. They are meant to help us wake up, to focus our attention and support us in remembering the essential impulse itself.

Linda: I guess I would express a different view, though I don't disagree with anything that has been said. Oftentimes groups will try to enter into dialogue without having a deep experience of it and when they find that they are not able to bring in the qualities that make dialogue dialogue, they become disillusioned with the process. So, I think attention to some of the skill areas can be useful as well as having people there who have had a deep enough experience so that they can bring in that intention to hold the space for others.

Meg: Well, my sense is that we're all almost done. Is that other people's sense?

Danny: This transcription will probably be longer than the book.

Meg: This dialogue has just been a wonderful confirmation of the joy of being and thinking and wondering together that is available to all of us, but it is not as often available in my own life as I would like. At least not with this particular group. And, so, I just had a wonderful time and it just felt very fruitful and soothing and wonderful thoughts that will keep circulating, so I would also like to express my thanks to everyone.

Danny: I sensed in the later part of our conversation the growing realization, or at least the increasing articulation, that people change out of experience. They don't change out of words or techniques or manipulation or policies, whether in organizations, or churches, or whatever. It is when you are grasped by something. And you said it, I think, Linda, that people need to experience dialogue to identify impulse. And, so, perhaps the thought is for us to give more creative, imaginative, playful musings about what kinds of things we could to do sort of help people experience what dialogue is about before launching into promoting and teaching it.

Peter: The last few minutes have brought back an awareness to me that I have had once or twice before, after what I thought were really quite profound periods of real dialogue, and that is an extraordinarily heightened appreciation of each person's voice. Literally their voice. I was able to close my eyes and each person's voice was so distinctive and so absolutely idiosyncratic and unique to them that I actually had the experience that I didn't need my eyes anymore and there were ways in which I could hear elements of the person in the subtleties of their voice which I had never heard before. And I was listening to each of your voices and I once again started to have that awareness, which is very unusual for me. It's probably a little bit like what it is like when you are blind. There is such richness in our voices, such uniqueness. Like so many things, we kind of skim the cream off the top and settle for this very superficial recognition. A part of us is not even present to hear the extraordinary tapestry that is present in our voices. I will remember your voices.

Glenna: I want to add, again, a thank you. Peter, you spoke of voices. And I think it is Rilke who speaks about singing the world and each other. I feel as though I have been sung, that we have been singing each other. And I know that I carry all of you and the conversation with me at very deep levels. I deeply appreciate the quality of everyone's attention, the questions, and the willingness to simply speak out. With each speaking it seems as though the container has grown larger. So, thank you for creating a context that I think will be of incredible service to the readers. I sincerely hope that through reading your words, they will, if they have not before, feel the impulse of dialogue, and that, as they move into the rest of the book they will find more food for thought and action that will amplify that impulse. Linda and I appreciate each of you and the energy you have gifted us with today.

Meg: If we have a moment. We started with Rilke. I would like to end us with T. S. Eliot. It is always humbling when a poet has said what you just struggled two hours to say, but here is T. S. Eliot.

So, here I am in the middle way, having had twenty years
Twenty years largely wasted, the years of l'entre guerres
Trying to learn to use words, and every attempt
Is a wholly new start, and a different kind of failure
Because one has only learnt to get the better of words
For the thing one no longer has to say, or the way in which
One is no longer disposed to say it. And so each venture
Is a new beginning, a raid on the inarticulate
With shabby equipment always deteriorating
In the general mess of imprecision of feeling
Undisciplined squads of emotions. And what there is to conquer
By strength and submission, has already been discovered
Once or twice, or several times, by men whom one cannot hope
To emulate—but there is no comparison—
There is only the fight to recover what has been lost
And found and lost again and again; and now, under conditions
That seem unpropitious. But perhaps neither gain nor loss.
For us, there is only the trying. The rest is not our business.

T.S. Eliot *Four Quartets*, East Coker. V.

OPENING THOUGHTS

Until three days ago, I was ambivalent about this book. It is a product of seven years' experience and one and one-half years of writing. It is a very different work than originally conceptualized; rethought and recreated many times through conversations with a publisher, three editors, and multiple readers. There is a lot of me in these pages. There is also a lot of me that is not here. Until last Saturday morning, the juxtaposition of these two truths was not okay with me. Today it is. Sitting in a white wooden-slat chair under a cottonwood tree at the Mabel Dodge Luhan House in Taos, New Mexico, I understood the essential nature of this book for me and it was sufficient. In fact, it was more than sufficient. It was good. What I saw in that moment is what I want to share with you now.

This book is about structure; a structure for powerful conversation, for dialogue. Yes, I did say structure, a word many associate with control, limitation, and lack of freedom and creativity. I, too, have experienced structure that way, as a prescription, as a way to keep me in line, within the nine-dots. But I've also experienced how structure can set me free; how I can range far and wide, exploring, trying out new things, without fear, knowing that I will be able to find my way home, thanks to a structure that grounds and centers me. Three day ago, in Taos, I was once again reminded that structure at its best encourages and supports exploration, moment-to-moment learning, and freedom.

I was at a writing workshop. It was Friday morning and I was sitting, listening to Natalie Goldberg talk to me and 58 others about writing. She had opened by saying she wanted to speak to us about structure. She paused to reflect on where she wanted to begin. I thought she was going to tell us how to outline a structure for a book. She had something much larger in mind. She began by speaking about how little exploration of the mind there had been here in the West until the 60s; specifically the exploration of how our minds move, how we create meaning, how original thought and feeling arise. She didn't think it was lack of interest. She attributed it to the fact that exploring the mind can be frightening. Without a practice or structure to both encourage and ground the exploration, explorers are at risk of getting lost, of "losing their minds." There were few such practices here in the West. Then came the 60s, when many took mind-altering substances such as acid, peyote, and mescaline. The chemicals unleashed their minds in ways they had not experienced before. Many became curious to learn more. Some traveled to the East where they became students of disciplines and practices such as meditation, yoga, and Zen.

Natalie continued. She spoke about Zen as an elegant example of a simple and powerful structure. At the core of Zen is a practice called sitting. Sitting is placing the body in a very specific posture, for set periods of time, and focusing on the breath. That is it. This simple structure is what permits you to stay awake to the exploration of your mind, to follow it without becoming overwhelmed and tossed away by it; no matter what surfaces, the structure is there to return to. Anger and rage—continue to sit—focus on the breath. Sadness and grief—continue to sit—focus on the breath. Life is disintegrating all around you—continue to sit—focus on the breath. Simple. Powerful. Structure. Within such a structure, exploration of the mind, of a territory that for many is one of the most frightening of all, becomes imaginable. Partnership with this powerful and creative dimension of ourselves becomes possible.

What does Natalie's teaching that morning have to do with this book? Everything. What I recognized that morning was that dialogue is another example of a simple and powerful structure. Like Zen, it is about the exploration of the mind but with a focus on collective or group mind. It is about waking up to how *meaning* is created whenever two or more people talk—meaning that shapes our lives, the decisions we make, and the results we produce. It is about a structure for open, authentic conversation about what matters most to us in life and work. This book is not about The Structure. There is still much work and learning to be done by many, including you, the reader. These pages are an offering of what we have learned so far, a place and a way to begin.

I remember the first impulse to write this book, over two years ago. I wanted to write about the heart and soul of dialogue. I wanted to write about the guts; about what turns you inside out when you sit with people in open conversation about things that are important to you; about how you never see the world quite the same way again once you have allowed yourself to listen, really listen, to people different than yourself. I didn't want to write about structure. I was stuck in the perception of structure as prescription, structure as a substitute for creativity and for being awake. It was this internal split that was at the core of my ambivalence.

Last Saturday, sitting and writing in Taos, I got hit right between the eyes. "Wake up, Glenna. The heart and soul and guts of dialogue are wholly interdependent with structure." It is structure that creates a container both open enough and strong enough to allow for the exploration of issues and questions that are important, for widely different options to be voiced and, even more importantly, listened to. It is structure that focuses our intention and attention in ways that allow us to range far and wide, to ask questions we might not have dared to, to allow the wild mind to express its crazy and far-out ideas, to loosen our grip on hallowed certainties and listen for new ways of putting together the pieces of our work and world.

Today as I write, I am content. I hope that you will read these pages, take in and mull over what we have learned, experiment with as many of the suggestions as you like, and above all LISTEN, LISTEN, LISTEN. Listen for the responses that arise within you as you consider our statements about what we think we know and the questions we continue to explore. Listen for what your own mind has to teach you as you stretch yourself both individually and with others. Listen for the subtle yet incredibly powerful interweaving of meaning being created moment to moment as people talk together about what is important. Listen for those moments when you feel free and fully awake. These are the moments when insights arrive through the open doors of the mind and relationships come alive. These are the moments when the magic of dialogue shines through.

In the spirit of dialogue,

Glenna Gerard
August 1997

✳

When I was eight years old, I took up the piano. I would wake up at six o'clock in the morning and practice scales and the classics for an hour every day. I continued this schedule well into my college years. I never considered myself especially talented or gifted, but this early morning discipline taught me a lot. It enabled me to acquire a strong musical and creative foundation and an understanding of how skills and capacities can be developed over time.

Some 30 years later when I discovered dialogue, I saw how developing skill in relationship with others is not unlike developing skills at the piano or any other artistic or athletic endeavor. The connection between practice, developing skills, creative performance, athletics, and relationship became obvious. If we are to improve the quality of our interpersonal life, just like for those of us in jazz bands, musical ensembles, or team sports, we need to practice and work out individually, but ultimately we need a discipline of collective practice. Otherwise the practice we do on our own has no place to fall and we get pulled back into habitual social behaviors. This is due to the powerful effect of culture.

As I became more familiar with dialogue, I began to see how it introduces certain qualities into conversation such as deep listening, reflection, and non-judgment. These qualities lead to high levels of trust and safety that are necessary ingredients in not only creative endeavors but also in healthy relationships. We can practice piano-playing skills, for instance, but if we want to allow musical inspiration to inform our playing or our songwriting, we must develop our intuitive sensibilities. These are more encouraged when we are in receptive, non-judgmental environments in which there is inner listening with no need for fixed outcomes. This is the kind of environment created by dialogue, and what is needed is also the same thing that is needed if satisfying relationships are to form at work or at home.

What has occurred to me over the years as I have been working with dialogue is that relationship itself is a kind of living art form. Too often we take our relationships for granted and miss this perspective. In the

West we can become so focused on the need for results that we miss the extremely subtle, creative opportunities possible in the dance of conversation. Our relationships offer us, if we let them, outlets for expression, exploration, and deep connection if we learn to perceive and appreciate them in artistic ways. If we want our relationships to be special, which lies at the heart of art, then making a commitment to a collective practice of conversation such as dialogue can be an essential ingredient. Dialogue helps us learn to treat one another with the honor and respect required for helping us all to feel special.

Why did I write this book? Plainly, it is that I *had* to. This book comes from a loneliness I have felt all my life. It comes from a feeling of deep disconnection and separateness that has run through my own life and in the lives of many others I have come to know personally or through my professional practice. This book is my heart going out to yours. All of us in the West are entombed in a shared culture that teaches us how to divide and conquer; to attack each other in order that we might save our own skins. We have been hypnotized from childhood to believe that the world is based on a Darwinian dog-eat-dog standard, and it is upon this foundation that our communication with one another flows. None of us escapes the effects of the out-of-balance, competitive, and individualistic culture we live in.

I wrote this book also because deep down I have always held open the possibility of hope that things can be different. I have known that there must be a way, if only we could find it, to be with each other in ways that nurture, love, support, and enliven us all. Perhaps my strong attraction for developing a discipline and practice of the piano sprang from this same inspiration.

In 1988 I began to serve the Center for Creative Leadership (CCL) as an executive coach in their *Leadership Development Programs.* I have seen over and over again that no matter how skilled and technically competent managers and business executives are, the main developmental issue they face revolves around a lack of and appreciation for solid interpersonal skills. The power of CCL's programs is that they help participants focus attention on personal strengths and areas in need of improvement. Since they do not stress the learning of skills, clients often ask me what they can do to enhance their ability to relate to those they work with. It has been frustrating to find the lack of effective skill programs addressing the interpersonal dimension. The reason is that though there are many such programs offered, few take into account the collective or cultural component and none, at least that I am aware of, emphasize a practice-approach to developing communication skills.

What typically happens if a participant attends a three-day communication workshop, is that what they learn in the way of handling conflict or developing listening skills is lost when they return to their usual operating environment. The culture pulls them back into the same old dysfunctional ways of being in relationship, coming out of the strong competitive norms and stress on bottom-line results that underlie most organizational cultures today.

Today I have little doubt that where dialogue is adopted and practiced broadly it will change the underlying culture to one that is more partnership and collaboratively based. I also see the potential that dialogue offers in augmenting and enhancing conventional organizational development activities such as team building, visioning, and large-group process.

I know that those of you who have picked up this book and are willing to try out the ideas and principles explored here will find out first-hand how the magic of dialogue can work to change lives.

In the spirit of dialogue,

Linda Ellinor
August 1997

I

THE JOURNEY
OF
DIALOGUE

"The ultimate source of the Susquehanna River was
a kind of meadow in which nothing happened: no cattle,
no mysteriously gushing water, merely the slow
accumulation of moisture from many unseen and
unimportant sources, the gathering of dew, so to speak,
the beginning, the unspectacular congregation of nothingness,
the origin of purpose.

And where the moisture stood, sharp rays of bright sunlight
were reflected back until the whole area seemed golden,
and hallowed, as if here life itself were beginning.

This is how everything begins—the mountains, the oceans,
life itself. A slow accumulation—the gathering together of
meaning."

James A. Michener
Chesapeake

D ialogue is a powerful communications practice that transforms those who engage in it. As organizations begin to integrate it into their operations, it will revolutionize how we work in the twenty-first century. Because dialogue brings into relief the hidden power of conversation and shows us how the shared meaning that accumulates over time is *the* source of collective action, its promise is to create conversations that matter and to expand the possibilities for creating and sustaining collaborative partnerships at work.

Like the Susquehanna River, dialogue has no traceable beginning. It has journeyed broadly throughout the course of human history and has had many contributory sources. Bridging our ancestral roots with our future, dialogue has been in evidence among the early Greeks, preliterate Europe, indigenous peoples, and is a part of certain spiritual traditions. The new sciences of chaos theory, self-organizing systems, and quantum physics corroborate and point towards its reemergence in organizations today. We see aspects of it in use wherever a premium is placed on personal healing, building relationships, moving past conflict, and sustaining creativity.

Where dialogue is taking root in modern times, it has largely been inspired by the visionary work of the late David Bohm[1], a quantum physicist and philosopher. Bohm combined ideas that draw upon ancient spiritual principles as well as modern disciplines of social psychology and quantum physics.

This book is written to capture your attention about the power of conversation. Its purpose is to inspire you and to move you in search of ways to engage in talk with more awareness. Learning about dialogue will not only change the way you think about conversation, it will help you move towards far more effective and satisfying action in the world.

Part I lays the groundwork for the rest of the book. In the first chapter, we look at how dialogue addresses discontent in organizations by surfacing dated norms and cultural habit patterns. The crisis of meaning that many find in work life today is due to the lack of ongoing reflection that helps to re-infuse work with new vitality.

In the second chapter, we describe the link between how we communicate, develop our leaders, and go about building cultures of collaboration and partnership. Dialogue is seen as the critical factor in all three areas. This chapter explains dialogue's value from an organizational development perspective.

In chapter three, we answer the question "What is dialogue?" and look at what are its essential characteristics and what makes it different from other forms of conversation such as discussion and debate.

Chapter four traces dialogue's historical roots and where it shows up today in modern contexts.

In chapter five, we explore the current practice of dialogue which was inspired by the work of the late David Bohm. We look at the theory behind the two essential modern-day elements of dialogue: "awareness of our thinking process" and working with "collective meaning."

Chapter six moves into how dialogue integrates findings from quantum physics, chaos theory, and self-organizing systems. As our worldview from the new sciences expands, so, too, do we need new ways of working in and finding order in chaos. Dialogue expands our ability to adapt to increasingly complex and rapidly changing conditions.

And, in conclusion of Part I, chapter seven asks the larger questions that the rediscovery of dialogue poses: What are the implications of its integration in organizational life for the future of our world?

1
A CRISIS OF MEANING

"Lord, the great cities [organizations] are lost and rotting.
Their time is running out.
The people there live harsh and heavy
Crowded together,
Weary of their own routines.

"Beyond them waits and breathes your earth,
But where they are
it can not reach them."

Rilke
Book of Hours

Many people have the sense that all is not as it should be in organizations today. Some say we are "hitting the wall" or the end of an era or a worldview and are no longer able to operate in the ways that have served us for so long. We seem to be gazing at how to move into the next century while steadfastly clinging to what we have known from earlier times. We experience a feeling of "being stuck" and for some of us an underlying ache of discontent.

At bottom is an accumulated buildup of ways of thinking, belief systems, norms, values, and shared meanings that take us away from what we say we want most from organizational life: high productivity, satisfying relationships, meaningful work. The roots of these problems that are causing our discontent are found deep within our individual psyches and the culture we share. They show up in a lack of consciousness towards relationships with others and in the confusion around ends and means of work. Ultimately, our problems come down to a crisis of meaning.

We can no longer afford to point a finger to forces outside ourselves for addressing what ails us. What is "lost and rotting" in organizations cannot be blamed on corrupt leaders or on those in power over us. Scapegoats will no longer serve as catharsis for the common problems and dilemmas of our times. It is to ourselves that we must look and to what resides in our shared mind-sets and what is found in our shared culture. The crisis of meaning we experience is rooted on our unconscious holding of outdated patterns of social behaviors.

A cultural norm in western society has been to focus attention on end results and productivity. We have been raised to measure progress by looking at material well-being and profitability. We use the bottom line as our singular tally for what is going well at work and what needs improving. These measurements of success and failure leave large gaps in a larger definition of what makes work satisfying in the first place. Because we generally assume that all is well when trend lines are moving up, we rarely place our attention on other factors such as the role of work in our lives and its by-products in terms of lifestyle, ecological sustainability, and meaning.

The pace of our work lives is speeding up. In order to keep up an acceptable standard of living, we work harder and yet find we are paid less due to cutbacks and downsizing. We stress ourselves out and yet are blind to both individual and collective exhaustion and approaching collapse. This is what we mean by "hitting the wall." This is what is meant by the "great cities [organizations] are lost and rotting" in Rilke's poem.

While we may be partially aware of a need for new ways of working together, we're not quite sure how to find them. To enter into a new worldview takes us out of our comfort level with older ways of operating[2]. We want to hold on to our need for control and our beliefs that we can solve problems by rational analysis alone. We think that the solution lies in fixing the parts of the system that we find broken rather than in considering what needs to happen in the system as a whole.

We do not see the forest for the trees. We say we need to see the forest, yet we keep using approaches that emphasize the trees. We have not figured out the key that can unlock the mysteries that would expand our vision and move us into new ways of being in the world.

Dialogue holds one important key to the mystery. Because it is both rooted deeply in our ancestral past—helping us remember the sacredness and value of relationship—as well as being aligned with twenty-first century thinking, it can be seen as the bridge between where we are now and where we want to go. As we learn to engage in dialogue, deeper and newer ways of thinking and operating will be a natural outgrowth. It focuses our attention on how work gets done through the shared meaning that develops through conversation. It builds our awareness of the importance of relationship in accomplishing work. Dialogue builds systemic perspectives and helps us approach complex problems and dilemmas that before confounded us. We move past simply adding up the individual trees to surfacing aspects of our culture and collective thinking that hold us back and limit us to dated ways of operating. Dialogue clarifies our mental maps and helps us see what underlies the end results we get.

In the past, our shared pictures of organizational life were largely taken for granted or ignored. When in earlier times we had a homogenous workforce and the pace of change was slower, it was easier to simply assume that everyone saw things the same way. The opinion of one leader or a few other observers was sufficient for moving into action.

But times have changed. Life has sped up, and everything in organizations is more complex and enmeshed. Dialogue answers our call for ways to unfold new patterns of order out of what can seem like chaos. It helps us see into complex situations by focusing our attention on relationships between the parts.

Through examination of our collective thinking, dialogue moves us upstream to where our belief systems reside. We explore what is important and what needs the focus of our attention. We move more directly towards desired results.

The crisis of meaning we experience in organizations today is becoming a strong catalyst for searching out new ways we can infuse our places of work with vitality. Dialogue at essence is about the search for new meanings. It meets the call of our times and is a powerful process for change.

In the next chapter, we examine three aspects of work life that often elude us: communication in general, developing leaders, and transforming organizational culture. Dialogue is a strategic way to approach all three and move the workplace into another dimension of possibility.

2

THE CONNECTION BETWEEN CONVERSATION, LEADERSHIP, AND CULTURES OF COLLABORATION AND PARTNERSHIP

"Eighty percent of the people who fail at work do so for one reason: they do not relate well to other people."

Robert Bolton
People Skills

The High Cost and Frustration of Poor Communication[3]

Millions of dollars are lost every day by organizations simply because of the limited and ineffective ways we have learned to communicate.[4] Think back to meetings you have attended lately that were long, dry, boring, and unproductive. Think of the countless numbers of hours that you sit in such meetings where nothing new is put forward, or certain members monopolize the air time, or everyone goes away with different understandings of what took place, or where power plays prevented any real or authentic conversation to take place. All of these and more are the repetitive norm in most organizations today. If you figure that we pay people a lot of money to engage in such conversations, think of the bottom-line ramifications of conversing in these ways.

Limitations in How We Develop our Leaders

Vast sums of money are also spent every year by organizations on executive and leadership development. Many organizations assume that because they pay their managers large salaries they ought to be investing in their ongoing growth and development. But, think back to the last time you attended a program of this sort. How much of what was covered were you able to apply when you returned to work? If you attended an outdoor or outward-bound program, you probably learned certain things about teamwork and the value of taking personal risks. Or, if you attended an awareness program, you may have been given insight into your strengths and weaknesses as a leader. Other programs stress leadership skills and theories that can be valuable. How much did any of what you may have learned affect your day-to-day behaviors when you returned? Can you say that you manage and lead differently now? Were the changes you made lasting ones?

The Difficulty of Building Cultures of Collaboration and Partnership

We talk a lot today about the importance of building collaboration and partnership in our organizations. We sense that a movement towards these qualities will make a difference in our ability to achieve higher productivity and a better quality of work life; but, with all the increases in workload on employees from downsizings, layoffs, and restructuring, we don't seem to be making much headway towards cultures of collaboration and partnership. These qualities don't fit into our short-term needs for handling the spiraling amount of work that must get done.

In fact, in our rush to accomplish rising levels of work, we rely even more strongly on what in the West has been our cultural mainstay: individual effort and heroism. With beating the competition, winning, and the Puritan work ethic pumping through our veins, we find ourselves unconsciously continuing to reward our workers based on *these* qualities rather than on the alternative norms of collaboration and partnership. Being pushed up against the wall for results creates ambivalence and confusion around any movement towards these later norms.

Even if we are clear about the need for change, it is often less clear *how* to bring it about. Weaving the qualities of collaboration and partnership into traditional competitive management practices can seem like mixing water and oil. We don't know how to do it.

We write what we want to see into vision and mission statements. We send individual managers to workshops that support the values we want to see in our firms. We make structural changes leading to more decentralized control. But after we do all these things, we realize that little has fundamentally changed. We still encounter the same old patterns in our meetings; the same competitive, uncooperative stuff, such as one-upmanship, the need to be right, the usual power plays that typify win/lose over others. "What is going on?" we ask ourselves. "Why aren't the new norms around teamwork and collaboration taking hold?"

Linking Communication, Leadership and Cultures of Collaboration and Partnership

A larger question may be how developing communication skills, leadership, and cultures of collaboration are all interconnected and can't be done effectively without treating them as one comprehensive whole.

By not seeing how they link and overlap, we address them piecemeal and overlook powerful ways they reinforce and impact each other. For instance, consider that the way we communicate is rooted in the shared norms we hold regarding competition and the role of the individual in getting the results we want. If we assume that in most organizations, competition and individualism still reign supreme, then it is little wonder that most of our meetings and conversations with others are chock-full of innuendoes and manners of speech that emphasize who is right, who is wrong, power plays, and gamesmanship. How could it be any different? We are so used to these ways of interacting that we just assume they are the natural order of things. We are not conscious of the underlying mind-sets that drive these ways of interrelating.

Communication is at the root in what needs changing in leadership development. We can help leaders see the value of teamwork and of motivating subordinates to higher levels of performance, but until we help them change the ways in which they communicate with their subordinates, little that is fundamental will be different. Theory, self-awareness, and outdoor activities that promote experiential learning are effective as far as they go. But, these forms of leadership development leave off where long-lasting behavioral change needs to begin. The behaviors that will make a difference are ones such as how leaders listen and develop the trust of others, and how they challenge team members to think productively together and surface problems before they become crises.

Think about leaders or managers you have known whose technical skills were extraordinary but whose people skills were lacking. If, in communicating with others, they always have to have the final say, if they ignore or discount others, or are disrespectful and arrogant, they will not be effective in their work with others. Eventually, such managers reach a plateau. They alienate people to the point where no one wants to work with them anymore. At this point they have three options available to them: 1) they can move to another job where they will most likely experience the same pattern playing out, 2) they can modify their job in ways that rely more on their technical versus people skills, or 3) they can bite the bullet and develop their people skills.

Finally, consider how communication itself is fundamental in the movement to a culture of collaboration and partnership. After all, it is in how we speak with one another that we experience respect from others and whether we are being heard. But, we can only speak in these ways if we have the corresponding attitudes and values about other people that support this kind of respect and integrity. It is our values and attitudes that drive how we speak and listen. They drive the overall culture that we create together through the ways in which we converse.

If we are to change the ways in which we communicate with one another, we must find a way to surface the underlying values and mental models that keep us locked into limited ways of speaking and listening. In the United States and other western-based cultures, this usually means examining our shared assumptions around competition and individual effort versus collaboration and partnership to see when and where we might be out of balance. Then we need to begin to practice behaviors that support the changes we would like to see, those that might give us more of the balance we desire between these two value sets. Dialogue is a process that can help us do just that.

An Answer for Our Times: Dialogue

For now, think of dialogue as a communications practice that actually bridges communication, leadership, and culture. It is a powerful form of conversation that helps us meet the dilemmas we face by transforming the consciousness of those who engage in it. Let's consider some key elements of this change process.

Relationships: The Critical Factor

Generally, it is the quality of our relationships that makes the critical difference in getting the results we are looking for at work. Having said this, it is also true that we are culturally blind to this critical factor. Why? Because we "attend" to the results of our work and not to how we get the results through working with others. Our relationships with others are often the last thing we consciously focus on. In our rush to complete our work, we may not realize the damage we do to some of the most important relationships we have.

Through ongoing practice of dialogue, we can breathe new life into our relationships. Dialogue helps us pay continuous attention to the ways in which we work with others. It safeguards the glue that binds us together in getting our work done.

It does this by building deeper and deeper levels of trust and understanding about who each of us is and how best we can blend and synchronize our work together. It helps us transcend the limitations of formal job roles and status. By seeing who each of us is *personally* and all that we bring to the table, we are able to take full advantage of all the relationships that help us get our work done.

Trust is built by taking the time to deeply listen to one another and to get to know one another. This is the secret of high-performance teams, whether they be related to sports, music, or work.

Moving Beyond the Level of the Individual to Our Shared Mental Models

Dialogue moves us beyond the individual to a focus on the larger social and cultural context in which we live and work. It is a natural evolution that expands on what has too often been a singular focus on the individual to the social systems in which work is actually being performed.

The larger core dilemmas of our times—such as alienation in the workplace, integration of diversity, running from one crisis to another, or making sense of increasing levels of complexity—can no longer be addressed piecemeal and only at the individual level. These seemingly intractable organizational problems can only be chipped away if seen through the lens of a system as a whole entity. Dialogue is by its nature such a lens. It works to bring integration and wholeness of perspective into the day-to-day decisions we make. By illuminating our shared mental models, dialogue helps surface and make conscious the shared underlying assumptions and belief systems that tie us all together into larger systems. We become more conscious of and have more choices around how we approach and solve systemic dilemmas.

Dialogue as Practice Field

Part of the power of dialogue is that it creates a practice field. Just as an orchestra or any performing art or team sport needs practice and rehearsal for peak performance, so do we all when it comes to changing and enhancing the quality of relationships that helps us get our work done. Practice is pivotal in developing competence around the new behaviors we desire. Practicing dialogue brings into relief our underlying behaviors and patterns of communication. We are able to see directly what works and what needs changing. From this place of greater awareness, we are then able to make the agreements we need with one another to move towards desired changes.

In the past, it has been common to send individuals off to workshops and programs that develop new skills and ways of working. Dialogue reverses this approach. In dialogue, we practice a set of skills and behaviors in the very groups and teams we work with. The more we practice dialogue in these intact groups and teams, the faster the behaviors, norms, and thinking patterns that support them begin to shift.

Bridging the Competitive Work Ethic with Collaboration and Partnership

Dialogue can help to dispel our ambivalence toward change. Coming out of a worldview that can hold the tension between competition individualism and collaborative partnership, it expands our notions of how organizations work. This expanded worldview arises from an understanding of how chaos theory, self-organizing systems, and quantum physics affect our concepts of social behavior. In nature, both competition and collaboration exist simultaneously, but collaboration is how most leaps in evolution occur. What are the implications for organizations? Competition is an appropriate strategy in certain contexts. But, if we want to see quantum leaps in productivity and results, we need to expand our repertoire to include collaboration.

Dialogue is a process that can help us embrace more of our human potential by learning how to bring in the qualities of cooperation and balance them with our natural urge to compete. In a sense, dialogue is a new way of "being" in relationship that will help all of us "be" more in whatever situation we confront. It gives us another approach for working together, for handling conflict, for making decisions, and solving problems. It also helps us create alignment in our visions of our work together. Altogether, dialogue can build more flexibility and scope into our organizations today. We can think of it as fitting into a natural evolutionary progression that moves us beyond strict reliance on competition and individual effort to cooperation between people.

Unleashing Motivation through the Re-infusion of Meaning

Dialogue provides ongoing forums for re-infusing the workplace with meaning, which drives motivation. Too often our workplaces become dry and sterile environments because we make little time for that which is human. Our meetings and conversations lack life because our attention is solely on the work at hand and the drive for results. We lose a fuller focus on why we are engaged in doing the work in the first place. In leaving time for the ongoing inquiry into the "why," we can re-enchant the workplace with the meaning that is needed for excitement and energy to come back where it may have been lost. Everyone who works as part of an organization or team today needs to feel how what they do is making a difference to the whole. In our rush for results, this is too often overlooked. Dialogue, when it is practiced routinely, can continuously keep our individual and collective juices flowing and the energy level high.

Building In Collective Thinking Capacity

Dialogue uncovers and makes clear the often unseen thinking patterns that block us from making lasting change in recurring problems. We usually see a problem occurring and rush into action before we have sorted things out more comprehensively. We get locked into problem/action/new problem cycles. We continue to get the same basic results, although we try numerous different approaches to solve it. Groups that practice dialogue over time actually develop a capability for collective thinking that can move them beyond this kind of vicious cycling.

Slowing Down to Go Faster

It is rare today that we provide the time and space for thoughtful and reflective conversations to take place. In our fast-paced rush to action, bringing in more thoughtful and reflective forms of speaking may seem somewhat odd or out-of-place. But, it is exactly because the pace of our lives is constantly accelerating, that dialogue is most needed. One of the greatest benefits of dialogue is that it slows the pace of our conversation down so that we can see what is behind all of the rushing around anyways. We stop fire fighting, stand back and consider what started the fires in the first place. Dialogue can help us see new and creative directions rather than just doing what we always have done before when there is no time to consider other possibilities for the future. Slowing down becomes a source of ongoing renewal and generativity.[5]

The New Sciences and Dialogue

The new sciences of chaos theory, self-organizing systems, and quantum physics tell us about the value of dialogue in the modern world. They point out how both the roots of, as well as the solution to, our current dilemmas spring from the very worldviews we hold. Images and ways of working based on seventeenth-century physics are now limiting us as we try to meet twenty-first-century challenges. The old, or Newtonian, views of how to organize and manage organizations are not only insufficient for facing our core dilemmas, but are, in certain cases, the cause of them. The new, or quantum, worldview tells us that the nature of our world is relational. Rather than being made up solely of parts, it is based on the interconnection between the parts. Reality is one seamless whole and cannot be reduced. Analytic/reductionistic ways of thinking about organizations that brought us fixed job descriptions and hierarchical chains of command can still serve us, but only in specific contexts and over a limited time frame. At a certain point, we need more expansive ways of operating that take paradox and shared meaning into account. The new sciences actually point to the absolute necessity of shared leadership if we are to take on the multifaceted, complex, and systemic problems of our day. Again, dialogue is a process that is tailor-made for this task.

The Overall Promise of Dialogue

None of us today can ignore the escalating problems we are confronting from expanding levels of complexity and the increasing speed of modern times. Nor can we continue to work in ways that alienate us from one another and from those we serve and manage. The new sciences tell us that the speed and complexity we are presently experiencing will only increase in the future. They tell us, too, that the only way we will be able to meet these challenges is to figure out how to unleash the full creative potential found within our human systems. The secret appears to be found in paying more attention to the quality of relationships and to the underlying culture and collective thinking patterns that help us get our work done. This is the promise of creating and sustaining cultures of collaboration and partnership through dialogue.

As dialogue is practiced over time, we discover 1) greater levels of authenticity showing up, 2) better decisions being made, and 3) improved morale and alignment forming around shared work. More personal initiative and leadership are exercised outside of the formal hierarchy. As people begin to see more of the whole of what is being accomplished together, they each see where he/she can add more value. People stop waiting for someone else to *tell* them what to do.

3

WHAT IS DIALOGUE?

"I give a meaning to the word 'dialogue' that is somewhat different from what is commonly used. The derivations of words often help to suggest a deeper meaning."

David Bohm
On Dialogue

Like a river that has no beginning and no end, there is no single clear definition of dialogue. Where aspects of it have sprung up in the past it has usually led to cultures that honor and respect individuals and the relationships that unite everyone into families and communities. The Greek roots of dialogue are *dia* (through) and *logos* (meaning). Although this definition may sound obtuse, it is the meanings that we share that form the very basis for understanding one another at all. It is also the root of our culture—all those ways of doing things, artifacts, symbols, and words and language—that tie us into a common heritage.

Dialogue helps us bridge the increasing diversity found within modern organizations today. It is through the exploration of meaning that we learn who each person is and how we can work together appropriately. Reflect back on a time when you may have been with people from a foreign country and didn't understand what was going on around you. You probably felt like an outsider, a bit in the dark and left out of things. Not only might you have experienced a language barrier, but a whole range of cultural meanings separating you from the others. Even if you spent a very long time with these people, studying their language and customs, you might still have felt like an outsider. This is because you have not been a part of their "meaning pool" or cultural experience over any significant period of time. Although an extreme example, this is the basis of what it feels like to be a part of a minority in any organization today where you have not grown up a member of whatever forms the majority. Dialogue can help us move beyond cultural stereotypes and develop a sense of shared meaning because then we learn who one another is authentically.

It's helpful to compare the roots of dialogue with the roots of a more commonly found form of conversation in organizations today—discussion. This comparison helps us understand dialogue by understanding what it is not. We generally do not find either pure dialogue or discussion in normal conversation; you might think of them as two poles of a conversation continuum. Although we tend to move between both, we usually are unaware of when we do so. We can improve the quality of our communication just by becoming more conscious of when and where to employ each one.

A Contrast with Discussion

The roots of *discussion* are the same as the roots of *percussion* and *concussion*. All three connote a fragmenting or shattering. The other root of *discussion*, "discus," connotes a disc being thrown against a wall and breaking apart. So, in contrasting dialogue with discussion, we can say that dialogue is about gathering or unfolding meaning that comes from many parts, while discussion is about breaking the whole down into many parts.

Think about the focus of attention in some of the meetings you have attended lately. Were people trying to learn from one another so that they could see what was going on from a larger perspective, or were they trying to justify, explain, or defend their personal perspective? When the underlying dynamic in a meeting is to learn and expand what is known about something or to generate new perspectives from the views of many, the conversation tends toward the dialogic end of the continuum. And, conversely, when the dynamic is about finding one solution or the best alternative among many, it tends towards the discussion end.

Let's look at the characteristics of what we might label as pure dialogic communication or pure discussion and its close, more extreme cousin, debate:

The Conversation Continuum

Dialogue	Discussion/Debate
Seeing the *whole* among the parts	Breaking issues/problems into *parts*
Seeing the *connections* between the parts	Seeing *distinctions* between the parts
Inquiring into assumptions	*Justifying/defending* assumptions
Learning through inquiry and disclosure	*Persuading, selling, telling*
Creating *shared* meaning among many	Gaining agreement on *one* meaning

The main question to ask yourself when you are wondering if the conversation is more dialogic or more discussion-based is whether the main intention of those taking part in it is to push towards closure and choose one perspective; or, if it is to primarily learn from each other and build shared meaning that includes all perspectives. When there is a strong push for a conclusion or to find one solution, people tend toward discussion. When there is no push for a conclusion or a solution, people find it safer to offer differing views without any need to justify "rightness," and it will have more of a dialogic flavor.

When and Why Would Dialogue versus Discussion Be Used?

Because most conversations include a mixture of both dialogic and discussion-based ways of communicating, it is a good idea to get clear on the different objectives or intentions behind both forms. In this way, you can engage each form, depending on the context in which you find yourself.

For instance, if you were calling a meeting together of your peers from different parts of your organization to talk about a joint problem that has arisen, you might ask yourself the following:

○   Am I calling the meeting to figure out what immediate action to take?

○   Or, am I calling the meeting to learn from everyone about the nature of the problem?

If it is the former, then people will naturally fall into discussion. If it is the latter, and people are clear that you are not trying to solve the problem at this point, you may notice more of a dialogic quality to the meeting.

What often happens in the above scenario is that since people are not consciously aware of the difference between dialogue and discussion, they will think that they have been called to the meeting for both purposes—to learn about the problem *and* to take immediate action. The limitation that this assumption imposes is that these two intentions don't mix very well. Like oil and water, they foster different dynamics and lead to very different end results. In most organizations today, if the purpose of a meeting is not made clear at the outset and there is something obvious to be decided, most groups engage in discussion rather than dialogue. Our need for action and immediate decisions make this so.

Divergent versus Convergent Conversation

Dialogue encourages an opening up about problems, issues, or topics. Because it *expands* what is being communicated by opening up many different perspectives, we call it *divergent* conversation.

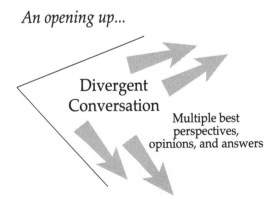

An opening up...

Divergent
Conversation

Multiple best
perspectives,
opinions, and answers

A narrowing down...

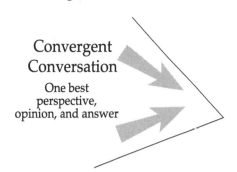

**Convergent
Conversation**

One best
perspective,
opinion, and answer

This is in contrast to discussion or debate that is about *narrowing* down the conversation to one end result. It is trying to come to closure so that everyone knows what to do. Because of this narrowing down, we call this *convergent* conversation. Discussion converges on one point versus dialogue opening to different points.

In most meetings held today in the West, we use convergent, or a discussion-based form of communication. And, when our objective is mainly to converge on the one right answer, we may be missing a large part of the whole picture as depicted below.

We depict the proportions in the following pie chart as we do because it is our strong intuition that if we spent more of our time in dialogic-based conversation first, we wouldn't need to spend as much time in discussion. We would have a larger vision or perspective about whatever it is we are trying to figure out.

Today, the pie is probably reversed with discussion taking up the major portion. Think how often in your experience there is a problem

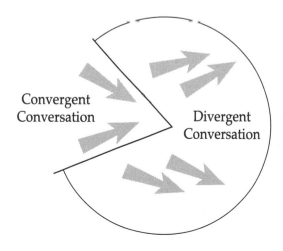

Convergent
Conversation

Divergent
Conversation

that has surfaced and everyone is gathered together to figure out what to do. Because the problem seems so menacing and urgent, little time is given to any kind of in-depth look at what is causing it, or how everyone is affected by it. Rather, in the rush to action, a decision is made that only later has to be aborted because it doesn't get at the root of things.

If a group or a team dialogues about such a problem or an issue first, by the time a solution must be selected, chances are the process will go more quickly. The choice may almost "choose itself."

Consider the amount of time that you and those you work with spend between the two. Are you constantly trying to rush to a decision and closure about whatever is "up" in your work situation, or do you take more time and explore what is the nature itself of what is "up"? If you reverse the proportions towards the latter, even though it may seem counter-intuitive to you just now, you may find things go a bit more easily in the long run.

TRY THIS: PRACTICE EXPANDING AND FILLING IN THE CIRCLE.

When a problem crops up, rather than trying to figure out what action to take immediately, build a bit more time into your decision-making process. Call a meeting of all those who are affected by the problem (or as many as practical). Tell them that you are not going to make a decision about what to do immediately. Ask them to reflect on what they consider to be the nature of the problem from their perspective and to be prepared to contribute this in the meeting.

When everyone has gathered, open by asking them to take turns speaking about the problem. Let them know that there will be no back-and-forth conversation until everyone has had a chance to speak at least once.

Depending on how much time there is available after everyone has spoken, open the meeting up for comments. Remind the group that the objective of the meeting is to learn about what the problem is about and not to make a decision. If you notice people trying to come to a conclusion, you may have to remind them of this objective. At the end, allow ten minutes to collect the key learnings. If you meet again with the same people for decision-making purposes, bring a copy of these key learnings with you to review before you begin.

Whether you meet to dialogue about a problem or about trying to come up with a new way of doing things to make improvements, you may notice a strong tendency to fall back into discussion or to converge on one solution. In western culture, this is common because of our "results and action-oriented" ethos. It is why it takes a while for groups to catch on. As people become accustomed to the difference in intention between discussion and dialogue, and they see the results they get after engaging in dialogue, it gets easier to maintain dialogue without unconsciously falling back into discussion. Participants learn to monitor themselves as to what conversational form needs to be used depending on the situation and need for a decision.

Advocacy and Inquiry in Dialogue

From what we have said so far about the distinction between dialogue and discussion, you might think that advocacy wouldn't occur in dialogue and that inquiry wouldn't occur in discussion. But, this isn't so.

What determines when and how these aspects of conversation show up, is the intention behind their use. In dialogue, advocacy is quite appropriate if it is to offer some perspective for the purpose of the group's learning. The intention is *not* to force the group to come around to your perspective as the right one, but rather to build shared meaning. It is just the reverse in discussion, where advocacy is intended to persuade and convince the others that your perspective is the right or best one, not just to add another perspective.

In dialogue, we use inquiry for the purpose of digging deeper into whatever we are talking about. We use it to ask about one another's assumptions and underlying thinking. We use it to clarify and expand what we know about something. Again, our overall intention in inquiring is to *learn* more.

Inquiry in discussion is used typically to learn enough about what the others are thinking so that we might better convince or advocate our own position. In this case, our use of inquiry is to gather enough ammunition to shoot down the other's opinion while elevating our own.

Other Defining Qualities of Dialogue

There are many other defining characteristics and qualities of dialogue. We speak more in depth about these in Part II. We list some below to give you a flavor for what is generally present when dialogue is practiced. None of these characteristics in and of themselves makes a conversation a dialogue. Rather, it is all of them combined that give it its unique feel and quality:

- O   Suspension of judgment
- O   Release of the need for specific outcomes
- O   An inquiry into and an examination of underlying assumptions
- O   Authenticity
- O   A slower pace with silence between speakers
- O   Listening deeply to self, others, and for collective meaning

The Many Faces of Dialogue

There are many forms and ways in which dialogue shows up in the world today. Some of them are based on the work of David Bohm, and others are not. While we (The Dialogue Group) largely take our inspiration from Bohm, we also recognize and draw from other disciplines and traditions such as Jungian and Gestalt psychology, western philosophy, eastern meditation practice, indigenous and Greek societies, Quaker religious and business practices, and others. And we, along with a host of colleagues and peers, are continuing to evolve new ways to work with dialogue. It is important to note that just as no two conversations are ever the same even between the same people, no two dialogues are ever the same in the same way. Each time dialogue is practiced, groups invent what works best for them.

What we have tried to do in this chapter is to give you a feel for what seems most universal about the many forms that dialogue takes.

Bohm's ideas have served as a platform for dialogue's current re-emergence in organizations. While it is not our intention to be inclusive of all those who are introducing dialogue into organizations, we do want to mention the work being done by The Dialogue Project out of MIT. Dr. William Isaacs, its director, has been conducting research, which is meant to advance what is known about how dialogue can be integrated into ongoing organizational practices, particularly in the field of organizational learning.[6]

There are other institutions and organizations that are also doing work with dialogue that go beyond the domain of the organization. Some of the contexts in which dialogue is being explored and practiced are interreligious groups, conflict resolution and mediation work, educational and public domain work, and therapeutic and small-group settings.

What all of these diverse forms of dialogue seem to share is the intention to promote learning, growth, understanding, healing, and renewal of those engaging in it.

4

WHERE DOES DIALOGUE

COME FROM?

*"The carpenter says to King Arthur: 'I will make thee
a fine table, where sixteen hundred may sit at once,
and from which none need be excluded and no knight
will be able to raise combat, for there the highly placed
will be on the same level as the lowly.'"*

Marcel Mauss
The Gift

Dialogic communication[7] in some form has been in existence ever
since the dawn of humanity. Otherwise, language and culture could
not have developed. Shared meanings form the bedrock of social
behaviors, which include such things as spiritual practices, artifacts,
architecture, art, symbols, and, of course, ways of speaking together.

Dialogue as a *practice*, however, is different. This present-day practice as described here is based on the work of David Bohm and is a
specific way of conversing, making it a subcategory of the more general form of dialogic communication. Today, dialogue has become a
distinct way of communicating in groups with the specific intention of
becoming conscious of the shared meanings we co-create. This intention is different from dialogic communication. Mostly where dialogic
communication has shown up over time, the intention has not been

explicitly stated or known among those who participated, but rather an implicit part of the cultural setting or context.

Although some say dialogic communication is new, it is important to realize the broad and deep roots it has had over time. It is as though it keeps returning and recycling throughout human history for reasons that we can only imagine. From preliterate societies to indigenous tribal councils, it has interwoven itself into numerous aspects of social life and in a variety cultures. Though not used as the distinct practice we are suggesting in this book, dialogic communication is found in many diverse social settings today where healing, understanding of differences, resolving conflict, and expanding creativity are present.

We can only ponder about the reasons for the renewed interest in dialogue. Perhaps it speaks of a deeply rooted impulse we have for conversation that directly involves us in meaning making. Or, perhaps it springs out of the isolation and fragmentation we feel from our culture's overemphasis on individualism and materialism. Whatever the source of dialogue's resurgence, it is important that we see how it connects with other age-old forms and ways of practicing dialogic principles. The interest in dialogue today is an example of an ageless, seemingly universal pattern of conversation.

To appreciate dialogue's traditions more deeply, we will first look at four historical contexts wherein dialogic communication was found. Then, we will turn to three modern contexts where aspects of dialogue are found.

Historical Antecedents of Dialogue

Indigenous Peoples

David Bohm would often share a story of what it would be like for a westerner to sit around a campfire at night with indigenous peoples[8]. Assuming that language was not a barrier, the westerner might think it was aimless talk, going nowhere in particular, covering many unrelated subjects. He might not notice any obvious thread running through the conversation at all. If the indigenous tribe were from the American plains, the next morning they might all get up and hunt buffalo together. Our westerner might see how well-coordinated their actions would be. Those participating in the hunt would know exactly what to do without any obvious structure or plan. How is this possible? From aimless talk? Where are their role definitions and who's in charge? When did they make their plans? This scenario makes no sense to our western ways of doing things.

We might speculate that the genesis of the dialogic form came from this kind of informal talk: our ancestors in small tribes, creating shared meaning through the spoken word. Sitting around at night when there was not enough light to hunt or work, sharing stories from their days' work and activities. Processing any tensions that might have developed and telling stories handed down to them from ancestors that came before them. All sowing seeds for how they live and work together in community. Acting as the glue for holding members together in a seamless whole.

This is one possible picture describing how language and culture began and developed over time.

One important artifact that modern-day dialogue inherited from the American Indians is the idea of the talking stick[9]. In Native American council meetings, a talking stick is often passed to signify who has the floor. It prevents cross talk from occurring, honors the words, and shows respect for the person holding it. We often use a talking implement in groups today to slow down the pace and/or to enforce one-at-a-time speaking.

Preliterate Societies

Riane Eisler in *The Chalice and the Blade* documents the work of the anthropologist, Marija Gimbutas and others who trace societies as far back as 7000 B.C. in old Europe. These were what she calls partnership-based cultures, built around a belief system that included the idea of the "equality of all life" and the "sacredness that resides in all its forms." Women and men were of equal status, and the societies did not tend to use force as a way to enforce compliance.

Because force or compliance was not prevalent in their culture, we might assume that dialogic communication was in common use among these early, preliterate societies. It is significant for us today that we find dialogic roots coming out of a Western European heritage. Eisler maintains that partnership-based cultures predated what she calls dominator-based cultures, which came from Aryan influences out of the north. These dominator-based cultures introduced ways of conversing that were probably more confrontational and closer to the discussion-oriented form that still predominates today.

The Early Greeks

Between 495 B.C. and the death of Aristotle in 322 B.C. in ancient Greece, "there was a novel cultural constellation, namely *democracy* that operated. It gave the citizenry ascendancy over the aristocracy. Every citizen had the right to attend the Assembly, where two to three thousand people at a time would come to vote and listen . . . never before or since has political life, within the circle of citizenship, been so intense or so creative." [10]

From this description of the political and cultural life of Athens, we might assume that dialogic communication was present. In fact, we might say that the dialogic form underlies our modern-day practice of democracy and that we have forgotten how deeply the original ideas influenced our current political structures. The irony of pointing this out is that the practice of dialogue is not widely used or known in most of our governing bodies today. What we would probably find if we were to watch how our politicians and leaders interact with one another in legislative and governing bodies is more along the lines of discussion and debate. Advocacy for the intention of persuasion and negotiation is more the norm than is listening and deep inquiry for the purpose of learning.

The early Greek philosopher, Socrates, lived during the years mentioned above. He used inquiry as a teaching device in dialogues with his students. These so-called *Socratic dialogues* were eventually written down by his student, Plato. While they might appear more to us today as monologues, Socrates' ability to stay with a question for a long time plays a powerful role in present-day dialogue. Socrates' use of inquiry helped his students tap into their own innate wisdom on such topics as beauty, truth, and justice.

The Quakers

The Quakers, also known as the Religious Society of Friends, evolved a unique form of Christian mysticism beginning in the seventeenth century from the teachings of George Fox. The key ideas that set the Quakers apart from other Christian sects arose from their belief that divine truth can be revealed from within. In their worship, as well as in their business meetings, their practice is to allow this "truth" to be revealed by any member present. They do not rely on a minister or priest in their spiritual services or a manager/leader in their business meetings. Rather, truth is revealed through what they call the "gathered meeting."

The collective nature of leaderless Quaker services and business meetings have a feeling tone that is very resonant with the current-day practice of dialogue. Especially in their business meetings, Quakers give us an existing model for how shared leadership can unfold in a larger community supported by a communication practice.

The idea of "truth" or "spirit" being drawn from an individual's inner knowing corresponds in dialogue to a practice of inner listening, as well as outer listening, that we will be explaining in Part II. Also, the Quakers emphasized trust in individual and collective intuitive ways of knowing, which is an important component of dialogue today.

Current Contexts Displaying Dialogic Qualities of Communication

Often, workshop participants will liken dialogue to other group experiences they have had. We list some of the ones we are most often asked about. It is important to note that while these modern contexts do share aspects in common with the practice of dialogue, they differ in their basic purpose and intention in that they are primarily focused on personal growth and relational healing.

Self-help Groups

Probably the largest and best known self-help group worldwide today is AA (Alcoholics Anonymous). There are many offshoots of the AA model, and the process found for communicating in most of these is similar. AA meetings contain several dialogic characteristics, such as one person speaking at a time, authenticity in the here and now, and deep listening to others. In self-help groups, the intention is on personal healing and growth (abstention from alcohol consumption or from other substance or behavioral addictions). In dialogue it is on becoming conscious of collective meaning unfolding.[11]

Community-Building

Best known in the field of community-building today is M. Scott Peck. His book, *The Different Drum,* and subsequent founding of the non-profit Foundation for Community Encouragement, paved the way for those specifically interested in how to create climates in groups that foster a spirit of community. There are many workshops and seminars, that provide participants with community-building experiences, wherein certain dialogic qualities of conversation can be found. As participants move through the stages of group development, dialogic qualities are experienced, such as respect for one another, deep listening, and one person speaking at a time. These aspects of dialogic communication become valued and used implicitly by the participants after moving through the conflict that occurs from encountering personal differences.

As we will explain in Part II when we talk about how the practice of dialogue works in groups over time, dialogue leads to the creation of community. But it does so as a by-product of its primary purpose of becoming conscious of unfolding meaning, or metacognition.[12] As we become more aware of our collective thinking process, we also learn to bring in the qualities in our relationships with others that encourage the spirit of community to build.

Sensitivity Training/Encounter Groups

Since the 60s The National Training Labs have offered small-group experiences, which many feel parallel experiences found in dialogue groups. These often intense, week-long relational programs focus on becoming aware of how the individual relates to others. Participants practice direct and authentic communication that leads to personal growth. Again, the focus is on the individual rather than on the collective.

Dialogic communication in one form or another has been with us since the beginning of humanity. It seems reasonable that its endurance and resurfacing over and over again speaks to some essential universal need. We propose that this need is the desire for meaningful conversation. We now turn to the current practice of dialogue.

5

THE CURRENT PRACTICE OF DIALOGUE

"Now if we think together, then maybe we can solve our common problems."

David Bohm
Changing Consciousness

There are several characteristics that distinguish dialogue as a practice today. These characteristics are a product of the conscious intention of the participants engaging in it. For instance, when a new dialogue group is formed, typically the participants make a conscious choice to:

- O practice *dialogue* as opposed to *discussion*,

- O practice periodically over an extended period of time (i.e., for several days in a row or for two hours every other week for a year or more, depending on the context), and

- O become conscious of their collective thinking and how they co-create unfolding meaning as they engage in the process.

These intentions originated in the work of David Bohm who was mainly concerned about the effects of what he called the fragmentation or limitations inherent in thought. In *Changing Consciousness* and other writings[13], he expresses his hope and vision for dialogue, which was to transform human society by helping it see how it creates what he calls incoherence[14]. Let's look into his original vision and then see how it might apply within an organizational context.

Our Thinking Is the Source of All Action

Everything that we do originates as some kind of idea or thought in our minds. If you were to decide to update your computer system at work, for instance, you would first have the idea to do so. Then, you might go to a supplier and talk about the various options available to you. You would think about what makes the most sense, given your computing needs. Then you would take action and buy it. It is the same when we take action together with others, only more complicated because it involves communication for coordination. An initial idea or thought arises somewhere within the group. It is talked about, and often the original idea is expanded or changed. At a certain point, people in the group implicitly or explicitly make choices to act upon it (or in some cases, not to act).

On the surface, this seems straightforward and obvious. But, hidden within its obviousness is the assumption that the thinking that led to the action won't have negative effects. Most of us live our whole lives based on this assumption. We want to do something, it seems okay for us to do so, and then we take action. No deep reflection seems required. Most of the time, this is probably so.

How Our "Thinking" Can Cause Problems

As the pace of our lives speeds up and our independent actions become complicated and have complex and interconnected effects on others, this assumption can get us into trouble. What if many people in the same office, for example, all decided to buy new computers at the same time without consulting one another? Later they would realize what they had done and that it might be too late to insure compatibility. They might not, for instance, be able to connect their computers for E-mail and for file-sharing purposes.

Suppose you owned a neighborhood computer store. For some unknown reason to you, there is a run on a particular brand of computer you sell. Let's assume that the manufacturer of this computer had created and run a highly successful ad campaign that surprised even them with its ability to promote sales. Some strange events might begin to unfold.

- ○ First, there wouldn't be enough computers to go around and you decide to increase your standing order for this computer.
- ○ As a result, the computer manufacturer decides to build more computers.
- ○ You keep getting computers in, but the demand seems to evaporate.
- ○ The buyers go elsewhere because an even more powerful ad campaign is launched by a competitive manufacturer.
- ○ The inventory of computers increases, but you aren't able to move them out.
- ○ Neither you nor the manufacturer understands completely what is happening! Because there is little communication about the potential success of the ad campaign and the potential risk, there is little awareness of how the whole system functions.
- ○ Other chain reactions occur as you now try to unload the over-supply and your buyers are drawn to the lower prices.

We could continue with further reverberations, but you get the picture.

How Thinking Divides and Fragments Reality

This computer story is one example of what Bohm meant by "fragmentation of thought." We think and take actions individually without concern for the whole or the long-term consequences. What we get is a lot of what he called incoherence in the world. By this he meant that since we do not "see" the impact of our thinking, we take actions and reap consequences we do not intend. In this example it would be supply and demand instability.

Another example of fragmentation of thought is a situation in which we make arbitrary distinctions between things and then forget that it was us who made them in the first place. Bohm would often use as an example borders around countries. We create borders, for example, between the United States and Mexico and Canada and come to believe that they have always been there. We forget our role in placing them there. We think of them as fixed and permanent, the way things are. We ignore the harm they may cause us when we face joint problems that cross borders such as environmental pollution and illegal immigration patterns. A business example would be ways we structure work around functional areas such as finance, marketing, and production. Once we make these arbitrary divisions, they seem permanent domains of activity, separate from one another and often with very different cultures. We forget that we were the ones who created the separations, and that it may be time to reconsider the current structure.

On the individual level, the fragmentation of thought can lead to consequences of immense proportion when looked at cumulatively. On the collective level, forms of fragmentation literally hide in culture. We all live and work in social settings with shared ways of doing things. We accept these things. That which was thought up in the past by others in our culture are givens. It would be rare for us to give them much reflection. Cultural norms, patterns, values, ways of perceiving (just like borders around countries) all become hardwired into our day-to-day actions.

Culture helps provide meaning and ways of organizing social life. But, what if certain aspects of our culture actually are doing us collective harm? What if by not reflecting on these things we discover that we are slowly creating the conditions that could lead to our global demise, or that we are boiling a collective frog to death and the frog is us.

The Way Out? Developing Shared Meaning and Shared Leadership through Dialogue

When groups come together in dialogue and converse deeply on a topic, they are learning to think together. This thinking together causes them to share in a common "meaning pool," which lays the foundation for taking coherent action together.

The shared meaning that comes out of thinking together precedes and leads to all action. We very seldom take the time to think together about the meaning our actions have for the whole system we are a part of. Neither do we often consider the long-term consequences of our near-term actions.

Bohm's proposal for dialogue was based on the idea that if we could become more aware of our collective thinking process and the meanings that arise from it, and all share in the leadership responsibility for acting coherently towards the whole, we could transform our world together.

Conversation, whether dialogic or not, *is* how most everything gets done in our organizations. Bohm would say that we should be giving conversation the attention it deserves instead of ignoring it as we do now. Since conversation is essential to all that we do, let's see it as foundational and act accordingly.

Thinking about Our Thinking

Bohm developed his ideas on thought and metacognition[15] through his many talks with the eastern spiritual sage, Krishnamurti[16]. Krishnamurti believed that humanity needed to make a fundamental shift in consciousness for transformation to occur in the world. He felt that war, environmental problems, conflict of all kinds were the direct result of the limitations of human thought. By becoming aware at the individual level of how we create our reality through our thinking process, he felt we could effect a change in the human psyche, leading to a change in the world at large.

The capability of becoming aware of our thinking process can be developed through the role of "witness," or a neutral observer. The witness is a part of ourselves that watches the stream of passing thoughts and feelings and thus becomes more aware of the internal thought process. In dialogue this core concept applies to the collective level. We learn to witness our collective thinking and unfolding meaning together—to become aware in real time of how our thinking and the shared meaning we create is impacting us in getting the results we desire.[17]

Social Therapy: Working on Issues and Problems We Have as "Collectives" of People

Bohm developed his ideas for working at the collective level through dialogue by coming into contact with the work of Patrick de Mare. De Mare is a social psychologist who has done extensive work in England, researching the dynamics involved in medium- to large-sized groups. His interest is in tracing the transformation of such groups over time as they engage in dialogic communication[18]. Over time, differences arise and groups move from animosity towards one another and conflict to what he calls impersonal fellowship. This happens as differences and conflicts are talked about and worked through in continuing dialogue.

De Mare believes that many of our most intractable problems can be solved only at the cultural or social level. In a sense he is suggesting a kind of "social therapy." Individuals can make progress on some psychological problems through personal therapy. But many other psychological problems are rooted in and caused by certain dysfunctional family or cultural norms and habit patterns. De Mare feels that these kinds of problems need to be addressed within the groups themselves and that dialogue is one way to go about doing this.

Specifically, de Mare proposes that people form groups to represent a kind of *microcosm* (a subsegment of society) of the *macrocosm* (the larger society) to which they belong. They agree to come together over time to observe their own dynamics and to work on what might cause social dysfunction. If many such groups formed, he feels that a fundamental change could take place in the whole society. This change could be described as a kind of impersonal fellowship, which would replace the tendency societies have towards conflict and social fragmentation (subgroups forming around group differences).

Putting "Thinking about Our Thinking" Together with Social Therapy

Bohm applied Krishnamurti's ideas on metacognition to de Mare's proposal of social therapy and came to his unique vision of dialogue. He saw that as humankind has grown and expanded on earth, limitations of human thought are becoming more and more critical. He felt dialogue could help improve our ability to make decisions in ways that lead to long-term sustainability and balance. Dialogue was his proposal for remedying further fragmentation and incoherence in our world.

Bohm's concerns were large ones. His interest encompassed the environment and the social and political life of our planet. Our focus, here, might not seem as large. Unless, that is, we recognize that the modern organization is *one of the most powerful institutions* on the planet today. If we do not take ourselves seriously in terms of the collective decisions we make, it is possible that our children's children will have to accept conditions of life that we would consider atrocious.

Quantum Considerations

You have probably heard about how the "quantum" worldview is changing the way we understand how our world works. Bohm was at the forefront of this changing worldview through his work with quantum mechanics. He spent the latter part of his life thinking about the philosophical and social ramifications of what quantum mechanics postulates. Dialogue was a natural outgrowth of these speculations. Quantum physics explains that we are all interconnected at a quantum level of reality[19]. Life is one whole, although it is difficult for us to perceive it as such. Reality is also constantly in motion around us, even though it may seem to be relatively solid and stable from our limited sense dependent perspective.

Something like dialogue is a way for us to begin to get in touch with all of the many ways we are interconnected and are part of one shared reality. It is also a way for us to perceive the ongoing nature of the changes occurring around us and to help us make sense or meaning out of what can seem like chaotic disorder. Dialogue can help us see the larger patterns that underlie our day-to-day lives.

We turn next to what all of the new sciences have to say about dialogue. From quantum physics to chaos theory to self-organizing systems, dialogue fits with our expanding understanding of reality. It also helps us get at formerly intractable problems as the speed and complexity of life continue to accelerate.

6

OUR EXPANDING WORLDVIEW:

FINDING ORDER IN CHAOS

THROUGH DIALOGUE

*"Think how many absolutely new scientific conceptions
have arisen in our own generation, how many new problems
have been formulated that were never thought of before, and then
cast an eye upon the brevity of science's career . . . Is it credible
that such a mushroom of knowledge, such a growth overnight as
this can represent more than the minutest glimpse of what the
universe will really prove to be when adequately understood?
No! Our science is a drop, our ignorance a sea."*

William James

The ideas that underlie and frame the practice of dialogue are similar to those growing out of an emerging worldview that comes from the new sciences. You may have heard something about the revolutionary nature of this emerging worldview, yet not be aware of how it impacts the way we think about organizations and managing human systems. Though the new sciences have been around for some time (i.e., quantum mechanics since the turn of the century and self-organizing systems from the last few decades), we are just now figuring out what it all means to us in practical day-to-day ways.

Basically, the revolution from the new sciences as applied to work is about moving beyond what we call *The Machine Model of Organizations*. This model is based on the following assumptions:

○ Organizations function as large machines with removable parts and in a hierarchic structure.

○ Workers are mere cogs in a wheel, removable, replaceable and expendable.

○ Leaders are captains at the helm of slow-moving ships.

Images from quantum mechanics and self-organizing systems theory continue to add new dimensions. We emphasize the word *add* because when we talk about these new images, we do not wish to imply that the older images of organizations as machine are wrong or out-of-date. From our expanded worldview, we might see them as limited or singular ways of perceiving more generalized and larger principles that we now know to be true. They are useful for organizing ourselves within specific ranges of experience, but limiting in larger contexts.

Quantum mechanics likens the organization to a hologram wherein all parts contain the whole and the whole is made up of unique parts. If we apply this holographic image to human systems, it becomes important that each worker, no matter at what level in the organization, have mental images of how the whole organization operates and knows what is important to it on a timely basis. Information becomes vital, communication between and among all the parts essential. What one part knows must be available to all so that the essential life of the organization is maintained.

Self-organizing systems theory likens the organization to a self-referencing system, which maintains itself around an evolving core identity. Adaptation to changing conditions is the norm. If we apply this image to organizations, we see that top/down direction needs to be supplemented with information moving to all parts of the organization through rapid networks of communication. Each part of the organization needs to be able to reference what all other parts are doing. In this way, the whole organization can adjust to changing internal and external conditions fluidly.

If we combine these two new images from quantum mechanics and self-organizing systems theory we might redefine organizations as "self-organizing holograms."

But how would such an image as "self-organizing holograms" help us in our day-to-day work? How would it combine with what we already do in organizations and piggyback onto the "machine model of organizations," the existing image we all carry around with us? Finally, how can this funny-sounding image add to rather than detract from successes we have had with existing organizational practices? And, what role can dialogue play?

We are all learning how to operate and dance outside our comfort zone, given these newer images from the scientific community. While many of us have understood the need to integrate these newer images into the way we organize and lead our organizations, we haven't always known how to do it. Dialogue, as we will see, is tailor-made for helping us meet this challenge. It provides a process that helps us take full advantage of what the new sciences tell us about the inherent potential for self-organization and generativity resident in human systems. All we need to do is discern when and under what conditions to employ dialogue. As we do so, we will be rewarded by more adaptable, flexible, and sustainable organizations.

Organizations as Self-Organizing Holograms: A Blending of the Old and the New Ways of Organizing and Managing

Consider the picture on the next page that depicts aspects of how we organize and manage coming out of a Newtonian versus a quantum worldview[20].

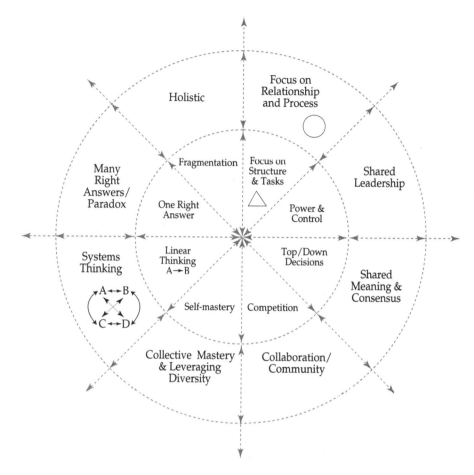

Notice that an inner circle is contained within an outer circle. Also notice the permeable boundaries separating the two circles with dotted lines pointing back and forth between the two circles and even beyond the outer one. This implies that while our worldview is expanding based on what we now know to be true about human systems from a quantum perspective, we do not have to give up on how we have been operating in the past. Not only are we are *not* throwing out the baby with the bath water, we aren't supposing that the quantum worldview is the last. Just as the quantum worldview builds and expands on what we know from the Newtonian one, we assume there will be additional worldviews that expand on what we know from the quantum one. We just don't know what they are yet.

Dispel any concerns you may have about giving up such structural ways of operating as hierarchy and top/down decision making, all contained in the inner circle. Over a certain domain, these Newtonian principles operate very well. The quantum worldview augments our capacity for meeting the challenges of today's world: the rapid acceleration of change and the greater, more complex reality that we are facing. It has more explanatory power and suggests alternative ways of working together. It also helps us address the core dilemmas that come about with accelerating change and complexity. The outer circle can help us engage and work with these dilemmas without throwing out anything from the past. Hierarchy can still be a useful organizing principle, though you may find it operating in service of a larger view. What we *are* suggesting is that you add a few things to what you already do and be prepared to discover new interweavings for structuring relationships emerging in the system.

Some of Our Core Dilemmas

Ways of operating in the outer circle also address many of the more intractable organizational problems that we face today, such as:

- o **The alienation of the workforce.** The lack of meaning and motivation and increasing levels of apathy that accompany downsizings, layoffs, restructuring, mergers, etc.

- o **The integration of diversity.** Our struggle to find ways for leveraging the full extent of our diverse workforce, while at the same time addressing the increasing conflict that often arises when cultural, racial, religious, and gender differences are encountered.

- o **The constant running we do from one fire to the next.** How do we stem the tide of crisis management when organizations face downsizing and cost containment at the same time?

- o **Making sense of increasing levels of complexity and size.** How do we move information up, down, and across large and complex organizations? How do we get it there in a timely way to those who need it most? How can we provide it in ways that help to make sense of what is going on in the organization as a whole?

○ **Creating alignment around vision.** As organizations decentralize and grow in size, how are they to hold themselves together through shared vision?

○ **Moving beyond one right answer**. As the world speeds up and the paradoxical nature of reality becomes more and more obvious, how do we hold multiple viewpoints and still move ahead with aligned action?

As our comfort level increases in moving back and forth between the two circles, we will find a larger capacity to address these core dilemmas. We will increase our ability to more rapidly adapt to problems as they arise and to face what has been coined as the "permanent white-water" of modern life[21].

Dialogue as a communication practice helps us navigate more effectively in the outer circle. As conditions warrant and we gain more capability, we will find ourselves naturally moving between both the old and new ways of working. Whether we use dialogue or another approach for operating in the outer circle will depend on the context and the nature of the situation we are facing. Whether we even move out to the outer circle at all will depend on many variables including how ready we are to engage in dialogue and its principles. Let's look at each of these pie slices one at a time.

Focus on Structure and Tasks
Focus on Relationship and Process

When we thought that reality consisted only of concrete matter[22], we divided ourselves up into discreet units and organized ourselves along specific job lines. We paid a lot of attention to how we structured the tasks that our work consisted of. We still do. Consider all the latest business books on re-engineering and downsizing.

From quantum physics and self-organizing systems theory, we know that reality is essentially

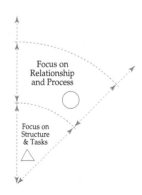

defined by relationship and process. Every one of us depends on and is impacted by the work, actions, and ideas of everyone else. We perform our work in tightly woven and interconnected webs of interdependent parts. In reality, structure often takes a back seat to the quality of the relationships that are present and the processes or ways we go about getting our work done.

To meet current challenges, we must explore building climates that support the development of quality relationships and how we can place more conscious attention on how we get our work done together. A communications practice such as dialogue can play a vital role in developing both of these capacities.

Power and Control
Shared Leadership

When all we knew was that organizations operated like machines, we vested our leaders with the formal power, authority, and control we thought they needed to ensure the results we were looking for. We believed that we had to do this because, after all, machines are inanimate objects without the power to do work unless we provide the initial thrust. And, machines need to be controlled because they cannot think for themselves. Our idea of leadership in this older view of the world says that the person at the top should act as the brains for the whole organization. Everyone else just does what they are told to do.

At times this is an extremely useful way of seeing organizations. Imagine what would happen if a fire broke out in a skyscraper. Would you want everyone to take their time coming to consensus about what is the best way to evacuate the building? Or, would you prefer that the person in charge quickly take control of the situation and order the evacuation plan ASAP? In some crisis situations, the use of power and control is essential.

But what if, on the other hand, we aren't facing an emergency at all? What if what we want is greater adaptability and creativity to reside in the organization? We can't order these highly-prized qualities. We have to take the time to build into our organization the norms for shared leadership that will get us there. We want to move towards a climate of collaborative partnership that dialogue can help us build.

Top/Down Decisions
Shared Meaning and Consensus

Top/down decision making works well with power and control exercised at the top. The flow of decisions arises at the top and is disseminated to the troops below. Easy and efficient, this method can lead to rapid results over the near term.

But what if what we want are quantum leaps in productivity? This implies more of a shared meaning, consensual process. We know that people work harder and are more motivated when they have been involved in making decisions affecting them.

This does not mean that we need consensus to order pencils every other month. This would be a silly waste of time. Routine, trivial decisions do not need to be consensual at all.

But when there is an important decision to be made that affects people in significant ways, developing shared meaning and consensus can be one of the best strategies to use for gaining the investment of all concerned. We all know that we have more incentive to change what we are doing if we have had a say in making the change itself. We also know that we tend to resist making changes when we are merely ordered to make them.

The use of dialogue is helpful when we are looking towards building shared meaning and consensus.

Competition
Collaboration/Community

Darwin's idea of survival of the fittest gave us powerful reasons to believe that the world operated on a dog-eat-dog basis. Beating the competition was equated with winning in life and everything that was good and useful about how to organize ourselves. It is deeply grooved into our western psyches.

From the quantum perspective, we notice the inherent limitations. Competition works within certain bounds, but does not meet all contingencies of life as we used to believe.

In the short run, competition can unleash incredible amounts of energy as individuals see what is at stake in beating their opponent. In the long run, however, collaboration will typically work better. When two individuals pool what they both know about a task and combine efforts, a huge leap in productivity is often the result. Think about two companies that currently compete. What could happen if they joined forces and became one combined company? In macroeconomic theory, it is postulated that at a certain stage of industrial development, prior competitors can maximize or make more efficient their joint productivity by merging efforts. In an early stage of development, however, its separate entities competing will allow each to differentiate themselves with respect to the other.

So, in the short run, we can see the value of competition with outside entities. And in the long run, it can be beneficial to combine efforts and collaborate. Witness all the industrial consolidations we are seeing lately. If we view this as a natural pattern of organization at a certain stage of development, then we can understand why there is also so much need for creating cultures of collaboration and partnership.

Competing internally against those whose work we depend on for task completion is counterproductive. Yet we do this all the time. We even reward each other in ways that perpetuate this kind of dysfunctional competition. Why so? Because we have used competition for so long that our behaviors are based on it. We aren't conscious at times that we have these kinds of disconnects in our organizations. If we *are* aware of them, we may not have the communication skills to support collaboration. We need to become aware of the results produced by communication patterns based on a competitive ethos. Otherwise, nothing we may try will move us closer to collaboration. Dialogue can play an instrumental role.

Self-mastery
Collective Mastery and Leveraging Diversity

We all know that it is hard today to get much done on our own. Work has become increasingly specialized and complex. This in turn creates increasing pressure on teamwork for desired results. Where we used to only develop individuals and called it self-mastery, we are now in need of developing whole teams and can call it collective mastery. Integration of tasks and seeing how everything fits together is key. Specialization alone without integration doesn't get us very far. Collective mastery builds on self-mastery.

Self-mastery

Collective Mastery
& Leveraging
Diversity

Once again, communication is essential. But, consider what is typical today in our organizations. We throw teams together to accomplish a complex task. We ask them to collaborate and to self-organize themselves. We provide them with little to no support in the way of interpersonal skills that would help them accomplish the task. Then we wonder what went wrong. We usually chalk it up to personality conflicts or poor management. We reorganize the team or bring in a team-building expert. We don't recognize that what it is we want them to do, they are not prepared to do. We don't see that the fundamental problem is communication. When a group of individuals come together who have few collective mastery skills, they continue to act as individuals—separately, with a lot of different and conflicting agendas.

Again, dialogue rests on the idea that we live in a world that is collective in nature with interconnected parts. Dialogue can help us see the interconnections in our work with others and can help build the capacity to leverage the team's inherent diversity. It can bring collective mastery to close-knit teams and task forces.

Linear Thinking
Systems Thinking

In Newtonian reality, we saw things as simple cause and effect. We prided ourselves on our ability to analyze data and to make projections based on trends and simple curves. From chaos theory and nonlinear-systems theory, we know that simple cause and effect is the exception rather than the norm. What is more common are complex interaction effects, which limit our ability to predetermine much in advance. These move beyond the simple *A* leads to *B* leads to *C* to consider how *C* also impacts and is impacted by both *A* and *B*. In other words, the arrows move in several directions rather than just from left to right.

What this means practically is that rather than spending so much of our time in planning for the future by extrapolating past trends, we could benefit from spending time in developing our ability to communicate about complex relationships and system interactions. Why? Because what matters is our ability to recognize the interplay between interdependent events, processes, and entities. Systems thinking is a step in this direction. A communication process such as dialogue can allow us to see into complex inter-relationships, a capability essential in meeting the increasing numbers of systemic problems we face today.

One Right Answer
Many Right Answers/Paradox

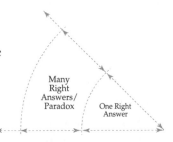

The Newtonian worldview has it that there is one right or best answer to our problems and that everything can be objectively determined. This idea was what created our experimental physical sciences.

Researchers became objective observers of life around them and sought to discover how the world works definitively.

What we now understand from the quantum worldview is that often what is so is paradox and many "right" or "best" answers. It tells us there are no absolutely objective answers, that the observer him/herself influences the answer based on the expectations or intention brought to the act of observing.

When faced with difficult choices where complexity and paradox are present, it may be more useful to entertain many answers and experiment with what works as we move along. To operate in this way, open-ended communication, such as dialogue, is imperative. Otherwise we narrow the field of potential choices and do not permit the largest view of reality to be perceived.

Fragmentation
Holistic

Based on Newtonian physics, we have been taught from a very early age to break everything down into smaller and smaller components. If something isn't working, we quickly analyze where the problem is and go after the cause to fix it. Just like a broken part in a clock, we might decide to replace a problem employee or redo a certain way we have structured a job assignment. For simple problems, this is often the best approach to take.

Based on the new sciences perspective, our world actually is one whole. So, for more complex dilemmas, such as are found in cross-industrial problems or in projects that cross functional lines, it is our ability to see problems within the context of a system as a whole that matters. To develop this capacity, once again, the ways in which we communicate are essential.

When we employ discussion, for example, we compete for which view is correct. We do not stand back and try to see the larger problem arising from the common threads of the various points of view. In dialogue, seeing these common threads is the intention. We are there to learn about the largest vision of what it is we are considering together.

> Shared meaning and shared leadership are the pivotal elements for operating in the outer ring of the model. Dialogue is a way to get there.

We have covered a lot of ground. If you were to remember just one key thing from this chapter that might help you operate in the outer circle it is this: *Pay attention to* shared meaning *and* shared leadership. *Both are essential in the creation and sustainability over time of* collaborative work environments. By learning and practicing dialogue, team members will begin to develop the capability to intentionally create shared meanings coherent with their actions and results. Alignment around vision and during task implementation will increase. Individuals will begin to share in the leadership function by taking personal initiative and responsibility for attaining the vision desired.

7

THE LARGER QUESTIONS

"Now we approach the difficult question
from the practical person — what is to be done?
What sorts of actions and programs do the
foregoing arguments suggest?"

Harmon Markeley

If you believe that the modern organization is the single most power-ful global institution in the world today, this alone is a powerful moti-vation to expand the ways in which we organize and operate. We are *the* carriers and shapers of world culture. The social and cultural ramifica-tions of how we operate and manage are essential in providing a model for organizations everywhere. All of us who work in organizations today need to be asking ourselves about how we treat people and how we make our decisions. Are we doing the best we can do? **Can we find ways for engaging in dialogue as a strategy for creating a more humane and sustainable world?**

Besides needing to be concerned with the cultural and social rami-fications of how we run our organizations, what about our need to con-tend with consequences of increasing technological sophistication? Our technologies are both valuable to us and are the source of many of our problems. We are facing worldwide crises coming from increas-ing pollution, environmental and ecological concerns, and increasing gaps between the rich and the poor. **Can we find ways for employing** *dialogue that will enhance our ability to make collective decisions that will more positively impact our shared future on earth?*

At a more micro level, we presently operate in ways that *actually* lead to the core dilemmas most organizations face: alienation and the lack of a motivated workforce; challenges in creating alignment around vision in increasingly complex organizational structures; leveraging diversity in a shrinking world where a homogenous workforce is no longer viable; and dealing with the problems of crisis management, uncertainty, and permanent whitewater. Behind these challenges is a value system that is in need of rebalancing and expansion. Competition, individualism, and the Puritan work ethic have served us for a very long time. Perhaps it is time we added to our repertoire. **How can dialogue help us rebalance and expand on these norms and move towards cultures of collaborative partnership?**

As you continue reading through this book, you might hold these larger questions in mind. All of us face different work situations and individual challenges. How dialogue can be of value to you and to me will not be the same. These larger questions, however, can serve as a framework for tying together those of us who work in organizations.

As the world continues to shrink and we increasingly notice that we share in a common destiny, it may be our willingness to hold these larger questions that will make the difference in future generations to come.

II

THE "LIVING TECHNOLOGY" OF DIALOGUE

Crafting Powerful Conversations

"What truly matters in our lives is measured through conversation."

Peter Block
Stewardship

H ow we converse with one another is fundamental to the way we work together, the decisions we make, and the results we create. Deep inside we all know this. The growing impulse for open and authentic conversation in our world today is a response to our desires for connection in the face of growing alienation and our need to make responsible socioeconomic and ecological decisions that ensure that there will be a twenty-first century worth living in. The impulse towards dialogue may well be an impulse towards survival for our organizations and our communities, both local and global.

On January 27, 1986, a conversation took place between two groups of people. The decision made at the conclusion of that meeting resulted in the launch of the space shuttle Challenger, the loss of seven lives and billions of dollars. The data was available; the people were intelligent, well intentioned, responsible human beings. What happened?[1]

NASA needed a successful launch; there were questions about the value of the program and suggestions of cutting funds. Morton Thiokol was the sole supplier on the o-rings for the solid fuel rocket booster, and NASA was considering looking for another. A multimillion dollar contract was at stake. The temperature at the time of launch was expected to be well outside the safety specification limits for the o-rings. There was no data to indicate what impact such a low temperature would have on the integrity of the seal provided by the o-rings. The engineers for Morton Thiokol relayed this data and their concerns more than once. They said that a decision to launch would not be in the direction of "goodness," a term that in engineering circles means "alignment with specifications" but also has strong implicit ethical meaning in our culture. NASA heard the words, but refused to accept them as the basis for a decision. The NASA team leader said that he would honor a no-launch decision but he would be shocked and concerned about the implications of such a recommendation. The Morton Thiokol project manager told his team off-line, "It really makes an impression on me when 'x' says he will be 'shocked and concerned.' " What veiled threats did the manager at Morton Thiokol hear in the words of the NASA team leader? Was the contract at stake? The unspoken is a powerful driver. The writing was on the wall. Morton Thiokol said they would go with the launch. When NASA asked if there were any dissenters to that position, no words were spoken.

Though a dramatic example, there was nothing going on that evening between Morton Thiokol and NASA that doesn't go on everyday in our organizations, our communities, and even our families. Smart people make poor and sometimes disastrous decisions even in the presence of adequate information because dynamics combine to create an inability to talk openly about what is important. Dialogue allows us to address crucial, yet often undiscussable, aspects of an issue or a problem so that we can make better choices for all involved.

Most of us have experienced similar conversations to the one described above. And, hopefully, we've all experienced conversations that lead to creative breakthroughs, shared visions, collaboration, and communication. What makes the difference? At the core of any conversation lie the intentions, behaviors, and skills of those involved; these create the environment and focus the way we speak and listen together. Part II is a series of chapters, each devoted to a closer look at these essential components and how they can support you in bringing the value of dialogue into your day-to-day activities.

A "Living Technology," Not a "Set of Techniques"

For many of us the word *technology* brings to mind mechanistic, machinelike images. So why would we choose to use such a word in the title for this section? Because much of this section is about looking through a different lens, rethinking our current and habitual ways of being in conversation, and remembering the art and beauty and deep satisfaction of well crafted conversation. The word *technology* derives from the root "techno," which carries the meanings "art, craft, skill." Dialogue is artful conversation crafted through the focusing of attention, attitudes and behaviors that support open authentic inquiry. We intentionally combined the word *living* with *technology* to help us remember that the art of dialogue is a living, interactive process. It is shaped by and shapes those who engage in it. The craft of dialogue is fluid. When we forget this, we run the risk of limiting dialogue to a set of fixed techniques or rules of the road.

There are many who think of dialogue as a technique, a set of steps or ingredients that you can throw into a bowl, mix up, and have the genie of dialogue appear. This is anything but the case.

Techniques and recipes are convenient. They allow us to move through the steps without paying too much attention. We don't have to think about what we are up to. Why do we add two tablespoons of sugar? We do it because the recipe in front of us says to. Techniques and recipes are good for reproducing specific forms, like chocolate cakes and aluminum cans manufactured to within 0.001 inch tolerance. But, by themselves they aren't much good for creating breakthrough thinking or listening for shared meaning in a diverse group of people. This requires a combination of skill, craft, and art. It requires listening without preconceived notions of what we are going to hear, a willingness to look through new eyes and see the world shift and move into new configurations.

Techniques and recipes can be helpful as guides to get one started. But they actually become dangerously limiting when we mistake them for the original creative impulse that they seek to express.

It is easy to focus on techniques and end up missing the meaning that is moving among a group of people, integrating their diverse thoughts and feelings into a larger and more complete picture. Meaning does not live in recipes but is heard through the artful listening of the "cooks" and artisans. We are all artisans capable of crafting extraordinary conversations. The behaviors and skills we include in the next chapters are important because they help to focus our attention on and reveal the meanings that move among us. They support us in following our natural impulse to be engaged in meaningful conversations. By remembering that these skills are always in the service of our intention to create open, authentic conversation, we can avoid the all too common trap of making dialogue just another formula and limiting its vast creative potential.

There Is a Landscape Larger Than the One You See

Consider how many times in your life you have been introduced to "the greatest thing since sliced bread," some process or thing that a friend or colleague felt was incredibly important. Your first response to their enthusiastic description may have been "What's so different about that? I don't get it." Perhaps it was only after experiencing it that you began to "get" what all the excitement was about.

Often the subtleties of a process and how they interweave to generate the process's inherent power are not immediately apparent. This can certainly be true with dialogue. For example, it is accurate to say that an essential ingredient of dialogue is listening. What is so special or different about that? On the surface, nothing. Yet, beyond that first surface impression, there is a vast landscape of difference. It is one thing to listen well, even so intently that you could feed back the words and meaning of what another has just said. To listen with a willingness to be influenced by what another says and to be willing to loosen your grip on hallowed certainties is quite another thing. In this section we delve deeper, beyond the surface of dialogue, into its larger landscape.

Weaving the Container

Any conversation or dialogue will be as powerful as the intention and skills of those who participate in it. One way to think of the relationship among the various components that create and sustain powerful dialogue is to picture a basket like the one shown on the next page.

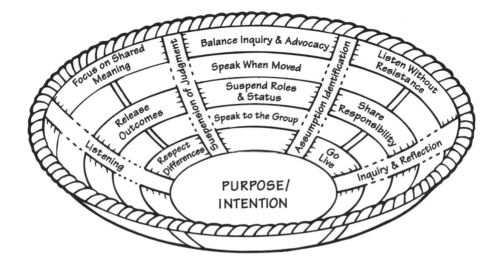

The integrity and strength of the basket are a function of the interweaving of the guides and skills. The more attention given to this interweaving, the more powerful the conversation will be. And, of course, no basket holds together for long if the initial core from which the weave began unravels. This is why we place purpose and intention at this center point.

Before moving to an in-depth view of the basket itself, be reminded once again of the importance of intention.

Dialogue Is Before All Else a Matter of Intention

No matter how proficient you become with the skills of dialogue, if your intention is unclear or more aligned with competition than collaboration, you will not be able to participate in the creation of true shared meaning nor build sustainable collaborative partnerships. You may be incredibly skilled at inquiry and listening; yet, if you use your skills to manipulate and unilaterally control a conversation or a relationship you will ultimately reap distrust and perhaps even retaliation. On a more subtle, yet just as powerful level, your intention shapes the tone and effectiveness of any conversation, because your intention guides the way you participate. If you are the person creating the agenda and leading a meeting, the impact will be even more power-ful. Your intention will shape the way everyone participates—the degree of openness, whether the focus is on digging deeper or staying at the surface, how much of a rush there is towards decision and action. As you read the following chapters on suspension of judgment, suspension and identification of assumptions, listening, inquiry and reflection and begin to practice these skills with others, keep your intention foremost in your mind. It, more than anything else, will determine what you pay attention to and the results you get.

I

SUSPENSION OF JUDGMENT

*"This is part of what I consider dialogue—for people
to realize what is on each other's minds without
coming to any conclusions or judgments.
In a dialogue we have to sort of weigh the question a little,
ponder it a little, feel it out."*

David Bohm
On Dialogue

*"If you begin to understand what you are
without trying to change it,
then what you are undergoes a transformation."*

J. Krishnamurti

We start with suspension of judgment because the ability to work with judgments provides the foundation for the other skills and guides in the chapters that follow. Without it, dialogue is not possible. Suspension of judgment is *not* about stopping judgments from occurring. This would be an impossible task. After all, judgments are the products of a process that is essential to the way our mind works, that is, "the forming of an opinion or evaluation by discerning and comparing." Good-bad, stupid-brilliant, yes-no, beautiful-ugly, safe-dangerous. We are judgment manufacturers. We turn them out in a variety of sizes, shapes, and intensities in a continuous production process that runs

24 hours a day, 7 days a week, no vacations. You could say we are judg-mentaholics.

Suspension of judgment is about developing the ability to observe judgments, your own and those of others, from a neutral position, remaining detached and unreactive. Why would this skill be essential to dialogue? No one likes to feel judged. Judgments shut down conversations and send creative thinking into hiding. They undermine the very openness that is required to create and sustain collaborative partnerships. And yet, we really have no choice; we cannot *not* judge. Judging is vital and useful to us. But it can also limit our ability to see a whole picture, shut down our listening, and stifle our creativity and learning. In this chapter we'll consider when judging is useful and when it is not. We will take a look at the impact of our judgments and explore ways of working with them in one-on-one interactions, group conversations, and dialogues.

To Judge or Not to Judge . . . Is Not Our Choice

Everyday I wake up and a judgment is the first thing on my mind. "I feel good." "I wish this day had never arrived!" "Who's the jerk that is already hammering away at six in the morning?" Two hours later I'm at work and the meeting to discuss the downturn in sales over the last few months comes all too soon and my judgments are definitely in attendance. "Is she crazy? We all know that production isn't keeping up with orders." "Now that's the first good idea I've heard this morning!" "Let's follow that line of thought." It all sounds so familiar.

There is rarely a moment in which we are not engaged in a "sort and judge" process. Each judgment, like a fork in the road, sets us walking in a particular direction. If you could trace the paths your judgments propel you along, similar to tracing the movement of particles in a cloud chamber, you might see something like the complex pattern on the following page.

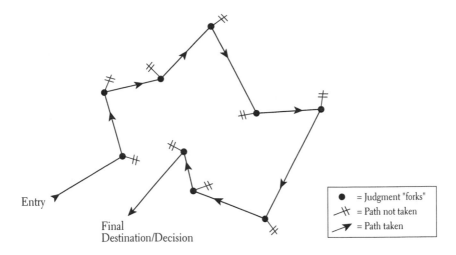

Entry

Final
Destination/Decision

● = Judgment "forks"
⚡ = Path not taken
➤ = Path taken

You take in data, sort, evaluate, and decide left or right, yes or no. The process repeats with lightning speed until after 5 or 500 of these events you arrive at some destination. Sometimes you are surprised. "What am I doing here? This was not what I had in mind!" But more often your judgments will propel you down the same recognizable paths over and over again, the result of repetitive, habitual patterns.

Useful or Not Useful . . . This IS the Question!

The automatic paths our judgments take us down can be both useful and not. *Useful:* I am riding a bike or performing some other fairly complex function that I want to be able to accomplish without too much conscious effort. I automatically collect data and make choices and ride along without much effort at all. *Not useful:* I'm involved in trying to find a creative new solution to a recurring problem in the plant, or to discover how people from two diverse cultures can most effectively work together. In this context my habitual judging process can limit my ability to move in new directions and discover new alternatives.

Our automatic judging process helps us with certain tasks and situations by reducing the effort required of us. It occurs very quickly, faster, in fact, than we can actually consciously think. The downside is that when the process moves at such high speed, the only options we think of tend to be those pigeonholes that already exist. There is little room or time to see new data and relationships.

David Bohm believed that for us to actually learn to think creatively, as opposed to simply reacting, we would have to slow down enough to see beyond our rapid-fire judgments, collect additional data, and formulate fresh alternatives. Bohm was fond of referring to judgments as thoughts that have been laid down in our memory banks. When any piece of data triggers these memories, they are acted upon automatically without any conscious thought. From the time we are born, we begin to collect the criteria for our judgments; from parents, friends, teachers, authority figures, mentors, etc. According to child-development experts, we collect the most important of these criteria within the first six years of our lives. From then on we simply build on these, reinforcing them with data collected from sources we respect and admire, often for no other reason than that they agree with our criteria. For the balance of our lives, we collect data, feed it through our criteria filters, and output the judgments that ultimately drive our decisions and actions. At some point most of us begin to realize that the judgments that have been so useful to us in many contexts are limiting us from moving into new territories. We become tired of engaging in the same conversations, finding ourselves at the same unsatisfying destinations. Often this is sufficient motivation for us to begin to loosen our grip on our certainties and begin to open our minds. We begin to notice new data, and wonder about new possibilities in terms of relationships and ways of working with an issue or a group of people.

Suspension of Judgment and Seeing the Whole Picture

The judging process divides reality into parts and then compares these parts as a way of knowing something about the whole system. It is not any surprise that we approach things this way. Hundreds of years of mechanistic science and the industrial age are grounded in this kind of thinking. Like our judging process, this mechanistic approach has been useful to us. Yet, there are two potential pitfalls that can dramatically impact our ability to build a larger picture of any issue that confronts us. The first is that when we focus on the parts alone, we tend to forget that they are not only connected and interrelated with one another, but that the system as a whole is constantly influencing the parts. This continuous dynamic interplay is completely ignored by the judging process, with its focus on comparing the parts to one another. It becomes virtually impossible to develop a system's view of any whole while deeply engaged in judging.

The second danger has to do with either/or and both/and thinking. Judging by its very nature is an either/or process. It cannot help but make evaluative choices between one or the other. That is what judging does and why it can be one of the greatest blocks to our ability to create collaborative partnerships. Either/or thinking fosters competition and exclusivity. We have all been on the losing end of an equation set up by judgment and have been in circumstances where it seemed impossible to find any win-win alternative because we could not see past the conflicting judgments of those involved. A "you or me" world does not inspire collaboration. Creating collaborative partnerships at work requires a high capacity for both/and thinking, to explore new ways of working with conflictual situations and learn to truly value and leverage diverse perspectives.

Judgment Listens Only to Itself

Whether you agree or disagree, your judgments will limit your ability to listen. Even agreement with another can limit how you listen. You simply reinforce your own judgments and don't hear or entertain anything different. In some cases you may not even pick up information from your environment that differs from the view you agree with: It is as if it doesn't even exist. In this way, judgments often provide support for and reinforce accepted views and behaviors.

By far the most damaging to your listening will be your negative judgments. Think back to any conversation you've been part of lately where you found yourself thinking something along the lines of "That is absolutely ridiculous. How can he not see it?" What happened to your listening? Ninety-nine percent of the time the accurate answer is that you stopped. You were no longer even a little curious about what the other's idea was except perhaps to gather information to help show him how wrong he was. If you were listening at all, it was to the voices inside your own head talking about how wrong the other was. You may have been preparing counterarguments or maybe you just checked out, figuring that it was a useless cause anyway, so why bother.

It is difficult, if not impossible, to be genuinely curious about someone's opinion and try to reach some deeper understanding of what the person is thinking when you've already judged it stupid or uninformed or even dangerous. The impact on creativity is no less striking. That's why one of the basic ground rules of brainstorming is "no evaluation—any idea is a good idea." Negative evaluations will shut a brainstorming process down faster than anything else a person can say or do.

Moving Beyond the "Box" of Our Judgments

While judging is sometimes useful, it can shut down dialogic conversations between people, making it almost impossible to engage with genuine curiosity and an attitude of learning. So, what can we do? We can learn to practice suspension of judgment. Suspension is the act of "holding in an undetermined or undecided state awaiting further information." We don't try to stop our judgments from coming up; we choose not to act on them in rapid-fire automatic mode.

At this point, you may be thinking, "Well, okay, but I already do that. I don't push my opinions on anybody. And I listen, even when I don't agree." We invite you to consider that you may not be particularly challenged until someone says something that runs counter to a deeply held belief of yours and then, suddenly, you will find yourself on "full autopilot" with not a millimeter of distance between you and your judgments. You will find yourself acting out your judgments rather than suspending them. You may not jump on the person or even strongly express your dissent, but you will most assuredly stop listening.

Practicing suspension of judgment requires that you be willing to release, at least temporarily, your certainties, your attachment to your judgments, opinions, and evaluations, even in the most trying of circumstances. To do this, you will need to begin developing a degree of detachment from your judgments, otherwise you will find yourself moved by them so quickly that your conscious mind will have no time to think and respond from a more considered vantage point.

Being detached does not mean that you are completely separate from your judgments or that you have no connection with them. Detachment is about creating an internal neutral observer that is not provoked by, and therefore not at the effect of, whatever judgments, thoughts, or feelings might arise in a conversation or dialogue. When our thoughts or judgments put us into an autopilot reactive mode, we lose most, if not all, of our ability to listen openly. In the East, many of the meditative disciplines use a practice of "following the breath" to help learn to observe thoughts and judgments moving through the mind, without becoming attached to or provoked by them. We outline an adaptation below that you can experiment with. The goal of the exercise is to help you 1) become aware of the reactive influence your thoughts and judgments can have on you, and 2) develop your neutral observer. This neutral observer will be invaluable to you in bringing more listening and a spirit of inquiry into your relationships and conversations, particularly in more challenging situations.

TRY THIS: FOLLOWING BREATH, THOUGHTS AND FEELINGS

1. Sit quietly and comfortably in an upright position. Close your eyes or fix them on a point in front of you. Bring your attention to your breathing. There is no need to change it. Simply focus on it. Notice the inhale, the slight pause, and then the exhale. Follow your breathing.

2. Now, simply bring to mind any current situation that is demanding a good deal of your attention at work. Once you've brought it to mind, release the thought and simply sit.

3. Notice how a steady stream of thoughts continues to move through. Some may catch you and off you go. Then along comes another and you notice your breathing changing or your jaw clenching or your mouth turning up into a smile. Notice each thought and each of your responses. Then release it and refocus on your breathing. Continue noticing and releasing, noticing and releasing, returning always to your breath.

Once you have begun to work with your judgments by observing them on your own, continue with the following activity designed to introduce you to the practice of suspension of judgment when you are engaged in conversations with others.

TRY THIS: PRACTICING SUSPENSION OF JUDGMENT

○ First say to yourself, "I am going to become aware of my judging process in the presence of others. Each time a judgment comes up, I will notice it. I will not do anything, simply notice." When you make this statement, you set a powerful intention in motion within your own mind.

○ Once you begin to become more aware of your judgments, you can begin to notice how they direct traffic and control how you listen and what you are willing and not willing to hear. Choose one conversation a day to practice with. At the conclusion write down the "big and loud" judgments and the effects you noticed.

○ Next time you are practicing and one of these "big and loud" judgments shows up and closes down your listening, imagine performing the following action. Pick the judgment up between the thumb and forefinger of your right hand and literally suspend it at a distance in front of you. Once you've suspended it, let it go. It will simply float there. Notice that you have created a space, an opening between you and your judgment, through which you can continue to listen, to allow the other person's words and reasoning to enter. How much longer can you listen? When the next judgment shows up (as it no doubt will), repeat the process.

○   When you begin the above practice, start with people who express judgments that are a little less challenging. Then as you continue to practice, increase the challenge. Your goal is to reach a point where you can listen with curiosity even to those with whom you strongly disagree.

If you practice this exercise with any kind of regularity, it is guaranteed to result in a deepening of your listening skills and your capacity to develop a larger picture of any issue, whether it be how to reorganize shifts at a plant or how to find a way to improve the working relationships between yourself and a co-worker.

Suspension of Judgment in a Group Dialogue

All that we've said above applies in groups as well as in one-on-one conversations. Yet in groups the impact of judgments and the lack of suspension of judgment have even more dramatic effects. When suspension is not present in a group, it is not uncommon for someone to express her opinion followed by someone making a disparaging remark or rolling her eyes towards the ceiling. Suddenly everyone knows it's not safe to speak freely. It is not the presence of judgment that is damaging; it is the recognition that group members are not committed to practicing suspending their judgments and listening. People generally respond to unsuspended judgments in one of two defensive ways. First, they shut down because they have decided it is unsafe to speak. Diverse perspectives are stifled. This can result in a form of group think where one opinion, usually one held by someone in authority, is expressed and everyone goes along, because no one wants to judge or be judged for having another opinion. Second, at other times the response is verbal defensiveness; everyone simply states their positions more loudly, competing to be heard and prove their opinion right. In either scenario, it will be impossible for the group to become aware of how they are thinking together, because they aren't. No listening is possible. There is no opportunity to develop shared understanding and shared meaning.

In a dialogue where everyone has agreed to hold the intention of suspending judgment, the scenario is potentially quite different. Judgments will still surface. But when they do come up, they are not acted on. It is like saying at a group level, "Okay, I know that I have a lot of random thoughts about xyz. I'm going to take the next ten minutes to suspend my judgments and just get all my thoughts out and see if I can see the larger picture here, so that I can make a better decision." For ten minutes you don't do or decide anything. You suspend your judgments. You are just seeing and clarifying what is there. When groups engage in this practice over time, they build trust and members are increasingly willing to speak directly and openly about important issues.

Speaking Your Judgments into a Group

Just as you can learn a lot from becoming more aware of your judgments and what triggers them, a group can also gain useful information by asking questions such as these: What are the judgments that the group shares? How do these provide information on mental models[3] that are influencing decisions and creative potential? For this to occur, all must be capable of voicing judgments aloud or suspending them into the group. This can be tricky. You will need to learn to discern when this will be useful and how you can do it in a way that is helpful, rather than one that shuts people down.

When a judgment continues to arise within you and you simply cannot release it, there may be two reasons to speak. First, speaking it may help you release the judgment and continue to engage in the dialogue. Second, many others may be sensing the same thing and feel unable to speak it themselves. A group can learn a lot about how it approaches certain issues by being willing to share the judgments that surface when the issue is talked about. Just as individual judgments can limit listening, creativity, and learning, judgments that a group shares can limit the group's ability to move creatively in new directions. For example, if the marketing group collectively judges research and development as incapable of understanding the current market trends, it will be almost impossible for them to work together creatively to discover and meet the needs of customers.

Two Kinds of Judgments.

When considering suspending judgments into the group, it is helpful to remember that there are often two types of judgments or thought forms we experience during a dialogue. The first is the yes/no, good/bad, or right/wrong variety. The second form is more complex judgments or assumptions about what is being said in the group. Of these two, the former, the good/bad variety, is death to dialogue. They shut people right up, especially if the person who makes them is in any kind of authority position in the group.

Let's suppose you and I are in a dialogue. You say something that I have an automatic negative reaction to. I notice how strongly I feel about what you say. I just know that what you said is wrong. If I can suspend my judgment long enough—pause—so that I am clear that this is just my reaction, I can bring it into the dialogue as a reaction that I had. I own it. It is my interpretation. No absolute truths here. I am just letting you know that this is how I am reacting, that this is an automatic way I think and feel. I am not forcing my judgments on you. I am open to understanding my own automatic reaction better and I am interested in learning more about your point of view. If I can't suspend my judgment long enough to detach from it in this way, I may strike back in such a way that the dialogue actually shuts down. Here are a few ideas to try the next time you notice yourself having a strong reaction and would like to bring it into the conversation.

TRY THIS: SUSPENDING A JUDGMENT IN DIALOGUE

○   Most of us never give ourselves enough reflection time before we respond, hence the old maxim "take a deep breath and count to ten." But counting to 100 may be more like it, and there are some useful things you can do while you're counting.

○   When you become aware of a strong negative reaction to something being said, pause. Simply sit with your reactions for a while. Notice if your reactions shift as the conversation unfolds.

○   Ask yourself: Where does my strong opinion come from? Who told me that? How did I come to believe it? What are my underlying assumptions about why it is so?

○   After a while, if you still feel strongly about your reaction, see if you can bring it into the conversation. Simply state it as one more perspective on what is being spoken about. Try not to refute what has already been said. Speak with the spirit of "here is another way of looking at it." Put your judgment out there and then let it go. Imagine extending your hand into the group, putting the judgment out there, and then taking your hand off it and remaining palm up and open to being influenced.

More often than not, individuals and groups will keep judgments under wraps because it feels too risky to reveal their thinking process. In the book *Radical Honesty*, Brad Blanton asks us to consider the impact of not speaking what we think and feel regardless of our reasons and the risks, real or perceived. He believes our "withholding strategy" results in compensating behaviors that range from "going to war" to passive-aggressive attacks when old baggage is brought into and acted out in current situations. He wonders if radical honesty could help us move beyond such conflicts. Although we don't expect his suggestions to be taken up by many any time soon, we do see the relevance to the process of developing shared understanding and meaning. Whenever there are scores of things that we cannot or will not speak about, it becomes nearly impossible to really understand what is happening in a whole system because large portions of it are being held invisible. Invisible, but not inoperable. Unspoken judgments can and do shut down a group's ability to engage in conversations about what is important and meaningful.

Here is an exercise meant to help people practice speaking and detaching from their judgments at the same time[3]. While we certainly wouldn't suggest you try this with just anyone, you might consider trying it with someone you have a high degree of trust with. The experience may be very helpful to you in other contexts where judgments are flying around. It strengthens your ability to hear judgments without going into automatic defensive mode.

TRY THIS: DEVELOPING NEUTRALITY IN THE FACE OF JUDGMENT

Sit facing your partner. First one of you speaks every thought that comes into your mind. No editing, no holds barred. Then the other person does the same. It is similar to the exercise of focusing on your breath and watching your own thoughts, only here you get to watch both yours and another person's.

When we learn to experience judgments without shutting down or retaliating, we begin to gain a vantage point where we can see beyond them. Seeing beyond our judgments is essential to reaching levels of understanding beyond those at which the problem was created. Suspension of judgment is fundamental to dialogue. Without a strong intention to focus on its practice, conversations remain superficial or turn into battlegrounds. It is vital that we learn to suspend our judgments both internally and with others if we are to create conversations where the information we need is available to help us learn about and move beyond our current thinking into new territories.

2

IDENTIFICATION AND SUSPENSION

OF ASSUMPTIONS

"Perception is a mirror, not a fact."

—From *Accept This Gift*

"Man is made by his belief.
As he believes, so he is."

—Bhagvad Gita

"The ability to perceive or think differently is more
important than the knowledge gained."

—David Bohm

Assumptions are the rationale behind the snap evaluations we make when we judge. "He is a good person because (assumption)." "That is a great idea because (assumption)." Every decision and action you take is the product of judgments that are grounded in one or more assumptions. Assumptions are the products of years of past experiences and teachings layered with judgments. They are the building blocks we assemble to make sense of our world and support the mental models, or paradigms, we live within. Assumptions are the way we make sense of our relationships, the strategies and policies of our organization, the projects we are involved in. Here are some examples. Assumption: It is not possible to create a culture of collaborative partnership within your department. Action: You don't try. Assumption: If I make my boss successful, I will be rewarded. Action: You put a lot of energy into a project that will mean exceeding short-term goals your boss set even though you think it may be harmful to the organization in the long run. Assumption: You can trust me. Action: You answer my question honestly. Assumption: You cannot trust me. Action: You communicate with me as little as possible. Assumption: I will not understand your point of view. Action: You don't bother explaining the details of your thinking to me.

Individuals and groups that are not aware of their assumptions are like planes on autopilot with no pilot in attendance. As long as things proceed according to plan, with little or no deviation, the journey progresses. But let there be a glitch in the weather pattern or unexpected air traffic in the area, and the same plane may find itself in danger. Leaders who have not devoted significant time to exploring the assumptions that underlie the infrastructures and flow of information in their organizations may find themselves unable to effectively navigate in turbulent times because they don't understand the basic assumptions that are driving the organization.

When assumptions take on the status of fact and truth, listening and learning suffer. People who hold widely differing assumptions because of their upbringing or culture may find themselves engaged in what appear to be irreconcilable conflicts over what is true and correct. Even team members who get along the majority of the time may find themselves in unexpected conflict with one another because their assumptions have come into conflict.

The more proficient you are at identifying assumptions and suspending them in order to enhance listening and learning, the more effective you will be. The same is true for any group, team, or organization. In this chapter, we consider the origins of our assumptions, our relationship to them, how they influence us, and the results we get. We see how our ignorance of them can lead to ineffectiveness, conflict, and inability to learn and think creatively. Finally, we suggest ways for individuals and groups practicing dialogue to work together to identify and suspend their assumptions for the purpose of enhancing learning and effectiveness.

"Assumptions Are Those Things We Think We Know."

The above words were used by a friend who was introducing dialogue to a second-grade class. The phrase is concise and to the point. Because assumptions are those things we think we know, we rarely question them. They are transparent to us because they are part of our identity, built into our thinking and perceiving. Just as fish might be the last to discover water, we are often the last to see our own assumptions, except when that popular saying "When you assume, you make an *ass* of *u* and *me*," becomes all too real and embarrassing. Here is a metaphorical story about assumptions, where they come from, and the impact they have on our day-to-day lives, particularly at work.

A STORY-METAPHOR

Imagine that at birth you are given a set of glasses. These glasses shift the angle at which you perceive everything by a one-degree angle, clockwise. By the time you are a year old, you've forgotten you even wear these glasses. They are part of you. You never take them off. Everything you look at you see through them. They have become an implicit part of how you interpret all data.

You learned to walk and run wearing these glasses. In fact, everything you know how to do incorporates a compensation factor for the one-degree shift in these glasses. As you meet people, you tend to gravitate to those who have the same glasses as you do, who see the world the same. You don't think much about this. It's just the way it is. When you grow up and go to work, you do most of your tasks by yourself, so it's not often a problem when someone sees something differently than you. It doesn't have much impact.

Then, one day your company decides that it can raise productivity and increase its competitive edge in the marketplace by having people work in teams. Suddenly, all the projects you work on are team projects. You're supposed to collaborate and come to consensus on how to go about things.

If this is such a great thing, why do you feel as if you've just arrived in hell? There are people on this team from "who knows where!" No matter how hard you try to explain the lay of the land, they just don't seem to get it. Whenever you try to walk down the same path together, you end up fighting about where you are going, what's the best way to get there, just about everything! You see everything differently.

Your team is not progressing as well as it's supposed to. Things have gotten so bad that your boss has asked someone named Paul to come in and see if he can help you figure out what the problem is. Nobody is particularly hopeful, but you've got to try something. You spend the better part of a day reading a case history about a group and then talking about what you read, how you interpreted it, what conclusions you drew, what assumptions you have about the characters, and, based on those assumptions, what you would do. Paul keeps asking questions such as "Could you tell us what specific statements make you think that 'x' is happening?" and "Could you explain how you interpreted that statement to mean 'y'?"

After a few hours of this conversation, a germ of suspicion begins to play at the corners of your mind. People chose the same statements as data to support their conclusions, yet they interpreted those statements in radically different ways. Some people chose different statements to support the same conclusions. People really saw things differently. You're curious to find out why.

Paul explains, "You've probably forgotten but when you were born, you were given a set of glasses. You've worn them all your lives. What no one ever tells you is that many of you have very different lenses in those glasses. Some of the lenses alter things by a degree or two. Others shift things about ten degrees. Still others add different colors. This alone is not a problem. The problem is that you've forgotten you have these glasses. You think that you are just looking at things the way they are and that the way they are is the same for everyone (your way). The reason you're having so much trouble is because you are all expecting one another to act as though you have the same glasses, but you don't. If you want to work together, you will need to begin asking one another about your different lenses and listening so you can learn to work as partners. If you listen well, you will also discover that there are unique benefits that each of the lenses has, and you can gain the advantages of the various lenses by learning how to 'see' and work with different individuals."

Well, things didn't go from hell to heaven overnight. But, at least now you knew what the underlying source of the problem was and you could begin to work with one another. Now, instead of saying "Joe, you are just plain wrong. How can you look at the data and make a statement like that?" you could ask, "Joe, what is it about the way you are seeing things that we're missing? Can you give us a tour through your thinking process? Help us see this through 'your lens'." Slowly, you began to learn a lot from one another. You've started coming up with better ideas as a group than you had as individuals. This focus on teamwork just might work out after all.

We all have multiple sets of assumption that act as lenses or filters for our perceptions. We began acquiring them at birth and we run everything through them. We even select data based on our assumptions so that, as time goes by, our perceptions tend to validate and reinforce our assumptions. We become more and more sure of the rightness of our worldview. We also forget how these assumptions came to be. They become fact, the way things are. When people with different assumptions meet, both needing to be right about how things are, there are bound to be fireworks.

Assumptions and Conflict

Just as there are no two people who are physically identical, no two people hold the same assumptions about how life works. Even children brought up in the same family environment can grow up with very different assumptions about life. This diversity is further magnified when people are from different cultures.

It is not so much the different assumptions that create problems, as the need to be right. The stability of our worldview depends on our assumptions being held as facts. Therefore, we will tend to judge as wrong any data or ideas that deviate from ours. The ability to suspend such judgments and take up a more neutral position, where we do not need to be right, allows us to begin to see our assumptions more clearly. Once you begin to identify your assumptions and trace the experiences and thinking that led to them, you will also begin to loosen your hold on your certainties and create openings for developing new levels of understanding with others. How do you start?

We've all had the experience of attending a meeting and then discovering later in conversation that there was a wide divergence of understanding about what occurred and what the appropriate course of action is. What is happening here? Selective listening? Different interpretations? Yes, combined with an assumption that we all hear and see the same thing. We may all share a similar thinking process, but the output is often vastly different.

Chris Argyris developed a useful tool for becoming more aware of our thinking and working to understand the origins of many misunderstandings and conflicts. It's called the "ladder of inference." An adaptation of one version of the Ladder of Inference in *The Fifth Discipline Fieldbook,* by Peter Senge, et al., is shown below.

Ladder of Inference

We couldn't have been at the same event.

Take Action

Adopt Beliefs

Draw Conclusions

Make Assumptions

Select Data & Add Meaning
[personal & cultural]

Data Pool

The ladder is a graphic representation of our thinking process. Whenever we enter a context or an experience, such as a meeting or other conversation, we enter at the bottom of the ladder and move upward. The speed with which we climb is incredible. It takes no more than a nanosecond to go from bottom to top. In fact, most of us are only aware of the top of the ladder. Everything below the "Take Action" rung is usually below the level of consciousness. We gather data, add meaning, make assumptions, draw conclusions, make decisions, and take action.

Example:

Take Action	I'm not going to give Sally responsibility for any key tasks.
Adopt Beliefs	Good team players adhere to norms and come to meetings on time.
Draw Conclusions	Sally is not going to be a good team player.
Make Assumptions	Sally thinks this meeting is unimportant.
Add Meaning (personal & cultural)	Being late is not acceptable behavior.
Select Data (personal & cultural)	Sally came to the meeting 30 minutes late. She didn't say why.

In the course of one meeting or conversation, we may climb the ladder hundreds of times. Everyone present is doing the same thing, climbing their ladder. And there the similarity ends.

Imagine the combined impact of people moving up their very different ladders around similar data. One possible graphic presentation is shown on the next page.

Imagine each rung of the ladder is a traffic circle that you enter and from which you emerge going in any number of different directions, depending on which exit you choose. At each rung on the ladder, you enter another traffic circle. By the time you and another reach the tops of your respective ladders, having been through multiple divergent circles, and arrive at decisions about which action to take, you could swear the two of you didn't even participate in the same meeting.

How I saw it

How you saw it

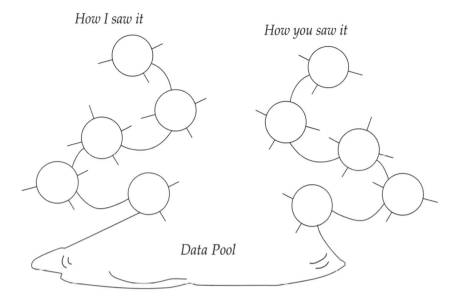

Data Pool

Moving Up Different Ladders

Becoming aware of how this process works allows people to work together to understand the thinking that led them to different positions and actions. This can alleviate tensions and open the way for creating new alternatives. It is also a key ingredient to understanding how decisions get made in groups and organizations. The next time you find yourself with a vastly different interpretation of events than a colleague, try using the ladder to gain some clarity. The most effective way to do this is to reveal your own thinking process and ask about the other person's. Remember to practice suspending judgment as you go.

"Walk-Talk" Conflicts

Shared assumptions glue us together. Opposing assumptions can rip us apart. Sometimes they even come in sets that simultaneously push and pull at us. When these divergent sets of assumptions show up, confusion is common, and, over time, demoralization, anger, and distrust often follow. Working with these conflicting assumptions is a high-leverage activity for enhancing alignment and energy within a relationship, a group, or an organization. It is one of the most power-ful ways for anyone to model alignment and integrity.

Examples:
- ○ "Team success is dependent on members supporting one another," paired with "People who can't swim on their own are probably not fit to be on this team!"
- ○ "We want all our employees to have balance in their work and family lives," paired with "Hard work and commitment to your job are valued here. If you are unwilling to put in 60 hours a week, it is unlikely that you will move much further in this organization."

Get the idea? You've probably got many other examples, from per-sonal and work life. These pairs are challenging because we have rea-sons for valuing both statements. When we peel back our thinking to reveal the supporting assumptions beneath each side, we find ourselves agreeing with them all to one degree or another. Of course, when we try to act in accordance with both sets of assumptions simultaneously, we often hear things like "She doesn't walk her talk." If we're leaders of a group, we can send double messages, which at the very best cause confusion and, at the worst, outright distrust.

Conflicting assumptions are at the foundation of some of our great-est dilemmas. As uncomfortable as they are to talk about, inquiring into them creates the potential for greater trust. By working through our discomfort and engaging in these conversations, we *can* learn from his-tory, see patterns that are no longer useful, and move beyond them.

Assumptions and Learning

A *true story*. A group of 17 managers sits in a follow-up dialogue ses-sion. In three hours, the director of the group will go to a board meet-ing where she will present the department's plan, objectives, and budget for the next year. People begin to speak about their annoy-ance with the procedure of compiling information that goes into the plan. One person says that they just threw together some numbers because "after all, the director will just put in what she thinks is appropriate anyway, so why go to a lot of trouble?" Others nod their heads. The director becomes very agitated. She reveals that she has taken the numbers as accurate and used them as the basis for the plan she will submit. The group is uniformly shocked and dismayed. The numbers will not realistically reflect what is possible and yet the group will be held accountable. (Their actions were based on assumptions from experience with past directors.) The director announces that she will go to the meeting but will not present the plan as final, so that there will be time to redo it. The group breathes a sigh of relief. There are offers to help put together the numbers that will be needed.

The group in this story discovered the power of what Chris Argyris calls "double loop learning,"[4] that is, of surfacing and working with assumptions before moving to important decisions. Double loop learning gets to the causal level of things, the thinking behind the strategies, decisions, and actions that produce results. Its counterpart, single loop learning, is more like a thermostat that automatically adjusts in one direction or the other based on programming. Too hot—cool. Too cold—heat.

Have you ever thought of a thermostat as capable of learning? Even with the latest in fuzzy logic chips, computers can only learn, or correct, within a bounded area. Single loop learning is based on automatic

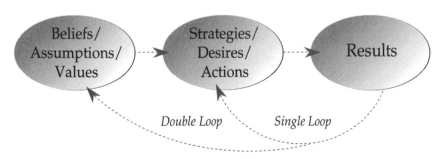

Single and Double Loop Learning

memory response. The complexity may vary, but it will always be pre-programmed. Sound familiar? Most of our responses are single loop responses.

Crisis management and fire fighting are all about single loop learning. If you and the group you are in are suffering from "repetitive problem syndrome," inquiring into the assumptions that drive your decisions (and produce the results) will get you closer to the root cause. Double loop learning moves you beyond surface signals to the assumptions and intentions that created your impulse to act. Unless you do this work, it is likely that you will continue to make decisions driven by the same assumptions and, even if your decisions appear to be different, you will probably get similar results. Double loop learning creates the potential for significant change and innovative problem solving.

So why don't we focus more attention on this high-leverage activity? Primarily, it is hard to get a handle on our assumptions. We don't particularly like to identify assumptions because we are accustomed to making facts of our assumptions. To identify a thought as an assumption is to somehow loosen our grip and acknowledge that what we think we know is based on interpretation of data rather than on some absolute truth about the characteristics of a process, person, or group. The word *assumption* implies a certain degree of probability and less than total certainty. In a culture where being right is highly valued, conversation about assumptions can be a risky business. This is one reason learning and a need to be right are incompatible. Learning requires a willingness to release some degree of certainty in order to allow new ideas and ways of thinking to emerge. We must be willing to shift our focus from amassing evidence to creating opportunities to "discover new lands by seeing through new eyes."[5]

Another reason it can be difficult for us to identify assumptions is because of the disconnection described in the metaphorical story earlier. We have forgotten that we are wearing glasses and that they impact our results. David Bohm often pointed to this disconnection between our thoughts and the results we obtain. One of the reasons he was so committed to dialogue was that he believed its practice could bridge the gap and bring us "real-time" awareness of this relationship. He described this awareness as "proprioception of thought." Here's a story that explains what he meant. As you read, notice elements that may seem familiar: experiences you've had or witnessed that are similar in interpersonal relationships, teams, your organization, or your community.

A *true story*. Dorothy had an injury that resulted in loss of proprioception. Proprioception means "self-perception." It is a term used to describe the physiological ability we all have to know how our bodies are oriented in space at any given moment. For example, I don't have to turn around and look to see that my bottom is sitting on a pillow on this chair. If I decide to lift my right hand from the keyboard and wave it around behind my head, I know where it is located, how it is moving, and that it is my hand without having to visually see it. That is because I have proprioceptive capacity. This story is about what happens when you lose this ability.

Occasionally, Dorothy would awaken from dreaming in the middle of the night. One such night she awoke very suddenly. She was disoriented. She felt a hand on her arm. She was being attacked! She lashed out at her attacker and hit herself! She struggled more, striking out repeatedly and still continuing to be beaten. When she finally awoke totally, she found herself alone. There was no one there. And she was bruised and battered.

Of course you can guess what happened. Because Dorothy did not have proprioception, she didn't know that the hand that she felt when she came suddenly out of her dream was her own, that the person she struck out at in fear and confusion was herself. Because she lacked proprioception, she ended up badly bruised and battered because she did not have the ability to self-perceive.

What experiences have you had or witnessed that are similar? When has the left hand unknowingly created disaster for the right hand? When have you shot yourself in the foot because you could not or would not see what was happening? Suspend judgment. We all have stories. Here's a rather personal, though not uncommon, one that has many corollaries in business relationships.

Rachel decided she wanted to be in a committed romantic relationship. In short order, she found herself in one. Time passed. Rachel began to notice she was unsure about a number of things, things that didn't seem like good signs. She noticed patterns that seemed familiar and deadening. The red flags were flying.

But, did Rachel take note? Of course not. She just worked harder, applied herself more. Then, a few months later when her partner tried to bring up some fears and concerns, did she listen? Of course not. She reassured. She turned concerns into possibilities. She was going to make a treasure out of this relationship.

What happened? Eventually the whole thing broke down and what had been present all along became visible. No, that's not accurate. It had always been visible, for anyone who was willing to look and see. Not Rachel. She was too busy creating.

Rachel created a relationship within a relationship. She ignored signals about what was going on. She reinforced her ideas about what was true. She looked for evidence to support her perceptions; where she couldn't find enough, she manufactured some. And she kept focusing on what she wanted. When the illusion could no longer shut out the power of reality, the illusion blew up. Then, for a period of time, Rachel pointed her finger firmly outward toward the source of the failure—her partner.

Rachel thought herself into a relationship, continued to reinforce its success for over a year, in the face of evidence to the contrary, and then when she finally had to acknowledge the failure, was quick to say "I didn't do that. This is mostly a result of my ex-partner's shortcomings." In retrospect, Rachel did see what was going on. She did take responsibility. But not in the moment, only in hindsight.

Rachel did not have proprioception mostly because she didn't want to see what was occurring. There is no dearth of similar stories in our organizations, communities, and families. Decisions are made that create value in one place with devastating consequences in another. For example, research and development continues to feed money into a project that sales knows is a dead end. Without proprioception, parts act independently with no regard or awareness of the consequences of their actions. The health of the whole often suffers, and the person or organization may find itself in precarious circumstances.

As long as we focus our attention on single parts or functions without developing a sense of how they relate to the whole, we will continue to unintentionally create results that do not serve us. This realization lies at the core of systems thinking. In reality, there are no separate, unrelated, independent parts. *Interdependent* is the appropriate word. Our sciences tell us this. Our marketplaces confirm it. And most important, in our gut, we know that all our experiences are the product of relationships; we are the sum total of our relationships. Individuals, teams, departments, divisions—we are all integrated parts of whole systems which, in turn, are parts of larger wholes, all irreducible. We believe this is one reason why the impulse to dialogue is showing up in so many places—for the increasing calls for shared responsibility and accountability.

Making Assumptions Visible

Proprioception requires the ability to identify your assumptions and the thinking behind your choices and actions. A first step in identifying assumptions is to learn how to notice the "lenses" you wear. There are questions and tools you can use to help unearth your assumptions, yet it is other people who will prove to be your greatest resource. Because I look from a different vantage point, it is frequently easier for me to hear an assumption you are making. You can do the same for me. We can help each other walk up and down our ladders of inference. Below are some useful tips for noticing your assumptions. Use them by yourself or create a "hunting buddy" and help each other track down the game.

TRY THIS: ASSUMPTION-HUNTING TIPS

To hunt assumptions, you need two things: the desire to find them, and perseverance and experience gained over time. When you hunt for game, you look for tracks, droppings, grazing patterns, signs that tell you game has been or is present. There are also signals that alert us to the presence of assumptions. For the next seven days, choose one group of signs and set the intention each day to notice these responses in yourself. You might even jot down a note each time you "make a sighting." Then, at the end of the day, before you go to bed, list the possible assumptions you think you've discovered.

You notice yourself making statements like:

- ○ That's just the way it is. (What is it about the world that makes you say this?)
- ○ If . . . then . . . (What is it that connects these two things?)
- ○ You can't do . . . (Why? What will happen or not happen?)
- ○ Are you nuts? That's the silliest thing I've ever heard. (Why would you think you were nuts if you had this idea?)

Internal dialogue with yourself

- ○ It won't do any good. I'll just keep it to myself. (Why won't it do any good? Why not say something? Why keep it to yourself? What will happen if you speak up?)
- ○ We all know how "so and so" is anyway. (What is it we know? What assumptions do we make about "so and so"? Who are "we"?)
- ○ It's never worked before. (Why do you think this is?)
- ○ I'm not getting into that one! (Why not? What do you think will happen? If it did, what do you suppose might be the reason for the response?)

Responding angrily to someone's opinion

Sometimes it's not until we rub up against another differing opinion that we discover we have a conflicting assumption. If you disagree strongly with someone, ask yourself why you have such a strong reaction. What is it about what this person said that triggered me? Is it what the person said? How the person said it?

What values or "shoulds" did the person violate? What assumptions must this person have to believe this? What opposing assumptions do you have?

Feelings of discomfort or fear

These responses often point to an assumption that there will be some negative consequence to an action, a statement, or an event. Where does this assumption come from? What data is it based on? Is this firsthand experience? What stories have you been told that reinforce your feelings?

A conclusion without apparent data

"In this financial environment, we won't be able to accomplish the task." Whenever you notice a cause-and-effect statement, ask what assumptions may lie within it. The example given might imply numerous assumptions: 1) We don't have money for this project. 2) All the possible alternatives are too expensive. 3) We've considered all options. 4) Cost cutting has created a morale problem that will undermine success.

Meeting people from different races, cultures, genders, sexual orientations

Notice your response when you meet people who are different from you. How does the difference affect your perception? What do you focus on? What makes you comfortable/uncomfortable? What assumptions do you notice yourself making? What questions come up for you? Can you identify the assumptions behind your questions?

Noticing assumptions about specific people

Name three people with whom you had some interaction today. For each person, list at least five assumptions that you have about that person, about what makes the person tick, what is important to him or her. Then consider how your assumptions influence the way you interact with that person.

Suspending Assumptions

If assumptions cause such problems, why don't we just take off our "glasses" and see without the distortions, additions, and subtractions? One of the paradoxes that confronts us is that our glasses both help us navigate our world and limit what it is possible for us to see. The same could be said of any structure we create to organize our reality: It is both useful and limiting. Just as with our assumptions.

An alternative to giving up your assumptions is to practice suspending them. Just as with suspension of judgment, this does not mean to stop having them. It would not be possible. When you practice suspending your assumptions, "hanging them out in front," you immediately get two big payoffs. First, you make your assumptions available for inquiry. When one or more people do this, the thinking and shared meanings within the group that are influencing decisions, actions, and results are clarified. The potential for better decisions and results takes a giant leap. Second, just as with judgments, when you "hang an assumption out in front," you simultaneously create a degree of separation between yourself and it, just enough distance to loosen your hold and begin to listen to others without reacting defensively. When two or more people can identify and suspend their assumptions, they gain the ability to "share meanings without the urge to defend them or conform to those of others."[6] Then, the creation of collaborative partnerships can move from wishful thinking to reality.

Teams that practice identifying and suspending assumptions soon discover which assumptions have served them well and which have not. They learn how to bridge the paradox of individuality and responsibility to and for the group—a key capability for creating organizational cultures and communities based on collaborative partnerships, where individual freedom is coupled with shared responsibility.

One of the most powerful exercises for uncovering and suspending assumptions both one-on-one and in groups is a variation based on the lefthand column work developed by Chris Argyris. "Lefthand column" refers to those thoughts, assumptions, and feelings that are present in our minds when we are conversing with others, but that we choose to not express for a variety of reasons. Distinguishing between what is said and what is not said in a conversation (or about an issue or a project) opens the way for inquiry into the assumptions behind undiscussed thoughts and feelings and their impact on the relationship and the results obtained. Learning to include some of this information in the conversation creates opportunities for expanded understanding and breaking out of old and often unwanted patterns of communicating. An adaptation of this exercise, along with some guidelines for suspending undiscussed assumptions into the conversation, can be found in the Appendix.

Shared Assumptions, Culture, and Organizational Learning

In the same way that individuals share sets of assumptions, so too do entire groups, organizations, communities, and nations. When we gather with other like-minded people and form collectives that hold the same values and behaviors as good and true, we create cultures based on collective agreements. These cultures reinforce the values and behaviors we choose to focus on. As time passes, the stories, values, and beliefs take on the status of universal truths. We look out at the world through these collective lenses of truth and all our decisions and actions align with and reinforce them. It doesn't occur to most of us to even think about asking where these guideposts of our culture originated. Cultures and the people who live within them become self-referencing and perpetuating loops. There is power here, and danger.

We have ample historical examples of the power of collective alignment around meaning. Unfortunately, many of them are demonstrations of alignment around separation, hate, and destruction: Hitler and the Nazi movement; the witch hunts of the Middle Ages; institutionalized racism and sexism. Yet our judgments about what we have created in the past do not alter the truth of the tremendous power for alignment inherent in shared meaning. The question then becomes how we intentionally create shared meaning that honors and integrates diversity and leads to healthy whole systems capable of collaboration and partnership.

We must begin to apply the skills we learn as individuals to a collective level. This is what the group practice of dialogue is all about. It intentionally creates conversations where we can speak about what has importance and meaning for us. By inquiring into our assumptions and listening for the shared meanings that emerge, we gain a vantage point from which we can observe ourselves in relationship to one another and the larger systems we are part of. As we become better at seeing the continuum of relationship between our experience, our thinking, actions, and results, we also gain the awareness needed to be more conscious participants. We can climb back into the pilot seat, turn off the autopilot, and navigate skillfully when needed.

When a group of people is able to attain this level of self-awareness, the payoff is tremendous. If you consider yourself a leader at any level of your organization, one of the most valuable activities you can engage in is conversation about the assumptions that underlie the structures and flow of information within that organization, the assumptions that drive all strategies, planning, and decision-making activities. Becoming aware of assumptions about the purpose of the business such as how business is conducted, how success is defined and rewarded, how information flow is directed, how the company relates internally and with the marketplace, how internal culture impacts relationships with customers may be the most powerful learning activity to which you as a leader can devote yourself.

Learning is about becoming more fluid and creative in your response to your environment. It requires the ability to reflect on your assumptions and make conscious choices about which ones serve you and which ones are incoherent or inconsistent with your purposes. The objective is to maintain a core identity while creatively evolving in relationship with your environment. It is no different for an organization. The degree of complexity may be more elaborate, but the principles and skills are the same. Dialogue is a powerful practice field for developing these capabilities.

In Closing, A Reminder

Whether at the individual, group, or organizational level, when we find ourselves in conflict with others, it may be time to suspend our judgments, open our listening, and walk up and down the ladder of inference together. When we think we have a handle on our goals and methods, yet continue to suffer unexpected consequences, we may be experiencing the result of our limited vision and a disconnection between our thinking and our actions. As the poet Rumi reminds us, it may be time to take another look at the assumptions and thinking behind our decisions and actions.

WHO MAKES THESE CHANGES?

> *Who makes these changes?*
> *I shoot an arrow right.*
> *It lands left.*
> *I ride after a deer and find myself*
> *chased by a hog.*
> *I plot to get what I want*
> *and end up in prison.*
> *I dig a pit to trap others*
> *and fall in.*
>
> *I should be suspicious*
> *of what I want*
> [and of what I think I know]

—Rumi[7]

3

LISTENING

"I think therefore I am ."

—Descartes

"I have been listened to therefore I am."

—Anonymous

"Dialogue is not just talking with one another.
More than speaking, it is a special way of listening to one
another—listening without resistance . . . it is listening
from a stand of being willing to be influenced."

—Sarita Chawla[7]

"To be able to really listen, one should abandon or put aside all prejudices . . .
When you are in a receptive state of mind, things can be easily understood . . .
But unfortunately, most of us listen through a screen of resistance.
We are screened with prejudices, whether religious or spiritual,
psychological or scientific; or, with daily worries, desires and fears.
And with these fears for a screen, we listen.
Therefore, we listen really to our own noise, our own sound,
not to what is being said."

—Krishnamurti
First and Last Freedom

It is nearly impossible to find words that will do justice to the role of listening in any conversation, and most particularly dialogue. Listening is the doorway through which we allow the world to enter. How we listen, to what and to whom we listen, and the assumptions we listen through all frame our perception of reality. Listening may be the single most powerful creative act we perform; we listen and create reality based on what we hear in each moment.

In group dialogue, the power of our listening increases exponentially because of collective listening and creation of shared meaning. With such power available, it becomes important to ask ourselves about the way we are listening. Are we listening from our past history, from our prejudices (prejudgments), from what we already know to be true and right, or from curiosity and a desire to expand our horizons, to see from new perspectives?

In this chapter we'll see how important listening is to creating collaborative partnerships, developing shared meaning, and participating in shared leadership. We will explore three dimensions of listening essential to dialogue, the relationship between suspension of judgment and listening, and the role listening plays in collective intelligence.

Listening, Collaborative Partnerships, and Shared Meaning

Without the ability to listen, collaborative partnerships cannot be born or sustained. Listening is an absolute necessity for the health of any whole, be it a work group, an organization, a family or a community. Consider our physical bodies, a prime example of a highly functional collaborative partnership. Every cell listens to its environment. If our bodies were not constantly listening, without the lapse of a single microsecond, we would die. When a part of the body loses the ability to listen for its relationship with the whole, disease such as cancer is often the result. A group of cells become a body unto themselves without regard for how their unlimited growth affects the health of the whole. The result is often death.

Without listening, our bodies would die. Without listening, dialogue cannot exist. In the absence of listening, the streams of meaning that move among a group of people become disconnected and often invisible. Individuals and subgroups within the larger whole begin to behave as if they were unrelated fragments. Collective learning and aligned action disappear from view.

Three Levels of Listening

For groups to develop collective intelligence and shared meaning, individual members must learn to listen across three dimensions simultaneously. First, you listen to others, to identify what you see as important and to expand your own understanding. Second, you listen to yourself, to your internal conversation and your own voice as you speak. Third, you listen for the collective themes, for the shared meaning the group is continuously creating and for new streams of meaning that may want to emerge. We'll consider each one in turn.

Listening to Another

Consider the impact of listening or its absence on interpersonal relationships. Have you ever met anyone who didn't want to be listened to? Who among us wouldn't like to feel that another person might stand beside us and look out at the world through our eyes, even if only temporarily. When we listen to others in this way, we acknowledge the value of their perspectives to a whole view.

Listening to another person is a powerful act. It is an act of respect, of valuing. Conversely, not listening is often experienced as disrespect.

> *There is a passage in the children's book* The Velveteen Rabbit *where a very tattered horse tells the newer rabbit how "love makes you real."*
> *"What is REAL?" asked the rabbit.*
> *"REAL isn't how you are made," said the skin horse. "It's a thing that happens to you. When a child loves you for a long, long time, not just to play with, but REALLY loves you, then you become REAL."*[8]

Substituting the word *listening* for *love* gives a flavor for the power of listening in relationship with another. When we listen with a willingness to hear what is real and important to another, both of us become more real. Listening adds color and life to our relationships. Not listening bleaches and flattens them, until they virtually disappear.

Among the most frequent complaints heard from people, whether in professional or personal life, are: "No one is listening. Sometimes I feel invisible in this group, like no one hears anything I say. Why bother speaking up? No one wants to hear what I've got to say anyway."

Why is no one listening? "No time. Don't want to hear. Judgments. Feelings of helplessness. I've got my own problems. If I really listen, they'll want more." Actually, from an early age we receive messages to not listen. "Pretend you didn't hear that." "We don't listen to those kinds of statements around here." "Don't listen to him/her."

TRY THIS: LISTENING TO OTHERS

o   When you are openly listening to another, what characterizes your listening? What things are important for you to be willing and able to listen fully to another? What behaviors do you display when you do listen fully?

o   Think about a time when you were listening fairly well, and then you stopped listening, or the quality of your listening changed. You became skeptical or your attention began to wander. What happened? What occurred that may have caused the change? What stopped your listening? What closed the door?

o   Recall a time when you were simply unable to listen to another person. You may have actually gotten up and left the room or you were looking at the person and hearing his words, but it was as if the words were bouncing off an invisible barrier in front of you, and there was no way they were going to get through. What things activated the barrier?

Reflecting on these questions always brings one face to face with the second level of listening.

Listening to Self

Internal conversation often makes it difficult to create and maintain a focus on what the other person is saying. It is often filled with judgments, doubts, preparation for what to say next, thinking up rebuttals, or wondering how much longer this is going to take. Perhaps no one speaks more directly and eloquently to this phenomenon than Krishnamurti.

Listen . . .

I do not know if you have ever examined how you listen,
it doesn't matter to what,
whether to a bird, to the wind in the leaves, to the rushing waters,
or how you listen in a dialogue with yourself,
to your conversation in various relationships
with your intimate friends, your wife or husband...

If we try to listen we find it extraordinarily difficult,
because we are always projecting our opinions and ideas,
our prejudices, our background, our inclinations, our impulses;
when they dominate we hardly listen at all to what is being said ...

In that state there is no value at all.
One listens and therefore learns,
only in a state of attention, a state of silence,
in which this whole background is in abeyance, is quiet;
then, it seems to me,
it is possible to communicate.

Real communication can only take place where there is
silence.

Krishnamurti

To listen deeply and fully to another requires focused attention and internal silence, to listen from a position of neutrality and detachment with a willingness to consider all perspectives. In many ways, this runs counter to our cultural experiences.

Consider that as we were growing up most of us were taught listening as a defensive skill. Listening was about getting clear on what was expected of us so we could remain in the good graces of authority figures.

When we were unsuccessful, it usually meant trouble. As adults, many of the dynamics within organizations, communities, and families continue to reinforce this kind of listening. We listen to discover what will help us fit in, keep our job, learn about how to deliver what someone else wants. We listen to figure out who has the power. We listen to anticipate possible danger.

Defensive listening can be a highly developed and tuned skill, honed by fear and an instinct for survival. It is also limiting. When we are fearful, we naturally strive to separate ourselves from whatever it is we fear. We build walls and peer over them. Listening becomes defensive information-gathering about the adversary. We use our active listening skills. We do perception checks, we paraphrase, with the goal of gathering accurate information. We might even invite our adversary to lunch. But never do we let that person beyond the walls, into our interior, into our operations center, not willingly. This is, after all, a matter of survival.

We have become accomplished at listening from a position of competition, of win/lose, of "it's me or you." Listening from this vantage point, our judgments become very important. We must be able to analyze incoming data very quickly, sorting for good/bad, useful/garbage. A capacity for rapid-fire judgment, decision, and action can be crucial to survival.

Now imagine a different scenario, where the focus is on learning and creating collaborative partnerships.

Example. We are members of a team sitting in a dialogue circle. I'm being asked to listen as a partner. This has been described to me as "listening as if we are all interrelated parts of a whole. Listening with the recognition that our individual well-being and the well-being of the whole are inextricably interconnected and are equal priorities. Listening as if what each person has to say, the view through her eyes, is important to my health."

So, I try. But the judgments simply will not stop coming. Judgments about whether a certain idea is good/ bad, useful/silly. Judgments about how someone speaks, how he didn't use the best words to describe something, how she forgot to include something important, how they're uninformed. It just goes on almost nonstop.

> Sometimes people say things I strongly disagree with. And, you want
> me to listen for wisdom here? Then give me some wisdom to listen
> for, not these crazy, off-the-wall, impractical ideas! Help! We're not
> getting anywhere here.

Not so easy, is it? It would be wonderful to be able to simply stop
our internal conversations, to quiet our internal judges, and then turn
them back on when we wanted them. But even people who have spent
their lives in a discipline of seeking inner silence, such as Buddhist
monks and contemplatives, find this difficult. Developing some degree
of mastery in suspending judgment and remaining open and willing
to listen is essential to discovering new possibilities in situations where
this often seems impossible.

TRY THIS: SUSPENSION OF JUDGMENT AND LISTENING

○ Decide that in your next meeting you will notice each time
  your judgments stop you from listening to another person.
  Simply notice.

○ We all know people in our work groups who are more difficult to listen to than others. The next time you are in a conversation with one of these people, make a point of first
  noticing when the judgment arises that stops your listening.
  Then make a very conscious choice to take a deep breath and
  continue to listen. See how long you can listen before the next
  judgment comes up. Take another breath and continue to listen. Notice what happens. Record any changes in the quality
  of your listening, in what you are able to hear.

○ The following exercise comes from our colleague, Sarita
  Chawla. She calls this a practice of "listening without resistance," and we are indebted to her for allowing its inclusion
  here.[10]

Listening without Resistance
Listening without defensiveness, that is, listening from a stance
of a willingness to be influenced by what is said. It does not

involve any requirement that one actually evidence this willingness by being influenced. Rather, one enters the dialogue with a
receptiveness to being influenced and changes only if that receptiveness leads one to willingly change. This requires temporarily
letting go of attachments both for and against your own and others' positions. This provides a space where thoughts themselves
can be examined and can creatively influence one another.

Defensiveness will sometimes show up in the body. Sense if
there is any tightening, change in breathing, stream of judgments,
or other sensations. Noticing them will help to dissolve them with
practice.

Practice (Duration: daily, for one month)

○ Imagine that you can invent an internal separation in your-
    self. Divide yourself into two persons, one who acts/reacts in
    life and one who just observes without judgment.

○ Using the questions below, begin to observe yourself in life.
    Observe quietly, with as little judgment as possible. Notice
    your internal states as well as what you show the world.

○ At the end of each day, scan through your day and note what
    happened and how you reacted. You may want to write notes
    so you can begin to notice patterns.

Questions

○ How effectively are you able to listen without resistance? How
    do you know that?

○ What emotions, reactions, and opinions arise when you sense
    resistance to what someone is saying?

○ Where do those resistances show up in your body?

○ What is the quality of listening when you do not resist?

○ What new understanding do you have of people and situa-
    tions when you listen without resistance?

○ What are you learning?

Listening for Collective Shared Meaning

Most of us have weak collective-listening muscles. We are not used to listening for collective themes or patterns in a conversation. We tend to listen like the blind men who found themselves positioned around an elephant. One had hold of the trunk, another the tail, and a third one the leg. Each described the reality they were touching as if its totality was simply a large version of the part they were in contact with. Of course, each described a very different reality. They did not listen to one another to see what reality might fit all three of their descriptions. The blind men were "listening" at the individual level. At this level there are two primary assumptions: 1) What I see, feel, hear, and perceive is representative of the whole, and 2) If someone else describes something different, they are talking about a different and separate entity.

Listening for collective meaning assumes that what we each feel, see, hear, and perceive is one window on a common reality. If we listen for the interrelationships among all the perceptions, the whole will become visible. We understand that we are each touching different parts of an entity that possesses a tail, a trunk, a large leg, and no doubt a number of other aspects, which when seen collectively are an elephant.

Listening for the collective view is not better than listening to others or ourselves. We need all the individual perceptions of members of our group, team, or family. It is these multiple views that add depth and substance to the whole image. When we listen using all three levels simultaneously, the interrelationships appear and the whole elephant is revealed.

Many of our organizations today are beginning to flex and develop collective listening muscles. One example of this is the increasing interest in systems thinking. Systems thinking is grounded in collective listening.

Example. A team is convened to solve a repeating problem. A series of individual events are disturbing upper management. Late deliveries have increased. The time for a salesperson to close a sale has increased. Billing errors have increased. Sales are off. Customer service staff is complaining of overload. Each department—sales, marketing, customer service — has a different idea about what the problem is and what they need to do to resolve it. In our example, management puts more pressure on sales by increasing the sales targets and encouraging them to make a greater effort. Sales responds. Not only do they need to make up for lost customers, but their bonuses depend on making more sales. Sales is even making sales that may be difficult to deliver. Service is irritated, because they feel that they have to clean up when sales are pushed through inappropriately; however, management is really pushing for new sales, so they decide they had better just keep quiet and do the best they can.

From your more neutral position as reader, you can probably see how all the efforts being made are interrelated and are in fact reinforcing the problems of all three groups. Each group is listening from its individual perspective and thinking they will fix the problem by working harder and smarter within their separate area. Sales is contributing to the problems of service, which are, in turn, resulting in lower customer service rates and loss of sales, which is pushing sales to do more of what they have been doing, and so on — a self-reinforcing loop. Only when they begin to listen collectively for the interrelationships among the events will they begin to perceive the whole reality and become able to work to create a healthier system.

Einstein spoke with wisdom when he said "no problem can be solved at the same level at which it was created." Many problems or dysfunctions stem from operating out of the assumption that parts, people, or departments are separate and unrelated. We may be diverse and distinct, but we are also interrelated. When we try to solve problems listening only with our individual ear, looking no further than our own back fences, we are addressing the problem at the same level of disconnected thinking it emerged from. When we begin listening for the collective meaning, expanded understanding and new possibilities become available.

Listening for shared meaning can also inform us about the culture of our organization or work group. It can reveal subtler webs of collectively held assumptions. If you want to learn about the norms and assumptions that guide your group's decisions and actions, listen for:

- ○   how people are rewarded;
- ○   the priorities that repeatedly gain the group's attention;
- ○   how the group spends its time;
- ○   whose presence is necessary for the group to function well and why;
- ○   how decisions are made; and
- ○   what the undiscussables, or taboo topics, are.

If you listen to the group's conversation and behaviors over time, you will begin to get a picture of the worldview or thinking that sits beneath the surface and drives the group's strategies and results. One way to explore this is to imagine yourselves as anthropologist observers who have been asked to write a report on the culture of your group based on its behaviors and conversations. What would your report say?

As a general rule of thumb, if you want to know what people believe about how something happens, if you observe them doing it, you'll be looking at their assumptions in action. What we believe is reflected in what we do and don't do, what we say and don't say. Here is an example of a conversation that took place at the end of a weekend dialogue. By listening for collective themes and patterns and observing our actions, we discovered a number of assumptions the group had about how intimacy and community are created.

A *reflection*. The weekend has been volatile and, for some, traumatic. There has been pain and disruption, talking it through, forgiveness, and mending. It is Sunday morning. Reflection time. Someone asks, "What exactly is it that we've been exploring this weekend?" The question asks us to focus on our collective listening. In the next few moments the elephant we have all been groping is unveiled. It is intimacy. We have been talking and acting out stories and assumptions about intimacy; how intimacy is formed; the roles of pain and forgiveness, separation, and reconnection. We begin to look more closely at the assumptions about intimacy and community reflected in our words and actions. Statements like "There's nothing like a crisis to pull people together" take on new meaning. Did we actually create crisis to experience intimacy and community? Perhaps. We begin to look at the connection between our own willingness to be open to another's pain. It seems easier (perhaps safer?) to be open if the other is in pain (perhaps they are temporarily less dangerous?). We've all heard stories about how separation creates pain. We begin to wonder what assumptions we may have about pain being a doorway to connection and how they might affect our behavior. We leave the weekend with many questions.

Collective listening leads to revelations and new questions. Each dialogue is like an act in a play. When we listen for the collective meaning, we reveal the plot we are enacting. Often there are many levels, some more subtly veiled than others. By becoming aware of our stories about how things work, we begin the process of reclaiming our ability to rewrite the plots, reshape the cultures of our organizations, communities, and families. We listen for what is and we listen for what may be wanting to emerge. We begin to intentionally participate in the process of self-organization that sustains our core identity in relationship with a continuously changing environment. *Listening for collective shared meaning informs us about who we are together. Listening for emergent threads of meaning speaks to us of who we are becoming together.*

TRY THIS: LISTENING FOR COLLECTIVE MEANING

- ○ The next time you are in a conversation where people are speaking from different and seemingly disconnected perspectives, ask yourself: What common reality could all these people be looking at? What assumptions might they share about what they see? What assumptions or lenses are creating this diversity of perspectives?

- ○ When you are in a dialogue, stop occasionally and ask: What are we hearing with our collective ear? What shared meaning or reality is our collective conversation revealing to us? What is the elephant we each have a piece of? What story are we acting out?

○   Ask the question: If there were one voice speaking here, what
would that voice be saying?

(There are a few selected exercises in the Appendix at the back of the
book that can be used to help groups heighten their awareness of listening and get a taste of how people listen when they are collectively
co-creating a conversation.)

4

INQUIRY AND REFLECTION

"Socrates changed an earlier method of discourse—designed for arguing and winning an argument—into a method for learning. And in the process he created the quintessential model for questioning and learning in western civilization."

—Sally J. Goerne
Chaos and the Evolving Ecological Universe

"In physics, reflection on the meanings of a wide range of experimental facts and theoretical problems and paradoxes eventually led Einstein to new insights concerning the meaning of space, time, and matter, which are at the foundation of the theory of relativity."

—David Bohm
Unfolding Meaning

Inquiry is about asking questions and holding an attitude of curiosity, opening the door for new insights. Refection is about holding the door open long enough for new perceptions to emerge.

When we inquire, we attempt to "see into" an issue or a person's thinking. We ask questions that create doorways into new levels of understanding. Such questions frequently delve into relationships, connections, and patterns. For example, let's look at Newton's discovery of gravity. One day an apple fell to the ground from a tree Newton was sitting under. He could have asked the obvious question, "Why does the apple fall from the tree?" But, he didn't. He asked a more fundamental question, "Given that the apple falls from the tree, why don't the stars fall from the sky?" This one question was what helped him discover the laws of gravity. It was a question that delved into the connections between different observations.

Inquiry creates openings for breakthrough innovation. It is also a necessity for effective problem solving and a mainstay of systems thinking where questions reveal the relationships among the parts that make up the whole. Take, for example, the actions of product development, marketing, sales, or manufacturing and service. They all combine to influence one another's effectiveness, and battles among them are not uncommon. Or the challenge of matrixed organizations where people often hold reporting relationships to more than one person. In both contexts, understanding the interrelationships among the parts and how they sit in the whole is essential to determining realistic expectations and ways of working together to accomplish both individual and organizational goals.

Reflection is about taking the time to observe more than one event and wonder about the connections between them, to formulate the questions that will take you to the next level. Newton was not racing anywhere when he crafted his question. Reflection is also about taking time to listen for the response to a question to emerge. For a clear reflection to form in a pool of water, the surface must be still. The more we can develop this same kind of stillness in our minds, the more likely we will be able to ask the powerful questions and to hear the responses that return to us.

Inquiry and reflection combined help us dig deeper into whatever important issues concern us, to see new patterns and ways of proceeding. In this chapter, we consider how this pair can lead to more productive and creative conversations, to what you will need to pay attention in developing these skills, and how you can incorporate them in both one-on-one conversations and group dialogues. We speak to the role of inquiry and reflection in fostering collective intelligence and learning and the importance of silence.

Inquiry

Those who have the truth are
both unable to learn and may expect others
to learn unreflectively in order to
reproduce their knowledge.

Peter Jarvis,
Paradoxes of Learning

The power of inquiry lies in its intention to go where we have not been before and see things with new eyes. It thrives on questions that carry the potential for moving beyond what we know to what we have yet to discover. One such question, raised at the right time, may be all it takes for a conversation to move into brand new dimensions, to a higher ground where you can see more territory clearly.

Questions that take us to new places tend to be the *how, when, where* and *what* questions. They are questions that *open* the field of conversation and encourage us to focus attention on relationships and the interdynamics among parts and whole systems. Either/or questions such as "Is intelligence determined by heredity or environment?" divide our attention and direct us along only one line of inquiry rather than considering how both might be related.

Whether you are working with a group looking for new solutions to a problem or engaged in a conversation with one other person whose position you are having trouble understanding, either/or questions will tend to result in separation and polarization. Try asking questions that reveal the thinking behind the positions or ideas. Experiment with questions that are curious about the other's thinking process, about the assumptions that led to a conclusion or statement. See if you can walk up the ladder of inference together. You may surprise yourself by seeing connections and relationships that were invisible before. It is these connections among distinct and different perspectives that often give rise to creative and innovative combinations. Once you've discovered one or more such solutions by using this approach, you'll know (more than just intellectually) that diversity is necessary for creativity.

Inquiring in a Group

For the most part, inquiry works in the same way for a group as it does for an individual. There is, however, one important distinction in how we direct our questions in a group. We ask questions into the circle, to everyone present, rather than directing them to one person. For example, something John said may have stimulated you to think of a question, but anyone in the group may have a perspective that will enhance the group's learning. Directing our questions to only one person rather than to the whole group tends to result in one-on-one conversation and make bystanders of everyone else. Collective intelligence owes its power to the contributions of all. No one person has all the answers. Even if John has a response to your question, he holds only one perspective of a vast array of possibilities. You may have heard about holographic plates. When they are shattered, each piece of the plate is capable of projecting the image of the whole that was imprinted in the plate. However, it is only with the added images from all the pieces that the image takes on full depth and perspective.

The Unasked Questions

Sometimes the questions we do not ask are as revealing as those we do. Experiment with asking the questions that you have not heard. At times we can get stuck in the rut of asking the same or similar questions over and over again. Try pausing and asking yourself and the group: "What questions have we not been asking? What have we not focused attention on and what might be different if we included it in our conversation?" Often, important aspects of an issue are skirted. Perhaps they are a little risky to speak about. Perhaps they get skirted because no one wants to ask a question that no one knows the answer to! How often have you been in conversations where people are asking about every aspect of a problem except one, the one that no one knows how to approach or assumes is impossible to approach? Often, these are just the questions that need to be asked to bring to light a missing piece of the puzzle or a fresh, innovative perspective.

At times, conversations seem to enter into repetitive cycles. You realize you haven't heard much new in the last ten minutes. Or perhaps
there are many ideas floating around without any apparent connections.
In both cases, you may feel as if the conversation is going nowhere fast.
Try asking these questions: "What is it that is trying to take shape here?
What is trying to emerge or come forth?" These questions make people stop and reflect on what is really going on, whether in a one-on-
one interaction or in a group dialogue. If the conversation is cycling,
the group will recognize this and can make a conscious choice about
how to proceed. If the conversation seems disconnected, the question
will help people focus attention on connecting threads of meaning.

Is More Better?

At a conference on dialogue, some of the people kept saying that they
were dissatisfied with the level of inquiry. It was unclear just what they
felt was missing. Was it the spirit of inquiry? The number of questions
being asked?

Inquiry is dependent first on intention, second on the type and quality of question, and last on quantity. Inquiry that deepens and enriches
a conversation is a matter of intention. If you ask few or no questions
and yet are genuinely curious as you listen to another, inquiry will be
present. If you offer your opinions with an openness that invites others
to ask about your thinking, your conversations may have more of a spirit
of inquiry running through them than one in which a question is asked
every minute. Ask yourself: Do I hold an intention of openness and
curiosity and a willingness to suspend judgment and listen? What questions can I ask that will help surface new perspectives and connections?

It would be appealing to think that all we have to do to increase our
inquiry skills is to ask more questions. But you can do just that and if
your intention is not one of curiosity and learning, the spirit of inquiry
will not be present. For example, take questions that start with "Don't
you think . . .?". What exactly is your intention? Are you trying to open
up the field? Commonly, this kind of question is more about telling the
other person what you think (advocating). The intention is validation of

your own perspective. This actually has the effect of converging the conversation, rather than opening it out. Other questions attempt to guide attention in a predetermined direction (leading). Salespeople are good at these kinds of questions: "Is the turnaround on orders acceptable these days?" versus "What is your experience with how orders are filled?" Although the primary objective is to gain information about the customer's experience with orders, the first question directs attention to one specific area, turnaround time, while the second is broader, allowing the customer to address whatever area might be of concern from his or her perspective. Then there are the *déjà vu* questions about specific issues or problems we've all heard and answered many times before.

Few of these advocating, leading, *déjà vu* questions will encourage new insights. Inquiry is not simply a matter of asking questions. If you want to increase the level of inquiry in a conversation, focus on intention and then quantity.

Imagine you are in a dialogue where one meaty question follows another. There is no lack of inquiry. But you're still frustrated. What is missing now is any time to ponder the questions you are hearing. Too many are fired in rapid succession. There's simply no time for them to settle inside you, for you to mull them over. Too many questions with no time to reflect is frustrating, sometimes even immobilizing. No question is useful without time to consider it.

TRY THIS: INQUIRY AND OPENING THE FIELD OF PERCEPTION

○ When you notice an automatic response arise within you to something that is being said, especially the kind of automatic response that is emotionally laden, practice suspending judgment and try changing your response to an inquiry. Or pause and, rather than responding, try to hear more of how others are feeling about what is being said. Notice if over time, as you hear more, you continue to feel the same charge around what you had wanted to say.

○ At the start of an upcoming dialogue where you will be considering a particular topic or issue, see if you can frame a question around it that is open-ended. In fact, all members might come prepared with a question they believe would open the conversation. You can open the dialogue by going around the circle and having everyone offer his/her question. No response is given at this time. This is a way to begin to open people's thinking. (If the group wants, you could have someone chart the questions and then leave them up on the wall during the dialogue.)

Reflection

reflect; to give back an image, to think carefully

—The Funk and Wagnall Standard Dictionary

"And if you ask a thousand questions, yet do not pause to listen and reflect on what emerges in response, how will you learn?"

—The Dialogue Group

Have you ever had the experience of reading a very weighty book and being grateful that you could put it down whenever you wanted? Unlike going to a talk or attending a meeting on some critical issue, you have the luxury of stopping and thinking about what you've been reading. Sometimes you might even stop after a single paragraph and wonder, "What does this mean for me? How might this change how I see and do things? Is this actually possible?" This desire to pause and think awhile is about the need for reflection. Whether reading a weighty book or engaging in a conversation about the reorganization of your department, thinking and responding effectively require time to let what people are saying soak in. Only then can you reflect on what you hear, perform a kind of inner inquiry or questioning process, and formulate your next question or statement. Without it, the proverbial "in one ear and out the other" takes over.

In the United States we pay little attention to reflection. In fact, statistically speaking, our western culture is primarily extroverted;[11] out there, talking. Because this extroverted tendency is so strong, we move quickly from one subject to the next, seldom pausing to reflect or ask questions that would help us move into deeper waters.

We also live in a culture in which we are expected to have a ready answer and hopefully the right one. This can be so strong that it leads to speaking with a certainty about something we may not know much about. Of course, fast-paced conversation with little silence in between speakers decreases the likelihood that anyone will be able to think too deeply about what we are saying and challenge us.

The need to have an answer, be right, and move quickly all influence the way we communicate, and run counter to conditions needed for an insightful conversation that fosters reflection and learning.

"Slow down, you move too fast.
You gotta make the mornin' last . . ."[12]

Reflection is directly related to the pace of conversation. In dialogue, there are often pauses, some quite long, between speakers. Words are spoken more deliberately; there may even be pauses between sentences. To an observer, everything might seem slowed down.

What's going on during these pauses between speakers? Why are they important? For learning to occur, new information must be processed. This involves relating it to what is already known, making meaning or sense of new data by connecting it into our knowledge system. This process is similar for individuals and groups. On how many levels we are able to make connections depends on how fast we are moving. With more time we are able to make connections at multiple levels, and our individual and collective learning deepens. Slowing down also gives us the opportunity to take ourselves off of autopilot and respond more effectively to what is going on around us. In complex situations this can be important for our survival, particularly long term.

Even in circumstances where our survival is not in question, if we do not slow down, we run the risk of spending our time jumping around

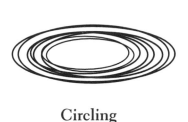 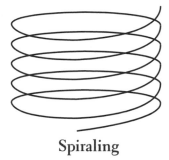

Circling   Spiraling

territory that is already known, skirting over the same old issues, wasting a lot of time and energy. We call this phenomenon circling and distinguish it from the spiraling that dialogue encourages.

We have all been in meetings and relationships where circling predominates. You leave the meeting thinking "We've had that meeting over and over again; same conversation, nothing new, getting nowhere." It is frustrating and a waste of time and energy. We all have examples in our interpersonal relationships, whether at work or at home. Here's a personal one from the home arena.

Example. In their marriage, Susan and Tom circled around the issue of when to eat dinner. Whenever the mealtime issue came up, they repeated well worn scripts exactly. Susan wanted to eat later rather than earlier, and Tom wanted to eat earlier rather than later. From replay to replay, the words might vary slightly, but the outcome was the same: conflict and ill feelings. They couldn't break through their strong preferences. Neither was willing to accommodate the other on a lasting basis. Nor could they accept their differences.

Although Susan and Tom invented a lot of rationales for supporting their personal agendas, there was never any real pause in these conversations, no real time and willingness to explore more deeply what seemed so essential to them both. This simple conflict defeated them over and over again because they just circled through the same conversation. They went on automatic pilot every time the subject came up.

You've probably had similar experiences with a spouse, child, or co-worker. This pattern of circling is so hard to break because our automatic assumptions and beliefs kick in quickly, like knee-jerk reactions. Because we don't slow down the pace long enough to actually see beneath the surface of what is happening, we do not descend the ladder of inference to discover what is behind our assumptions and actions. We don't inquire into the other's point of view, nor do we bother to reflect on our own. There is little time allowed or effort at learning anything new. We continue to repeat the same story line based on what we already know or want. You might say that circling is the ultimate in single loop learning.

Circling often happens in tightly coupled relationships, whether personal or professional. We get so used to the other's arguments and agendas that we don't see what might be new. There can be a host of obstacles that prevent us from seeing or doing much about this circling. Fear of our own vulnerability or of being proven wrong are two of the more common blocks.

If we can get ourselves to stop long enough to reflect and inquire, double loop learning becomes possible and we can move from circling to a much more productive spiraling pattern. Spiraling is the product of the combined collective intelligence of those involved. But, this collective intelligence is not available to us until we begin to inquire with curiosity, pause and reflect, and allow for the connections that will reveal new ways of approaching the issue at hand. Only then will we begin to move upward to new levels of understanding and possibility.

Fostering Collective Intelligence through Inquiry and Reflection

"Organizations that can't learn, can't change. Organizations that can learn, can transform themselves into new entities capable of greater heights of achievement."

Robert Fritz, *Corporate Tides*

The capability for inquiry and reflection is essential to the perception of collective meaning and learning. What do we mean by collective intelligence? Do we mean two heads are better than one? Well, yes, that and more. We've all had experiences when working with one or more people has resulted in a better product than we could have come up with by ourselves. But, we've also had experiences where more heads have created confusion and chaos. What makes the difference? How can we tap into the power of collective collaboration and partnership? How can groups focus their attention in ways that lead to an ability to learn as a collective entity?

The roots of the word *intelligence* come from the Latin *inter* and *legere*, which mean "to gather in-between." Collective intelligence is about gathering the meaning(s) moving among a group of people. Practicing inquiry and reflection at the same three levels we spoke of for listening is essential. When you ask a question of another or of the entire group, ask it also of yourself. Reflect not only on what you are hearing but how it is affecting you. Listen for the patterns that emerge in people's reflections and questions. What collective themes do you hear emerging? If you were listening to the group as if listening to the voice of one entity, what would that voice be saying? What question would it be asking? What whole view would make sense of the many diverse perspectives you are hearing? What questions could you pose to further clarify the shared meaning that is emerging?

Groups that develop the ability to weave individual thinking into collective intelligence can learn together. When we use the term "learn," we are not talking about simple rote memorization, such as learning the alphabet or multiplication tables. We are referring to new ways of thinking about how the world works, to the kind of learning that changes our perceptions and our behaviors.

This form of learning requires collective "soak time" to integrate diverse perspectives and new information. The group will need to learn how to honor the different paces at which its members reflect and integrate. Both individuals and the group as a whole will need to move together through a reflection and inquiry process, considering questions such as: "What does this mean to me and to the group? How are they the same, different? What are the ramifications for me, and for the group? How might it change how I/we do things or how I/we interpret the world? What new connections and understandings are emerging?"

This capability for collective inquiry and reflection is what leads to quantum leaps and breakthroughs in a group's thinking. There may even be times when a group finds itself reaching beyond the boundaries of current understanding into a place it cannot find words to describe.[13] At these times a new knowing is emerging, but the ability to articulate it has not yet caught up. These are the experiences of arriving at the frontiers of our thinking and looking upon lands yet to be explored. Often the result is a new model or way of viewing relationships that, in turn, leads to such practical things as innovative products and processes or new approaches to working with important issues.

TRY THIS: REFLECTING ON CONTENT AND PROCESS LEARNINGS

At the end of every dialogue, set aside 10 to 15 minutes to reflect on and talk about what you noticed and are learning from the dialogue. This is a very practical way to "gather in-between" the collective intelligence of the group. The reflection can be divided into two parts — content and process.

- The *content reflection* will contain key themes, ideas, questions, and new insights that emerged during the conversation. It is useful to distinguish between insights around the topic and any observations about what you may have learned about the thinking behind people's perspectives. Two useful questions are: What conclusions did you draw that would be useful to move forward? What did we learn about our thinking process?

- The *process reflection* is focused on what you noticed about how the group worked together; how the various skills were used, what the pace what like, what worked well for you, what the group could pay more attention to the next time.

Three questions are: What supported us in moving to new levels of understanding? What hindered us? What would we explore doing differently?

Such reflective sessions are a crucial part of a group learning to develop skills on a collective level and gain the ability to tap into the power of dialogue.[14]

Silence: The Ground from Which Inquiry and Reflection Arise

"In order to tap the human resource of wisdom, it is necessary to practice the art of listening. Periods of silence and solitude allow us to obtain more clarity, objectivity, and discernment, the qualities inherent to wisdom."

—Angeles Arrien

Is music the arrangement of notes or of the silent spaces in between? *Yes.* Is shared meaning the product of collective thinking or the silent spaces out of which questions and thoughts emerge? *Yes.* Without silence there would be no works of art, nothing discernible. Silence is the backdrop against which we perceive the notes of a musical piece; ask questions, listen, reflect, integrate, and learn. There is no conversation or dialogue that cannot be enriched by attention to silence.

Silence is essential to the practice of dialogue and the development of collective intelligence. It allows more subtle levels of meaning and relationship to come forward; we see more of what our collective conversation is about. Silence is often the key to new insights and breakthroughs in thinking. It is for this reason that we often work intentionally with silence. The following words from a seminar participant's journal illustrate the richness of perception that is often experienced within extended silence.

We've been in silence since last night. No phone calls. No television or radio. No conversation. Morning has come. People are entering the dining area to have breakfast. One by one, they enter, pick up their trays, make their food choices, and move to tables. Separate tables. They do not sit together. I am curious. Why aren't we sitting together this morning? Is it the silence? Why do we sit with others? Observing this scenario one would conclude that the only reason is to speak. No words. No sitting together.

I clean up my dishes, get a cup of coffee, and very intentionally go sit at a table with Elizabeth. She is eating cereal. We share the table. But not much else. We only initially make eye contact. Smile. Nod our heads in greeting. Then we both look elsewhere. I stare out the window. She focuses on her cereal. As I sit looking out the window, a strange thing happens. It is as if a two-dimensional scene becomes three-dimensional, and then four. Even the air between the trees takes on substance. I feel I can reach out and touch the house across the lake. The trees are vibrating with fullness. I can see tones of brown in the bark, shades of green in the tiniest leaf buds. I can see the wind moving through space. It is as if in the silence, seeing becomes some fuller version, SEEING.

I turn and look at Elizabeth. I am fascinated with the way she is eating, the way she moves the spoon through the cereal and fruit and milk and lifts it to her mouth. The way she chews. The intervals between spoonfuls. Her whole body seems to pulse. Her skin has the same luminescent quality as the light outside. I turn and begin to look at the people around me in the same way. It is not easy, because it requires a steady, open looking, the kind you often see babies engage in, unafraid of offending, judging, discomforting. I am uncomfortable, but I continue to look. It is as if a veil has lifted. People become fuller, more radiant, quite beautiful. They become "bigger than life."

And then I SEE. This is how we really are. Large and full and fascinatingly unique. Not some weak imitations that have become flattened and dulled by fear of judgment, hidden amidst the noise and busyness of our day-to-day lives.

That day I thanked the silence for its power of revelation. I didn't want it to end. As the bell rang to close the silent period, I said a prayer that I would be able to maintain the silence within me as I continued. I wondered what additional dimensions I would be able to see at work, with my family.

Silence is a paradox for many of us. When the noise and busyness of our lives overwhelm us, we crave silence. Minute to minute, we discard silence as non-useful and unproductive. Often, we actively avoid it. The ability to work with silence, with the pauses in which we listen and reflect, is a capacity few people have developed. A group that has learned to sit together in silence for more than a few minutes at a time is most likely a group that has developed a certain level of trust among members and in itself as a learning community.

QUESTIONS FOR REFLECTION_____

○   What is your personal relationship with silence? When is it comfortable? Uncomfortable? What makes it so?

○   What value does silence have for you? What benefits does it provide?

○   What is different about being in silence with other people than alone? In a work group, what additional dimensions add to the discomfort of silence? Imagine how some of the values you personally derive from silence could be translated into a group setting such as your work team. One small step at a time, think about little ways that silence could add value. What possibilities can you imagine? How could a group use silence to help discover its own internal rhythm?

TRY THIS:

○   Experiment with starting any conversation, whether with one other person or with a group, with a moment of silence. The time can be used to formulate personal questions or reflections and then the dialogue can begin.

○   Periodically incorporate a moment of silence within a conversation as a way to slow things down and give all participants a chance to reflect and integrate what has been said to that point.

○   You've come together with a group of people to consider a very important issue. It could be a recurring production problem. Or perhaps you've been charged with coming up with a way to implement shared governance on your college campus. Or your family is faced with a decision about a move and you want to hear from everyone. Whatever the case, once you are all together, pass out paper and pencils and allow about ten minutes of silence during which each person can write down whatever thoughts and questions he or she has about the issue in question. Then take a moment for everyone to read selected portions of what they've written. Conclude the reading with a moment of silence and then begin your conversation.

○   Set aside a period of time within which you will not speak to others, take phone calls, read, listen to the radio, stereo, or TV. Allow yourself to simply experience being in silence. What occurs? What do you notice?

○   Many couples report that setting aside a significant period of time, say, 1 to 4 hours, to be in silence yet in the same location with their partner, is a fascinating learning experience.

Listen to the Silence

"Out beyond ideas of
rightdoing and wrongdoing
there is a field
I'll meet you there
When the soul lies down
In that grass
The world is too full to talk about."

(Rumi)

Listen.
The silence is not empty
A universe rests within
There is a landscape
Larger than the one you see.
A symphony between the notes.

Listen
The sounds of silence can be
The loudest call you've ever heard
Stopped, midway in your speech
By the profundity of revelation
You fall off the edge
Into infinity . . .

Listen.
You cannot hide in silence
Even a deaf man will hear you,
A blind man see you,
Only a dead man would not.

Listen.
If a tree falls in the forest
And no one hears it
Did it fall?
If no one hears your sound
Do you exist?

Listen.
We are so busy talking
We cannot hear ourselves
If we do not hear each other
We join the procession
Of the Living Dead.

Listen.
The din is terrible
We all are shouting to be heard
Too busy to listen
We are killing each other.
Committing collective suicide
Because we are deaf to
Each other's sounds.

I hope
Soon
We will fall silent
And our dialogue will begin.

—*Glenna Gerard*

NONVERBAL COMMUNICATION
AND DIALOGUE

"I believe in all that has never yet been spoken.
I want to free what waits within me
so that what no one has dared to wish for

may for once spring clear
without my contriving."

—Rilke,
The Book of Hours

Dialogue has been practiced and explored almost exclusively as a verbal medium. We communicate by talking with one another, by using words. We think in words, so what more appropriate medium could there be for exploring our thinking around issues that are important to us? Yet it is also true that when people are trying to communicate profound and meaningful experiences, they often find themselves at a loss for words. Words cannot always hold the totality of what is meaningful and significant.

Just as there are times when words are limiting in terms of expressing what we are experiencing, we suspect that words may also limit the amount and character of what we are able to receive from our environment. During the years we've practiced dialogue with various groups, we often find ourselves wondering what perceptions and distinct views of reality might literally be filtered out from our conversation, simply because they do not "fit" within the realm of words. In the hope of expanding the range of both our ability to perceive information and to express it, we began incorporating nonverbal forms of communication into our work with dialogue. These include music, movement, art, meditation, forms of visualization, and dream work. Each provides a different and unique lens through which to look at reality. Often, using one of them will yield an insight that leads to an innovative way of working with an issue or a challenge.

Developing a capacity for listening through nonverbal channels is a powerful addition to dialogue. We consider it right up there with the capacities for suspension of judgment, identification and suspension of assumptions, listening, and inquiry and reflection. In addition, the nonverbal channels are primary ways of learning and integrating for many of us. For this reason we devote a chapter to this material. If, however, you are feeling a little overwhelmed at this point, or just feel the need to move on, you may want to skip these pages and return to them at a later date. Reading them is not essential for your understanding of the remainder of the book.

Whether or not you continue through this chapter, we do encourage you to keep your sensors open to the nonverbal components of any conversation. At a minimum, this includes being aware of others' body postures and movements, although it is advisable to always check out your interpretations before deciding and acting on them. Even more than attending to the body language of others, it can be particularly useful to pay attention to your own body signals. When do your shoulders rise up or your palms begin to sweat? What do these signals mean for you? You body is a powerful listening device; it can provide you with invaluable information.

Nonverbal Doorways

Our capacity for sensing through nonverbal channels is high though mostly forgotten and/or dulled by the almost exclusive focus on verbal communication in our culture. We believe you will be pleasantly surprised at the added depth and richness these doorways will make available to you. We hope the following experiences and suggestions will inspire you to explore opening some of these doorways. Even cracking the door open just a bit may delight you.

The format for this chapter differs significantly from that of the others in Part II. All the activities we describe were developed in the context of dialogue programs. We begin with a statement of the purpose of each and commentary about what the experience was like, followed by suggestions for how to adapt the activities for the workplace.

Collective Art

Purpose/Intention

To create an opening for intuitive, nonverbal information to emerge and be integrated into the conversation. To explore the collective interweaving of nonverbal symbols as a way of listening for collective meaning.

Commentary

One of our first experiments with collective art was as an opener for a dialogue on power and love. We created collective pieces of art using power as the theme and then love. The art from each one was very different. It was illuminating to look at them side by side and ask, "What do we notice within ourselves as we look at this art?" We learned a lot about our thoughts on power just looking at the finished pieces. There were different perspectives, and there were common themes. There was a jaggedness, lots of straight lines, a sort of staccato feeling to most of the paintings. There was little or no white space left on any of the pages. The colors used tended to be darker earth tones, along with black and some red. There was very little yellow. If you were "reading" our art, what might you say about our images of power?

Some of us spoke about power as simply neutral energy available for any use. But our art spoke of darkness, distrust, and was not very comfortable to look at. The dialogue that followed provided many insights into how our experiences of power shape our current perceptions and behaviors, the role power plays in our culture. The paintings of love were very different. Brighter colors, more playful, much more white space. People really got creative with their additions, changing the original idea completely. Placing the power and love pieces side by side provoked some interesting questions: "We speak about the power of love, yet look how different our artwork is. They don't seem to go together in the consciousness that produced these paintings. How does this dilemma play out in our day-to-day life?"

WORK APPLICATION:

Suppose you have a particular systemic problem that has been plaguing you for months. You can use this exercise to help uncover fresh insights and perceptions on the issue. One person will need to lead the group, keep time (in 60-second intervals), and ring a bell (a spoon on a cup will do). The leader will also be participating, so make sure you're familiar with the steps before you begin.

Sit around a table with a piece of white paper in front of each person (18" × 24" is a good size). You'll need a selection of colored markers, crayons, paints (whatever you can get your hands on) in the center of the table.

Before starting, ask everyone to focus inward, becoming aware of their breathing and of themselves sitting in their chairs with their feet firmly on the floor. Ask that each person allow the issue to take shape in their awareness. Ring the bell. This begins a 60-second round during which each person allows an image to come to mind and then transfers it to paper.

Don't worry if you can't translate it exactly; simply let your hands choose a color and move on the paper. You don't have time for perfection anyway. After 60 seconds, everyone stops and passes their paper one person to the right.

The bell rings. This time you ask yourself, "What wants to be added to this piece?" Then add it. After 60 seconds, the bell sounds. Papers pass and the cycle repeats until each person has back in front of him/her the piece of paper they started with.

Now you are ready to begin your conversation. Place all the collective art in the center of the table or circle, take a moment of silence to simply look, and then begin. What do you see? Try to allow the information to speak to you. What common themes do you see? Patterns? Any particular piece that is very different? Ask questions. What are you curious about? Listen. Suspend your judgments. See how many new perspectives you can gain. What have you learned about the issue?

Materials

- ○ Paper for each person (preferably at least 18" × 24")
- ○ Watercolors, colored markers, water-soluble paints, crayons (whatever art supplies are available). The necessary paint-brushes, cups of waters, etc. The more variety, the more fun, but colored markers alone will do.
- ○ A timer or a watch with a second hand.

Art Can Speak to Us

Purpose/Intention

To develop a capacity for listening to the environment as a source of symbolic information that can enrich the conversation, adding previously unconsidered perspectives.

Commentary

We sit in a room. All around us are pieces of art. Wood carvings from Bali. Elephant gods, goddesses in various poses, two-headed dragons, mother and child, lovers, weavers; all kinds of wonderful wooden people surround us. We are asked to take a few moments, walk around the room, and gaze upon the pieces of art. If we notice a piece that we are drawn to in some way, we pick it up. It may be that we find someone else who is also drawn to the piece. After a few minutes we all move into self-selected groupings of between four and seven people. We sit and speak about how we are drawn, what we feel, what thoughts are evoked, what questions come up. What we learn about one another and about ourselves is fascinating.

To take this to the level of the collective, we ask the question, "What do our stories tell us about this particular group?" The indigenous peoples have a saying that when a circle of people gather, they are together because as a whole they have "medicine," wisdom, for one another. What wisdom does this collective bring?

WORK APPLICATION:

A variation on this theme is aimed more at gaining information about specific issues or questions. If you work in an environment where there are pieces of art that are movable, you can take advantage of it, but if not, use this variation, which focuses on everyday items in your surroundings as symbols that can yield information. Here's what you do.

Sit down. Focus your attention in your body. Put both feet flat on the floor. Become aware of your breathing. Now allow whatever it is that you want to gather more information about to enter your consciousness. If you have a specific question, state it to yourself. Now, open your eyes and look around the room you are in. Notice the first object that draws your attention. It could be a fly on the wall, a palm plant in the corner, a mirror, a sentence on a flip chart. It doesn't matter. Just notice where your attention settles. Now consider the object a symbol. You are going to interpret it. Free associate. What does this symbol mean to you? What associations does it evoke? Memories, feelings? What might these have to do with the issue/question you wanted information on? The symbol is giving you information. What is it telling you?

While we realize this may seem "way out there" to many of you, try it a few times. It's really quite amazing what you can learn from yourself by noticing what symbol captures your attention when you open your eyes. If you have focused first on your issue or question, then there will be a relationship and it shouldn't be too hard to uncover.

Materials

- Any environment where there is either art or a diversity of composition, such as plants, pictures, or paintings. Outdoors also works well since nature tends to provide lots of variety in any given setting.

Meditation and Prayer

Purpose/Intention

To bring your attention fully present and to ground it in your own center point in preparation for conversation. To invoke those qualities that are important to us for meaningful conversation. To give thanks for the conversation we engage in.

Commentary

Morning Meditation. It is the second day of a dialogue program. We gather in the circle, each of us finding our place, saying hello to those around us. The chime rings, calling for our attention. We all rise for a centering meditation. We stand with our feet shoulder-width apart. As we move through a pattern of breathing and subtle movements, we allow our focus of attention to move first inward, into our bodies. With each breath we move towards and settle into our center point. We allow ourselves to become aware of our contact with the floor or ground and rest into it. Then, while maintaining this internal center, we allow our focus to move outward into the group. The chime sounds. We take our seats. We will now attend, listen, and speak from a different place than we would have five minutes ago.

WORK APPLICATION:

On the agenda for your next meeting or at your next dialogue session, set aside five minutes for someone to lead the group in a meditation. There are many variations possible, and you may want to refer to the mediation section in the Bibliography for books that contain examples. Here's a simple one.

Have everyone get quiet and settle down. Become aware of how you are sitting in your chairs. Place your feet on the floor. Your eyes can be closed or open. Begin to focus your attention on your breathing. Don't change anything. Just notice your breath. Notice how the air moves in on the inhale. Notice the pause between the inhale and the exhale. Notice the air moving out on the exhale. Continue to attend to your breathing for at least another five breaths. Now, go inside yourself, and internally state your intention for your breathing to begin to move with that of the other people in the circle, like clocks synchronizing. You don't have to do anything. Just state the intention and remain focused on *your* breathing. Follow your breath for another ten breaths. At this point most groups are actually breathing together.

Now, whoever is leading reads the following few lines (or some other reading that they find inspirational and that speaks to the importance of the group in the work that will follow).

> *Let us all leave behind our individual concerns, safe beyond the Circle. Let our thoughts draw towards our Center. Let us be warmed by our Common Purpose. For, you and I may differ, may fall to blows between us. Yet, if our thoughts turn toward the Center, I and you — and as many others as there may be — may yet build our Central Fire, create and sustain its energy, recognize our Common Purpose. Let it be so.*
>
> —Paula Underwood,
> *Who Speaks for Wolf?*

Close the exercise by asking everyone to open their eyes (if closed) and return their attention to the room. Start your meeting, or dialogue. This exercise will slow people down and center them both within themselves as well as with the group.

Evening Prayer. [When we use the word *prayer* here and above, we do not necessarily mean traditional religious prayer, although we certainly include it. Prayer is an invocation, an invitation, to the consciousness of wholeness.] It is evening. We are in a sweat lodge. Sweat lodges are used for purification and prayer by the Native American peoples. We have entered in ritual and now sit in the dark. The sweat lodge flaps are closed. Water has just been added to the hot rocks. The next round of prayer begins. This evening there are four rounds, corresponding to the four directions, North (power), South (love), East (vision), and West (wisdom). We offer prayers of love, for those we love, for wounds that need healing, to know the grace of love entering and living in us, our work, our families. We offer prayers for the earth and all our relationships upon it. Many of us are moved by the prayers. Each prayer is an acknowledgment of love and our pain at being separated from it. The round is over. The flap opens for air and the bringing in of more hot rocks. Twice more we pray and then close with a round of sound. We have been moved within ourselves by our prayers and the power of the ritual. Most important, the movement within has taken us beyond, into renewed awareness of our relationships. Sweat lodges are often doorways into the mystery. Tomorrow our dialogue will carry in it tonight's experience.

> WORK APPLICATION:
> The next time you begin a meeting or dialogue, start with a round of invocation. Ask each person to speak of a quality he/she wants to bring to the conversation to deepen it and increase its value. Listen. At the end of the meeting, ask for a round where each speaks one thing he/she is grateful for receiving from the conversation. Such an exercise helps to focus people's attention on shared responsibility for the quality of the upcoming conversation and reminds us of the value of our learnings.

Materials

○ Any of a variety of meditation exercises, visualizations, readings. Books on Zen Buddhism are rich sources. Another is *Full Catastrophe Living* by Jon Kabat-Zinn.

Movement

Purpose/Intention

To develop a capacity for listening to the rhythm of your body. To access information based on associations with diverse movements and rhythms.

Commentary

The Rhythms of Life. It's afternoon. The trees outside are moving in the wind. Inside we are moving to a selection of musical rhythms. Flowing. Staccato. Chaos. Lyrical. Stillness. As we listen to each and allow ourselves to move, we are carried through a cycle not unlike what we might experience when we make love. First a flowing, slow, round, soft movement begins to move us. Smoothly, we glide around the room. The energy begins to shift, takes on a bit more urgency; the movements become quicker, excited, enthusiastic. Then the energy becomes so much that any pattern dissolves and there is pure, unconfined, unorganized movement. We touch all patterns, but hold to none. Can we sustain this? We begin to leap and dance like a smile moving us through the air. Our feet want to leave the ground. We want to travel up on the next sunbeam, higher, higher. And, finally, we rest. All is still. We bask in the glow of an internal silence that holds us close to our hearts. We are at peace.

As we move with the rhythms, first we find the rhythm inside ourselves. Then we explore moving in this rhythm with the group. We are continuously shifting our focus to include both our own center and relationship with others.

When we have concluded, we begin our dialogue. People usually begin with insights that the different rhythms evoke. Movements may remind them of certain experiences. We all notice there are some rhythms we are more comfortable with than others, and this varies from person to person. Most of our questions are about how we move in relationship with others and how this shifts with each rhythm. The movement has brought forth into our consciousness material that we might not have been able to express verbally.

(We express our thanks to here to Gabrielle Roth[15] whose work with movement and rhythms has added so much richness and depth to our work.)

WORK APPLICATION:

Select one or two minutes each of three to four different pieces of music that embody different dynamics, ways of relating, and feeling states. What you choose for your focus will depend on the issue or topic the group is exploring. You may be able to use some of Gabrielle Roth's rhythms because they are such essential representations of ways that we move both internally and in relationship to others.

Play the pieces. Which one do you think is most representative of your perception of the issue? If you are doing this in a group, have everyone choose and then do the remaining steps.

Play the piece you chose and move your body to the music in a way that expresses what it is about the music that made you choose it as related to the issue.

Reflect on what the movement felt like. Ask yourself what changes you might make to the movement. How would you create new possibilities/solutions/approaches?

If people choose different pieces of music, play each one, have everyone move together with the music, and then talk about what ideas and/or new understandings they have as a result.

Materials

○   Equipment for playing audiotapes or CDs

○   Tapes or CDs with music you choose to experiment with

Mandalas

Purpose/Intention

To listen for internal individual and collective images and symbols associated with wholeness and health.

Commentary

We first came to the idea of using mandalas when we were designing a "Deepening the Dialogue" program. Mandala is the Sanskrit word for *circle*. It is a symbolic pattern making the invisible visible.[16] We had been searching for a focus of attention that could provide both a thread of continuity and a doorway into expanded consciousness at both individual and collective levels. What follows is a recounting of that experience.

The program has begun. Our first mandala exercise will take place on the morning of the second day. After briefly laying out the road map for the next few days and giving a short introduction to mandalas, we begin. A meditation helps each of us open to our first symbol, one that represents healing and wholeness to us personally. We begin to put the symbols on paper. We finish them individually in the afternoon. That evening, we move over to the mandala wall. The wall is covered with black paper. In the middle is a circle about four feet in diameter. This will be the collective mandala. We tell the stories of our mandalas and place them around the outside of the collective mandala circle. Some of us are astounded by what we have drawn, by the symbology and what it says to us about who we are and what represents wholeness for us. The wall is an awesome collection. We talk a little about similarities, ask one another questions. Mostly, we listen and learn much more about who is in the room with us.

On our final evening together, the group travels on a journey to bring back a symbol for the collective mandala. When we complete the journey, we begin a period of silence that lasts through the evening and breakfast the next morning. We continue in silence as we work on the collective mandala. With the sound of the chime, we enter into a conversation about our mandala and the experience of its creation. People speak about dreams that brought them symbols that didn't mean anything to them, only to see the fit when they placed them on the wall along with the symbols of others. Some of us received symbols that we don't have words for, yet we have drawn them knowing they are important to our collective. At one point, one member of the group is drawn, like a magnet, to the wall. She says she feels compelled to erase the white circle that separates the individual mandalas from the collective work. We all realize the deep significance of this as we sit back and look. Some people are upset. They want the boundary there. The woman who removed it reports that she was afraid to remove it. She realized that her fear was associated with the fear that without the boundary the individual mandalas might become lost in the collective. We know we see this same fear every time we work with organizations or groups that are struggling with the tension between team and individual, between collective excellence and acknowledgment of individual contribution. Individuals fear groups, particularly powerful groups. But, the experience reminds us that the boundary between individual and collective is arbitrary. It is necessary for our differentiation as unique individuals. But, at this stage of our evolution, we need a consciousness that embraces both the individual and the collective without losing sight of either. Erasing the boundary was a reminder that it is of our own creation, it is an arbitrary separation that we create for distinction. When we forget this, we become locked at a level of consciousness dominated by separation, which makes it very difficult for us to create partnerships and work together.

The entire week, starting with creating individual mandalas and culminating in the creation of the collective mandala, was one of the most powerful nonverbal experiences this group engaged in. The depth of insight into both individual and collective consciousness and the dance between them was profound. The silence was too full for words. When we said good-bye, no one spoke of loss. Many spoke of how unusual this was and speculated that it was because they felt full and had a knowledge of our wholeness that would leave with them.

WORK APPLICATION:

You might consider creating either individual or collective mandalas in the following scenarios.

O A systemic problem has been plaguing you for some time. You'd like to expand your understanding of how many aspects of the problem are interrelated. You are looking for a solution or guidance as to how to approach the issue to create a healthier system overall.

O You are creating a vision for a new operation. You'd like to create a collective picture of what would be important things to consider in creating a structure that will support individual creativity, partnership, and integration throughout the many departments.

To create the mandalas, each person will need a piece of black paper and some way of drawing a circle in its center. A dinner plate is about the right size. You will also need a selection of colored markers, pencils, chalks, and crayons.

Begin by focusing people's attention on the issue/vision you will be working with. It is often useful to frame a question such as "What is needed for us to create an environment in our new operation that will support us individually and in partnership with one another?"

Each person will then enter a short meditation or period of silence within which he/she will ask to receive a symbol that addresses the question. It is important not to question the symbol, but to simply translate it as best you can to the paper in front of you. You may not understand the symbol until you reflect on it or another person in the group speaks of what the symbol evokes for them.

After all have completed their mandalas, do a round where each person speaks about what they have received and created. You may want to place all of the mandalas together in the middle of the table or up on the wall, where you can reflect on them as a collective set of images. Are there any repeating themes? What have you learned from this activity that will be important for you to carry forward into your work?

Materials

- Black paper and colored markers, chalks, pencils, and crayons.
- Mandalas are created using colored pastels on a black background. The effect is quite striking. An excellent source of information is the book *Mandala* by Judith Cornell.

6

GUIDES FOR CREATING AND

SUSTAINING DIALOGUES

guide: *(n.) one that leads or directs another's way;*
(v.) to provide support and direction

—Funk and Wagnall Standard Dictionary

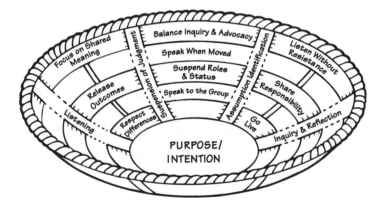

Remembering

We've devoted many pages to considering how focusing your attention on specific capacities, such as suspension of judgment, assumptions, listening, and inquiry and reflection, can help in crafting powerful conversations about questions that matter. To grapple with the dilemmas that face us all today requires an environment that supports all our voices in speaking and being heard. Earlier in the introduction to this section we spoke of creating a container for such conversations, a basket woven of the capacities, attitudes, and behaviors that support open, authentic conversation. We come now to a description of some of the attitudes and behaviors that many groups of diverse composition have found helpful. We offer them as *guides* rather than guidelines, thanks to a participant in one of our seminars who pointed out to us that the word *guidelines* sounded too much like rules. The comment brought us face to face once again with the power and importance of intention.

If these, or any other guides or guidelines, are put forth with the intention that they are the "rules of the road" and reflect a right way to be in dialogue, they will almost certainly end up being rallying points that divide the group and limit participation and creativity. If, however, they are named and held as supports to remembering the natural impulse to dialogue that lives within all of us, if they are offered in the spirit of remembering what you already know, then they will be invaluable to you in focusing your intention and attention, even in times when the going gets tough.

Ritual is a ceremony utilizing a combination of speaking, action, and listening to help us remember what is essential. Though most often associated with religion, we would like to suggest that if you work with these guides, or whatever ones you develop, in the spirit of ritual, if you let go of the concept of rules and focus on what is essential to sustaining your internal knowing of what is needed to be in dialogue, you will find yourself in the midst of powerful and transforming conversation.

Focus on Shared Meaning and Learning

This guide could be a purpose statement for dialogue, designed to help us remember that dialogue is about learning from and with one another and increasing our capacity to respond creatively to our environment. As we build a larger picture by inviting in diverse perspectives, we gain access to a collective wisdom far greater than that of any one individual. To do this requires that we learn to open our field of perception and tune all our receptors to maximum.

Anything that narrows the field of listening will not be useful. For example, when we focus on determining what is the right or best

answer, our conversations tend to be filled with persuasion and evaluation and the pitting of one perspective against another. Remember times
when you've been set on being right and how this impacted the way
you listened and learned. By focusing on learning, you open the scope
of your listening and create the possibility of developing shared meaning with others. Creating and sustaining collaborative partnerships is not
something that any one of us knows a lot about. We all have much to
learn and our best source is one another. This guide reminds us of where
we need to maintain our focus of attention if we are to be successful.

Release the Need for Specific Outcomes

This is one of the trickiest things for us to remember and, hence, one of
the most important guides. Living in the results-oriented culture we do,
it is difficult for us to release the need for a specific outcome. We tend
to equate this with having no purpose, with aimlessness and wasting
time. Yet, in dialogue we actually do have a purpose: to develop collaborative partnerships, to expand and deepen our understanding, and
be more intentional about the forms of shared meaning we create
together. In reality, we are focused on an outcome of some magnitude.
So what do we mean by release the need for a specific outcome, and
why is this so important? *Specific* is the operative word here. Anytime
we focus on a specific outcome, we create a convergent conversation;
all questions and thinking converge towards that one outcome. This
severely limits the creative process of dialogue. Rather than expanding
our thinking in search of new possibilities, we evaluate all input with an
eye towards selecting the best one to accomplish our specific outcome.
We stop seeking out different perspectives and a larger whole view.
Learning and creativity are at high risk of being sacrificed to getting
on with it and finding the right answer in the shortest time possible.

In real life. Suppose you have an important issue on the table such as
the reorganization strategy for a new company as a result of a recent
merger. Consider the following structure. You begin your work by
convening a dialogue. Because this is a very important issue, you set

aside a whole day to develop some shared understanding around the challenges, the diverse cultures involved, the assumptions people have about what is going on, what is needed, and what is possible now. One of your guides is to not move into solution, to stay with the task of creating as full a view of the picture as you can. At the end of that day, you engage the group in reflecting on the day and recording learnings, insights, and understandings that it will be useful to take forward into tomorrow's meeting. Your outcome is the content of your reflections and the increased knowledge you have of one another. Setting aside the need for a specific outcome or decision is what allows you to develop the understanding that will ultimately lead to a better quality decision when you move to that stage of the process.

This guide is a crucial reminder that within dialogue the task is *not* to reach a decision. The task is to enhance understanding and build a shared view that includes diverse perspectives and creates the possibility for decisions made later to be better informed and possibly even of breakthrough quality.

Listen without Resistance

Although we've already said a lot about listening, we reiterate here because most groups will want to put something about this skill into their list of guides to serve as a powerful reminder of the importance of listening without resistance, particularly when the other may be in disagreement with your viewpoint. This guide encourages you to stretch beyond your usual goals of listening for content accuracy and understanding to a request that you be willing to set aside your own certainties and open yourself to receiving what others have to say. The image is one of letting the meaning of another's words shine through into you, rather than listening through the tightly guarded doors of your own opinions and judgments.

Respect Differences

It is our differing assumptions and the judgments we make based on them that most often separate us. Differences show up in all groups over time. Although differences can certainly be a source of conflict, they also create the zest, the renewal of the group's energy and spirit. Without differences, most groups are flat. Yet, in our culture, we have a very limiting attitude toward differences. We have been conditioned to think that it is better to focus on our similarities and shun our differences for fear we will be judged unworthy or undesirable, or end up in conflict. We have equated belonging and peace with being alike.

A respect for differences is considered the heart and soul of many spiritual traditions and lies at the core of most belief systems, regardless of culture. Respect has its roots in the Latin *respicere*, to "look back" or "look again." Think about times when you have consciously chosen to listen again to something said that at first seemed off the wall to you, simply because the person who said it was someone you respect. Respect lies at the heart of the ability to truly value diversity. It is hard to imagine how shared meaning that includes diverse perspectives can be built without it. Disrespect often excludes and at the very least minimizes the contributions of others, shrinks creativity, and fosters distrust. Respect is essential to any conversation that seeks openness and the advantage of an expanded view.

Suspend Role and Status

Roles and status weigh heavily on how we view and interact with people; they can make it almost impossible to create a level playing field where differences are respected and contributions are not limited by expectations associated with role and authority. Even in groups of peers, there will be unspoken roles and authority relationships. It is very difficult for us to hold them lightly or leave them at the door. And yet, to the degree that they limit us in speaking or listening openly, they limit our learning and the development of shared meaning. While status most often limits our speaking and/or causes us to confer more weight on what someone says, roles limit our perceptions of the value of someone's contribution. For example, if you hold someone to her role as director of marketing, you may unconsciously discount her ideas about research and development for a new software package.

Roles and status considerations do not magically disappear. Their influence is too ingrained by experience. Only over time, with the accumulation of different experiences, do we become able to suspend roles and status and not replace them with other versions.

> *In real life.* Suppose you are a member of a team that has worked together for some time and you are just beginning to explore dialogue. Within the group there are several levels of management. The lowest-ranking employees aren't too sure about speaking any more openly than they have in the past. The burden is on those with the most status: If this describes you, you will need to be aware of how you may unwittingly reinforce your role and status in the group. Behaviors such as judging the input of others, speaking more and expecting to be listened to more, giving directions and strong opinions, or not sharing the floor equally will all limit the participation of others. Behaviors that will help include considering everyone's opinion important and inviting participation, revealing your own uncertainties and questions, and contributing your thinking in ways that invite others to take ideas and creatively play with them to build something better.

How do roles and status positions influence the way you think, behave, and communicate with others? Reflecting on this question will make your own assumptions and behaviors more visible and enable you to make more conscious choices in your interactions.

Share Responsibility and Leadership

Where roles and status are suspended, leadership becomes the shared responsibility of the whole group. This can be very uncomfortable because it fundamentally alters power relationships in the group and disrupts habitual patterns of reliance on facilitators and/or leaders for the success of the conversation. Shared responsibility means that all members are now called upon to listen and respond in ways that support everyone's participation. You can't just space out and let a designated facilitator or team leader be the only one tending to the process. Constant attention to both what is being spoken about and how it is spoken is required.

When groups first begin to work with shared leadership, they often end up creating a vacuum into which no one is willing to step. This happens because leadership roles are traditionally well-defined in organizations. Everyone is supposed to know how much responsibility and leadership authority he/she has. When someone oversteps the bounds, intentionally or not, disciplinary action is swift. From the day we are born, we begin to learn about boundaries that limit our sphere of responsibility. There is always someone to whom we report—parents, older siblings, bosses, politicians. Self-determined responsibility is often neither expected nor desired of us. When we become managers and parents, the coin flips. Now we are the only ones who are responsible. We live in a culture where responsibility and leadership are carved out and distributed. Some have it and others don't.

To access the power of dialogue and create true collaborative partnerships requires the leadership of all members. Without shared leadership, it is difficult to avoid the trap of collapsing the many diverse views needed to create shared meaning into the significantly more limited view that results from focusing on conforming with the opinion of one designated leader or authority figure.

To develop this capacity in a group, everyone will need to break out of customary ways of thinking of leadership. One of the traditional leadership roles in group conversations is that of facilitator. The objective in dialogue is for the role of facilitator to reside within the entire group; for there to be no official facilitator; for each participant to share in the responsibilities that would normally be attributed to the facilitator. For example, if things aren't going well or if your needs are not being met, it is your responsibility to bring it to the attention of the whole group. This does not mean the group will immediately stop and shift gears to suit you. Honoring requests involves listening and considering all information provided when making informed choices about behaviors. Every group has its own rhythm and way of incorporating the voices of all its members. It is only through the continuous feedback loop created by all members offering input that the group can discover the unique combinations of behaviors that work for it. When a group has found its own collective rhythm, the full power of dialogue emerges.

In the beginning, a facilitator may be helpful, even essential, to support group members in developing skills and learning how to self-facilitate. But the desired end point is for the group to build its capacity for self-facilitation.

Speak to the Group

Dialogue fosters collective intelligence. When you think about a group, do you think of a collection of individuals or a collective entity? When you speak to people in a group, where do you tend to focus your attention? Most people consider groups collections of individuals and focus on one person in a group when they speak. In dialogue we shift our focus to consciously speak to the entire group. This can be difficult at first since we are used to speaking one-on-one, even in a group.

Sometimes, it can be confusing if you are responding to another person's question or asking one yourself. Remembering the purpose of the guide helps: *to support a conversation that includes everyone and allows the group to tap into collective intelligence.* One-on-one conversations tend to create spectators of those not involved. Questions and statements addressed to the whole group invite the participation and insights of all present. If you want to initially address yourself to one person, do so and then turn to include the group.

Speak when the Spirit Moves You

The origin of this guide is found in Quaker spiritual and business practice and is at the foundation of dialogue. Often, those new to dialogue ask, "How do I know when to speak?" This knowing is the result of learning to listen both within yourself and for what is moving in the group. Some people describe having a physical feeling as though they are compelled to speak. If you are uncertain, simply sit and continue to listen. If the idea or question or feeling continues to arise within you, then it is a good bet that it is time to speak and that it may be of value to the group. You'll often discover you are not the only one thinking or feeling the same way.

Also, learn how to discern what is true for you and to trust yourself to bring it into the group. At times it may be a very tenuous insight, something that springs out of an intuitive knowing. These can be the richest meanings, and they can also feel risky to share, especially if they seem far out or divergent from what has been spoken. Again, it is the practice of listening to yourself and to the group simultaneously and learning to tap into and trust your intuition that can result in contributions that open doors into new levels of understanding within the group.

Go Live

This is borrowed from a course developed by Jim Shipley of Interaction Associates. We particularly like it because it is a simple reminder to speak from your own experience and stick with what you are thinking/feeling/wondering about in the present moment rather than going over old territory again and again, or talking only about what others are saying, thinking, and doing. By focusing on the present and the thinking of those participating in the conversation and by holding an intention of moving beyond the way it has always been, you will spend less time circling and increase your chances of moving up the spiral to new levels of understanding and innovation.

Balance Inquiry and Advocacy

Inquiry, as we stated earlier, is one of the primary skills of dialogue. Yet advocacy is just as important. Both are needed to build shared meaning and sustain a powerful conversation. This guide is a reminder to be aware of the intentions behind your inquiry and advocacy and to balance the two.

Without advocacy we could not hear the different views in the room needed to build shared meaning. The ability to share something that you feel strongly about with the group is important. The problem arises when the way you share your view puts others on the defensive and/or shuts down conversation. The impact you will have depends on the intention with which you put it forth. If you advocate with the intention to persuade, control, or manipulate others, the group will instantly fall out of dialogue. Advocacy spoken with the attitude of "I am right" squashes listening and triggers defensiveness, aggression, and/or withdrawal. In such advocacy, there is no invitation to hear and learn from differing perspectives. There is no invitation to inquire. Only agreement is appreciated. If, on the other hand, your intention is to offer your perspective as one of many contributions to building a fuller picture of the issue and invite inquiry, then your advocacy will support the development of the group's collective intelligence.

We are all experts at advocating from an "I am right" stance. In fact, we are so good at it that we've even learned to ask questions to disguise our advocacy as inquiry. We mentioned such questions in the section on inquiry and reflection. They tend to start with words like "Don't you think . . . ?", rather than "What do you think . . . ?" Again, it is all a matter of intention. Questions can be interrogations with a "wrong until proven otherwise" message. They can be for the purpose of gathering ammunition in order to rebut another opinion. In dialogue the intention that motivates inquiry is to expand understanding, to build a more inclusive view of the whole. Such questions inquire into the relationships between ideas and ponder the patterns that may be emerging. They stretch our thinking and create openings for seeing in new ways.

Both advocacy and inquiry are needed. This guide reminds us to listen for our intention and a balance between the two. When you notice a lopsidedness or feel that you and others are using advocacy and/or inquiry to defend or push a position, here are a few suggestions. First, simply let the group know what you've observed. It will help increase the group's awareness of the conversation. Second, make your contributions in a way that acts to create more balance. If the scales seem tipped towards advocacy, try asking a question that helps refocus attention on inquiry and reflection.

Some Closing Thoughts

To guide or not to guide.

Most groups don't set aside time to agree on guides. Many never even speak of them. Perhaps they assume they are operating under a common understanding and that guides are unnecessary. Often such assumptions break down and misunderstandings develop in many forms from outright conflict to domination of the group by a few and lack of participation by others.

Group development of guides is essential in dialogue. The nature of the conversation you are creating is different from your everyday communication patterns. The primary purpose of guides is to help you to stay aligned with your intentions. For this reason it is important that they be crafted by you, the people who are engaging in the conversation. You may start with a few suggestions, such as those we have listed. But don't assume appropriateness or acceptance without checking it out with your partners in dialogue.

Once is never enough.

Because dialogue is a continuing practice, groups need to revisit guides and talk about unspoken norms that may be emerging. There is no hard and fast list of what will work. As your group develops, the guides may need to change to reflect ongoing changes.

Guides are a shared responsibility activity.

Shared responsibility is key to development of a group of equals. It is essential that all members reflect on whether the guides, as they currently stand, are serving the group or need changing. The more you and others can bring what is not working to the group's attention during the dialogue, the better. Reflection periods after the dialogue are useful, particularly in the beginning, because they provide a designated time to reflect and speak about the process itself, encourage continuous learning, and help avoid perpetuation of ways of interacting that are not useful.

Bringing the power of ritual to your dialogues.

The power of ritual derives from the respect with which people approach it and the shared meaning that it helps them remember. Ritual is a way of creating and stepping into an environment simultaneously. Introductions in workshops are simple informal rituals. The intention is to hear the voice of everyone in the room before proceeding. A ritual for evoking the qualities of conversation that you wish to bring forward in dialogue can be as simple as each person speaking about the quality they intend to bring forward and focus attention on. You can add to the power of this sharing by asking people to bring objects that symbolize those qualities of open and authentic conversation they wish to have present.

A FEW QUESTIONS FOR REFLECTION

- ○ What distinct elements would be important in your specific group/team to create dialogue?
- ○ What additional guides from your own culture might be useful in creating and sustaining dialogue?
- ○ Which of the above guides might you focus on as an individual to enhance your interpersonal communications?
- ○ How do you envision yourself acting to bring the guide(s) you are focusing on into your conversations with others?
- ○ What simple ritual could you create to serve as a way of calling forth the kind of environment and conversation you wish to create?

PUTTING IT ALL TOGETHER OVER TIME

*"This instrument can teach, it can illuminate; yes,
and it can even inspire. But it can do so only to the extent
that humans are determined to use it to those ends."*

—Edward R. Murrow
(about television, and true for dialogue)

*"In the beginning, people were expressing fixed positions,
which they were tending to defend, but later it became clear that
to maintain the feeling of friendship in the group was much more
important than to hold any position. Such friendship has an
impersonal quality in the sense that its establishment does not
depend on close personal relationships between participants.
A new kind of mind thus begins to come into being, which is
based on the development of common meaning that is
constantly transforming the process of the dialogue."*

—David Bohm
Unfolding Meaning

All the skills and guides we've spoken about so far can be practiced singly or together, in one-on-one conversations and in groups. Engaging in dialogue once, twice, or a handful of times will yield more meaningful conversation around important questions. If practiced on a continuing basis, it can produce significant shifts in the culture of the group or organization.

In Part I, reference was made to two primary aspects of dialogue: 1) building our capacity for metacognition, or the witnessing of our thinking process and the way we create meaning, make decisions, and take action; and 2) coming to an impersonal fellowship or spirit of community through a focus on relationship and how we are together. Experience has shown us that these two are so closely interwoven that no matter which one you initially focus your attention on, you are likely to end up experiencing both. The skills and guides focus attention on both aspects simultaneously. As you learn to suspend judgment and inquire into your assumptions, you become more aware of your thinking process and cannot help but see better ways of relating and working together more effectively. As you listen deeply to one another and reflect on both the diversity and the shared meanings in the group, relationships improve. The value of speaking openly about what is important and meaningful to building shared understanding and alignment is reinforced.

Through the practice of dialogue, the capacities for collective thinking and community develop side by side. As this occurs, it is common for both group and organizational culture to be affected in three noticeable and interrelated ways: 1) behaviorally, 2) experientially, and 3) attitudinally.

- ○ *Behaviorally.* The practice of new skill sets directs attention to different ways of conversing and working with others, leading to new cultural norms.

- ○ *Experientially.* The skills and guides set up conditions for experiencing metacognition and community. These experiences reinforce shifts in behavior and thinking. For example, as a new group you may find yourself in an atmosphere that has the feel and many of the characteristics of community early on, before you have had the time to get to know one another well. This experience gives a taste of what is possible and is a strong motivation for continuing the exploration. You may also find the experience of witnessing your thinking and the patterns of thought that influence your decisions and actions creates a powerful shift in how your group approaches issues. You will find yourselves more apt to inquire into your thinking in search of more comprehensive understanding and better decisions. You may also find you are more open to challenging your own certainties and seeing diverse alternatives.

○ *Attitudinally.* As you experience shifting behaviors and ways of thinking, a profound change begins to take place in the group's worldview. Attitudes of competition and individualism begin to give way to a focus on collaboration, partnership, and shared responsibility. People begin to seek out diversity in order to increase the quality of decisions. Beliefs around the value of the collective strengthen.

The diagram below depicts how the practice of dialogue creates changes in awareness and behavior that ripple out from individuals and groups to impact organizational culture. The ovals in the center represent possible applications, or practice fields, for dialogue that bring value to day-to-day activities. We will consider these more in depth when we speak about strategies for bringing dialogue into your work environment in Part III.

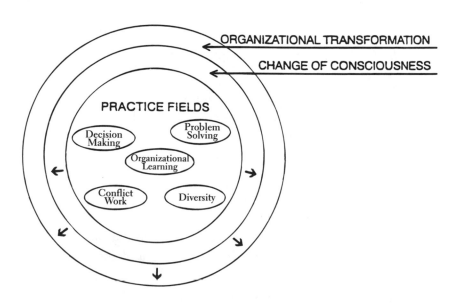

The Practice of Dialogue and Group Life

People often ask us if there is a pattern that groups follow as they learn and practice dialogue. We find both similarities and distinctions between the dynamics experienced in other group processes and dialogue. It is the distinctions that are more interesting to us. We'll return to these after a brief description of where the similarities lie.

Group process research and theory assures us that all groups move through a basic development sequence over time if they remain together. We outline this briefly below.

Stages of group development

Forming, inclusion, or pseudocommunity.[17]

You are getting to know one another. More attention is paid to similarities than to differences. You are discovering what fitting in means and making decisions about how "in" or "out" you want to be. One word characterizing behavior during this stage might be *cautious*.

Storming, control, or chaos.

You begin to explore your differences—styles, opinions, pacing. You are no longer content to agree with one another. You are discovering how control is exercised, by whom, where you fit in the control and influence circles and what will be needed to advance yourself and your ideas. One word characterizing behavior might be *challenging*.

Norming, or emptying.

You begin to look for the group's collective identity, determining what norms will work for everyone. The emphasis is shifting from individuals knowing what is best and being in control towards a realization that collaboration might be beneficial. One word characterizing behavior might be *inquiring*.

Performing, openness, or community.

You have found your collective identity, at least for the moment. There is agreement on norms that work for you as a group. A level of trust has developed such that you feel comfortable speaking freely with one another and can work with any conflict that may surface without withdrawing. You are able to benefit from your diversity. One word characterizing behavior might be *collaborative.*

The above stages may overlap from model to model. Groups practicing dialogue will, in general, experience similar dynamics. One description has been offered by Bill Isaacs of MIT based on his work with the Dialogue Project. He describes the four stages as they relate to the development of dialogue and what he calls "cool inquiry."[18] The stages are: 1) instability *of* the container, 2) instability *in* the container, 3) inquiry in the container, and 4) creativity in the container. The container is similar to the basket we've described as holding and facilitating the conversation. Stages one and two correspond with what we describe above as the appearance of chaos and differences and the move to working with them, using the skills that support dialogue. Stage three corresponds to the time when certainties are released and inquiry takes hold. Stage four, if it is attained, is where the capacity for collective thinking and creativity emerges. This model fits most observations from our work as well. However, as we said earlier, it is the distinctions that we've noticed with the practice of dialogue that are of most interest to us. We move now to a description of the primary ones we've experienced.

Going for Depth

To what depths are people willing to go? How much will they open up and speak what is on their minds? And in what time frame? If we were to draw a curve that represents roughly how groups commonly move into deeper conversation, it might look like this.

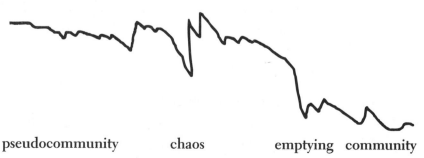

pseudocommunity　　　　chaos　　　　emptying community

Generally, people will reserve talk about what is most important to them until they have moved into the emptying and community stages described above. In those stages, it may be safe to risk deeper water. In most organizations, it is the exception for conversation to reach this degree of openness and depth. Most groups tend to cycle between the first two stages of group development—pseudocommunity and chaos. The exceptions to this pattern are groups that have made a commitment to work thorough their differences. Such groups have usually engaged in team-building activities or have been pushed into collaboration because of a crisis they have had to confront.

A group that is practicing dialogue often has a different experience. The curve might look more like this.

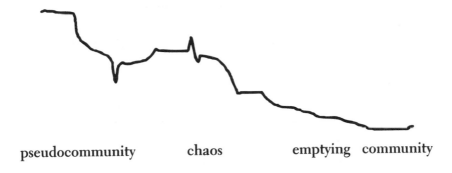

pseudocommunity   chaos   emptying   community

Agreement to use the guides and practice the skills for dialogue creates a significantly different environment than most groups experience when they first come together. While you may still deny major differences, there is usually some ability to raise diverse perspectives. There is an intuitive sense that more open conversation may indeed be possible with the skills and guides as aids. You will at times find yourselves going deeply into important issues early on. You may even be surprised by this and remark on it.

Hanging In There and Moving Through

As with all groups, when strongly held differences begin to emerge, there is usually chaos and discomfort. These will cause many groups to delegate issues to committee, table them, spend hours or even months cycling in the chaos, or even disband altogether. Occasionally, chaos may result in a leader deciding to push a group forward using more confrontative types of team-building activities designed to break down the barriers and create unity. When this path is taken, progress may be made but often it is only for the short term. The greater risk is that people may be injured emotionally and withdraw permanently.

It is here, in chaos, that the skills of dialogue can provide a way for you to work with what often seem to be irreconcilable differences. Suspending judgments, inquiring into the thinking behind assumptions, listening to all voices all combine to create the possibility for expanded understanding and alternative ways of moving forward. Because dialogue is about inviting, rather than pushing, and all members share responsibility for the pace, any progress made is usually built on solid ground. Dialogue helps make the inevitable chaos feel not quite so out-of-control. As you are able to work effectively with chaos and differences, these take on new meaning; they come to be seen as the seeds for creativity.

As your group deals with chaos and develops a capacity for valuing differences, you will find yourselves entering the norming/emptying stage. You will have begun to loosen your hold on hallowed certainties and move towards shared understandings and ways of working together. This process of letting go and moving on is often a time when old ways may need to be mourned. It can be a time of ambiguity and uncertainty as new, but not yet fully developed, ways of thinking and behaving emerge and grow stronger. This is a critical time to sustain the practice of dialogue. You need the ongoing support of a group working with the skills together to avoid reverting to old patterns. As you let go and move on, you will find yourselves in a field of impersonal fellowship, community, and openness. Performance and creativity usually reach new heights.

Continuous Renewal

At this point your group has fully developed both its metacognitive/learning and relationship/community abilities. You are flying high. Other people are asking you what you have been doing, how you can be so energized and creative amidst all the chaos and stress. *Now is not the time to stop.* Now is the time to recommit to your practice. Too often we arrive at our destination only to find that our destination is continuously moving under our feet. This is particularly true in group life where people work and learn together. New issues will surface new assumptions, new hallowed certainties, new differences to be worked with and integrated. The maintenance and constant renewal needed by a group of people seeking to be fluid in their thinking and learning is significant. Taking your accomplishments for granted is one way to guarantee that you will soon be in search of them once more.

Dialogue is meant to be an ongoing practice. By integrating the skills into your day-to-day activities in ways that create value for the group, you ensure the opportunity to develop and renew your capacity for collaboration and shared leadership on an ongoing basis. This integration is key to seeding more widespread cultural change within the organization. Most interventions used to improve group effectiveness are just that, an intervening or interruption in the group's day-to-day functioning. They are events. Then you go back to work in the same environment and structures that contributed to the development of the problem or dysfunctional patterns of communication in the first place. To shift culture, day-to-day norms must begin to shift. This will occur when you see a payoff in your everyday activities and not before. Approaching the practice of dialogue strategically can help create this kind of movement. In Part III we'll explore the challenges and possible strategies for bringing the principles and skills of dialogue into the workplace. Hopefully, the discussion will permit you and those you work with to move steadily into collaborative partnerships and shared leadership.

III

BRINGING
DIALOGUE
TO WORK

---

*"In dialogue a group of people can explore the individual
and collective presuppositions, ideas, beliefs, and feelings
that subtly control their interactions . . .* [Their
conversations] *can reveal the . . . puzzling patterns . . .
that often lead them to avoid certain issues or,
on the other hand, to insist, against all reason,
on standing and defending their opinions
about them."*

—David Bohm

T he power of dialogue can create profound shifts within individuals, groups, and entire organizations. Yet, as with many things, it is beginnings that are often the most challenging. Should you take one giant step forward or a series of small ones?

Our intention is to offer you a menu of strategies that will help you as an individual leader encourage and support the natural impulse for meaningful conversation and dialogue that lives within all of us. We hope that in bringing the principles and skills of dialogue into your workplace, you will find yourself increasingly in learning conversations and less often in the kind exemplified by the Morton-Thiokol-NASA story.

We do not offer these strategies as The Answers. Rather, what we propose here is a collaborative partnership. As we describe how dialogue and its principles can support you as leader, it will be your job to use your experience and knowledge to identify key leverage points for integrating dialogue within your particular context. In Chapter 1 we describe underlying values and conversational patterns experienced in most organizational cultures today. Chapters 2 and 3 propose strategies for creating conversations that support collaborative partnerships. Chapter 4 offers you a glimpse at some of the ways that dialogue is being brought into real-life everyday settings.

A *word on strategies.* In our history, "strategy," defined as "the art and science of conducting a military campaign to gain advantage,"[1] has been almost entirely associated with the competitive ethic and war. What we are proposing is that collaboration and partnership be pursued with the same tenacity, with clearly developed intentions and thoughtfully considered actions, to gain advantage for *all.*

1

CONVERSATIONAL VALUES
AND PATTERNS

"SEE, DO, GET.
Repeat what we see—get more of the same.
Look again—choose differently—create breakthroughs."

—Glenna Gerard

How we talk with one another is fundamental to our ability to think and learn together and make appropriate decisions. What follows is a collection of brief descriptions of some prevailing beliefs, values, and behaviors that shape conversations in organizations. They are intended to bring to mind real-life memories of conversations you have been part of and start you thinking about what is needed to create powerful conversations that support collaborative thinking and learning. The strategies in chapters 2 and 3 are the product of reflecting on this question.

And the Curtain Rises on Yet Another Day at Work

It's all about being right! We come to meetings to *advocate* our answers, our agenda, or to determine whose agenda we should adopt in order to be in the favored camp. Learning from one another through the exchange of ideas is not the top priority. There is always one best answer;

you win when it is yours and lose when it is not. Challenging questions demonstrate strength. Revealing a lack of knowledge is a sign of weakness.

In search of agreement, not input. Leaders often arrive for the meeting with a solution or destination already firmly rooted in mind. If opinions are invited, all those at odds with the leader's solution are met with counterpoints. Integrating new and different perspectives is too much work. Besides, the leader already knows the best way to go; isn't that what she is paid for?

Up the ladder in search of answers. It is safer to look to leadership for answers than to come up with one's own. Many of us will state our opinion only when we know where those in power stand. Leaders are validated for providing answers rather than listening and/or asking questions to help others find their own answers.

Escaping the gray zone. Ambiguity is confusing, uncomfortable, and to be avoided. When an answer is not obvious, there is a high degree of pressure for someone to "make the call" and whoever does becomes responsible. This means gray zones are risk zones. To escape them, we tend to see alternatives as black and white, right or wrong, winners or losers, when in actuality they are not. We may even find ourselves defending a course of action in the face of all evidence to the contrary.

We are all actors in a play. Though people are much more than numbers, functions, or roles, we come to meetings cast as sales managers, production supervisors, accounts receivable, customer service, marketing, shipping, legal, etc. We contribute ideas and questions from our assigned perspective; we play *our* role and expect others to play theirs. Crossing boundaries into other territories is not often done and can be dangerous. What does a salesperson know about production or vice versa? Roles allow people to focus attention and develop depth of experience in a specific area. They also fragment and limit the scope of what people observe, how they think, even how they are allowed and willing to contribute. A team becomes quite literally the sum of its parts/roles rather than a gathering of multidimensional people. Some teams end up as a functioning whole, others don't. If roles are too restricting, most of us just check out of the conversation. Our bodies are sitting there, but our energy and creativity remain elsewhere. Sometimes you can feel the "Why bother?" attitude in the room.

People are not trusted to make appropriate decisions. Control often substitutes for shared understanding and a feeling of ownership. Without shared understanding, flexibility and decentralized decision making seem dangerous. As a leader you might find yourself challenging decisions you delegated and looking over people's shoulders. Your questions may take on the flavor of interrogation. The relationship between flexibility, responsiveness, alignment, and effective decision making becomes unclear. Willingness to take on and share responsibility diminishes among team members as they decide that it is more efficient "to just go to command central before it comes to them."

You are not like me. We say diversity is a resource, but we often think the opposite: It is a pain in the neck. Are you in or out? Being different is not safe. It can make getting along with others difficult and make authentic conversaton seem risky.

Agreeing to disagree. Surely you jest! Sounds good, but in a culture where it's all about being right, and being right requires getting agreement, how realistic is this? Different styles and values tend to become either right or wrong. Most often, agreeing to disagree results in the separation of disagreeing parties or stalemated conflicts, both of which decrease open conversation and collaboration and minimize chances for aligned action. Suspension of judgment and listening are the exception. Questions are aimed at determining who is right rather than in revealing underlying interests to build shared understanding.

There is no time! Reorganization at multiple levels is the rule. Team membership changes day to day, yet you are expected to perform a nonstop stream of tasks, figure out how to integrate new people and create new structures and processes with no more time than you had before. Crisis management rules, and fire fighting is a 24-hours-a-day, 7-days-a-week activity. There is no time to talk about what is important, create shared meaning, and do what it takes to make informed versus reactive decisions. Conversation is totally task focused. Shortcuts are frequently taken to reach decisions. We say we want alternative and innovative thinking, but questions and new ideas are often unwelcome because they require time for consideration. People are either burnt out or edgy and volatile. Conflicts erupt, getting by becomes the norm, and creativity becomes equated with more work.

Why are we solving this problem for the umpteenth time? We "go fast to go fast" and often find we have "gone fast to go *very* slow." We find ourselves talking about the same problems and challenges over and over because so many of our solutions are single loop in nature. They take into account a change of action but rarely address the beliefs, assumptions, and motivating values involved. No one is amused when an old familiar enemy shows up yet again at the weekly production/marketing/customer service meeting. "If there is anything we learn from history, it is that we don't learn from history" can be a disappointing and expensive reality. And still we hurry to the next fix.

Mission/Vision: inspiration or demotivator? Imagine: one hundred top leaders, three days, a very fancy package with video clips, overheads, and multiple modules that you are supposed to present to everyone in the company. And it's really worse than useless because it's all based on the wrong questions and the people in the front lines know it. The mission statement tells us what we want to be but never stops to ask why we aren't that, why we aren't the best healthcare or manufacturing company around. The vision is too far removed from reality. People are disillusioned, even angry. Often those who are supposed to implement the vision were not even consulted.

Show me the money! The bottom line on the profit-loss statement is the driving force in most organizations. It drives downsizing, almost nonstop reorganizations, rapid cycles of hiring and layoffs, mergers, and on and on. You might assume that a focus on the bottom line would provide a common goal for alignment, but it can just as easily create chaos. When the bottom line is the prize, individuals, teams, and even divisions will move into competition with one another at the drop of a hat. Competition for resources and a singular focus on competing goals can rapidly create a house divided and undermine the overall health of the organization.

Values and Conversational Patterns

There are common themes in the images we've just described. They are values, beliefs, and assumptions. Though not always spoken out loud, they are indelibly etched in us all by experience and determine the nature and quality of our conversations.

- ○ Decisions and action create results. Reflection and soak time do not.

- ○ Attention to relationships and quality are secondary to quick decisions and action.

- ○ *Agreement = closure and getting on with it* is more important than shared understanding of what is agreed upon.

- ○ Fast equals efficient equals good. Slow equals inefficient equals bad.

- ○ Being right and being certain are strengths. Not knowing is a weakness.

- ○ Diversity creates problems and is not efficient. Similarity and agreement lead to fast, predictable results.

- ○ It is better to act as if those in power know best even when they don't.

- ○ We all have specific roles and will be evaluated on that basis.

- ○ Responsibility without power/control is undesirable.

The patterns of conversation that arise from these values and beliefs can be readily observed in our business cultures today.

- ○ high levels of advocacy with the intention of convincing, persuading, selling

- ○ low levels of inquiry, mostly directed at challenging or validating a position

- ○ little willingness to risk addressing undiscussables or suggesting alternatives different from the majority position

- ○ high levels of debate, with occasional chaos and conflict, as people compete to be right

- ○ cutting people off in mid-sentence
- ○ high levels of judgment of others' ideas, styles, interests
- ○ ignoring or denying others' views
- ○ low tolerance for examining assumptions, except as evidence in support of a position
- ○ low tolerance for silence, reflection, or any other activity that is not directed towards closure and action
- ○ listening primarily from an adversarial stance

None of the above is surprising, nor does it reflect a right way or wrong way to be in conversation. There are advantages and disadvantages to all these patterns, depending on your intention. Conversations are mirrors of the cultures they take place within. The above patterns are in complete alignment with the hierarchical, competition-based, individual-focused cultures that exist in most organizations, at least within the United States. The question that is important for our purposes is: *"What actions would help you create more powerful conversations and support collaborative thinking and learning?"* In Part I we talked of expanding our worldview rather than passing judgment on or throwing out current ways of working. David Bohm proposed that "observed thought changes." Rather than mounting a military campaign against current patterns, we suggest creating an environment for dialogue. This will naturally bring forth our inherent capacity for collaboration. Dialogue helps all of us see more of what is present so that we can make more conscious choices about how we talk together, think, create meaning, and take action.

2

CREATING THE CHANGE

YOU WISH TO SEE

"What got us here won't get us there."

—Executive at Silicon Graphics, Inc.

*"Definition of insanity: doing the same thing again and again
and expecting different results."*

—Anonymous

This chapter is the product of our work with businesspeople at various levels of leadership and management with whom we partnered in crafting approaches for using dialogue. Our joint purpose was to create more powerful conversations that would foster collaboration and shared leadership.

Our work together taught us much about moving toward collaborative partnership and shared leadership—first and foremost, that it is serious business. The good news was that the power of groups that learned to think and work together was nothing short of awesome. The bad news was that this capacity for collective intelligence and the power it brings with it can be perceived as threatening to the status quo.

Collaborative partnership is countercultural in most organizations. This is not surprising. A fundamentally competitive culture might be expected to perceive collaboration as a threat. Collaborative partnership could change how people are recognized, rewarded, and promoted

—the very definition of success. If you already know the rules of the game called Competition and are pretty successful, collaboration and partnership may not appear to offer you anything of value, particularly in the short run.

Collaboration and shared leadership shift the power dynamics of the game. As you consider the strategies suggested here, it will be helpful for you to do so with an awareness of this shift and some of the ways it may impact you. If you are prepared going in, your chances of successfully embracing and working with these challenges will be that much greater. So, here is a very short preview. We will return to this issue in the last pages for a closer look once you've made a first pass through the strategies.

As leader, moving towards partnership can feel like losing some measure of control. Or even worse, it may seem as if you are still responsible and accountable for everything but in control of nothing. Your visibility will change. People will challenge you in ways they never have before. You will hear things you would prefer not to know. You will find that people have expectations of you that you cannot meet, and vice versa. You will discover people who don't want to share responsibility with you. You will find people who want to share responsibility and find *you're* not sure how much you want to delegate or let go of. You may find yourself out of step with your peers in other parts of the organization.

All these challenges can be positive forces if you are prepared. With some forethought you can minimize the unexpected surprises that can put you on the defensive and make it tempting to revert back to business as usual. Working through your own discomfort and continuing forward in the spirit of dialogue will open people's minds to see that a different way of working together may be possible.

The strategies we propose have all been designed to help you bring the principles and value of dialogue to your day-to-day work with others. The intention behind them is *"to foster and support powerful conversations that will help create and sustain collaborative partnerships."*

We begin by speaking directly to you, the individual leader. Your attitudes and behaviors will be the single most powerful support or obstacle to fostering dialogue. The circle is then widened to consider two essentials for dialogue: 1) creating a safe environment where all can speak their truths, and 2) shifting towards sharing responsibility and information. From here, more specific aspects and activities of group life, such as diversity, conflict, vision/mission, problem solving and decision making, are dealt with. Ways are suggested in which dialogue can bring value to each. Two final strategies help you reflect on what support you, as a leader, will need and consider your approach before diving in.

✖ Strategy 1 ✖

BE THE CHANGE YOU WANT TO SEE IN THE WORLD.

*It is said that one day a woman came to Gandhi and asked
that he tell her child to stop eating sugar. Gandhi replied
"Come back tomorrow." When she asked why, he said
"I cannot tell another to do what I have not done.
Tomorrow I will have stopped eating sugar."*

This is a small story with a large message. Gandhi knew that we all *always* lead by example. In every meeting, every performance review, every planning session, you will lead by example. You have no choice. The important question is "What example?" This strategy is based on the recognition that you are the change agent. What will impact people is how you show up, what you say and the actions you take in one-on-one interactions, team meetings, in the cafeteria, or walking on the manufacturing floor. You are the most powerful tool at your disposal for bringing the principles and skills of dialogue, or any other process, to your group and organization.

Karen, chief operating officer to a large health-care provider, described to us how she first came to this realization. When Karen accepted her position, her charter was to get a troubled operation back on its feet in an environment characterized by crisis management and total demoralization at all levels. When she sat down to assess her role in accomplishing this mission, she found herself repeatedly pointing the finger of responsibility squarely in her own direction. Whose responsibility was it to provide some initial structure to get the organization stabilized? Hers. What about improving morale and the relationship between management and other employees? Her responsibility. Creating an environment where people could begin to entertain other ways of operating? Her responsibility. Karen didn't think she was going to do it all alone. She simply recognized that if she didn't do her job in a way that demonstrated that things could be different, then nothing new was going to happen. For the first time in her career, she realized that her superior abilities as an individual would not get the job done. Her success was going to depend to a high degree on her relationships with others, her ability to influence, and her willingness to be influenced in working collaboratively. There was no way around it. Karen was going to have to be the change she wanted to see.

We all pay much more attention to what people do than to what they say because deep inside we know that actions reflect a person's true thinking, values, and priorities. When there is a lack of alignment between what you say as a leader and what you do, the results are often confusion, frustration, demoralization, even anger and sabotage.

> *"There are three principles in a man's being and life, the principle of thought, the principle of speech, and the principle of action. The origin of all conflict between me and my fellow-men is that I do not say what I mean and that I do not do what I say."*
>
> —Martin Buber, *The Way of Man*

Three Key Focal Points

Of all the behaviors that support collaborative partnership, there are three crucial ones we want to draw your attention to: balance task, process, and relationship; schedule unstructured time into your calendar; develop a focus of curiosity about others. All three are directly aligned with the principles of dialogue. They commonly receive little or no attention because they are countercultural. They are all capable of creating significant shifts in the way people work together.

Balance Task, Process, and Relationship

Most leaders and managers are task proficient to one degree or another. Organizational cultures emphasize task and results and base most rewards and promotions on them. In the last 25 years, there has been an increasing interest in examining the processes by which results are obtained. The total quality movement and re-engineering both focus on process. What has been largely missing is any focus on relationship and its importance in producing quality results. Even the current emphasis on process is not about human process, the dynamics of how we work and communicate with one another. Many leaders actually avoid focusing energy in the area of relationship. They say it is personal and, therefore, does not belong in the work environment. Relationship is relegated to the realm of the soft stuff, the feelings, the stuff that gets in the way, that is better left at home, and is only dealt with if it becomes a big problem.

This presents a dilemma because, in actuality, nothing gets done except in relationship. Task, process, and results depend on it. Action does not occur in a vauum. At some point, every one of us was taught that for every action there is a reaction. Ignoring relationship and its dynamics is ostrich behavior of the most dangerous kind. Dialogue is a powerful practice field for learning how relationship, process, and results are interrelated.

Schedule Unstructured Time into Your Calendar

Make a task out of setting aside a given amount of time each week that is devoted to being in conversation with those you work most closely with, with no agenda and no predetermined outcome. Your only goal is to learn more about them personally, about the work they do and how you can support each other in the work you do together. Particularly in our culture, all conversation tends to be task focused. We ask about the family after we talk about the report if there is time left. One of the few professional relationships where this may be reversed is in sales-customer interactions. There seems to be more awareness that developing the relationship correlates directly with the success of the task. Getting to know those we work with helps us develop the relationships we need in order to work effectively together. It is no coincidence that the strongest teams have the strongest relationships. That doesn't mean they necessarily see each other after hours socially (though they may). It means that they know each other well and understand how to leverage their relationships to get work done.

Develop a Focus of Curiosity About Others

Being curious about people allows you to learn what makes them tick, how you are different and similar, how you see issues, what is easy, what the challenges are. Genuine curiosity evokes open conversation. Ask people what is important to them, what they feel passionate about these days in their lives and at work. You'll discover where their energy lives and how you can engage it. Practice being curious about very different points of view. Inquire into others' thinking. Use the ladder of inference. Find out what assumptions are behind their conclusions. And be willing to reveal your own thinking without being defensive. Often, when you disclose your ladder of inference and see the differences between you and another, you both begin to understand each other at a deeper level. You'll be surprised at how far curiosity and inquiry can take you in creating collaborative partnerships with those you work with and for. You may also be surprised at how challenging this is. Being genuinely curious when what you would like to do is tell the other person why he/she is wrong takes real commitment and practice.

Self-inquiry and Reflection: The Key Capability for Being the Change You Wish to See

What are the driving values in your life and work? If you are going to act with intention and awareness to create an environment for collaborative partnership, it is imperative that you know the *unedited* answer to this question.

One of Socrates' most important legacies was: *Know thyself.* Without this self-knowledge, Strategy #1 will always remain elusive. The practice of dialogue begins with a process of self-inquiry and self-reflection. Listening for one's own assumptions and most deeply held beliefs and values is essential in dialogue. Below are some questions worth reflecting on. They will help you become familiar with your own mental models and how they impact your ability to be the change you wish to see.

TRY THIS: A VALUES AND TIME INVENTORY

There is a saying that if you want to know what a leader values all you have to do is look at how she spends her time. Take a few moments to consider the following questions for the sake of what they can reveal to you about your personal focus of attention. As you reflect, practice suspending any judgments you may have about what comes up and simply work on noticing what is so. The more you suspend judgment, the clearer the picture you will get and the more useful this reflection will be.

1.   What are your day-to-day priorities? Make a list of the main activities you engaged in over the last week. Be specific. How was your time distributed among them? What do they tell you about what you value? For example, if you treated a colleague to lunch for his birthday, you might say that you value friendship or relationship. What percentage of your time do you devote to each value?

Activities	Values they reflect
% time	

2.   When activities compete for your attention, how do you make decisions? What values sit highest on the priority list? Check your answer against what you actually do. For most of us, they are not always the same.

3.   What is the balance of time you spend between "unstructured activities" versus "task- focused goals"?

4. If you were to create a list of activities for an ideal day at work, how would it differ from how you actually spend your day? How would your values shift in priority?

5. What blocks you from living your ideal day?

6. What choices will you make based on what you've learned from this reflection?

Moving Beyond Patterns

We are all programmed to behave and respond in certain ways; it is part of the enculturation process that ensures we will be able to survive in the environment we inhabit. Different families' cultures have different norms. Your birth order and early family experiences were among the first influences to shape your future leadership and management styles. Schools, religions, sports teams, fraternities/sororities, and the military provide values and beliefs about leadership, authority, and belonging to a group. It should be no surprise that you have developed patterns of behavior from these experiences. The question is: "How aware are you of these patterns?"

There are multiple personality indicators, self-assessment tools, and processes designed to help you build awareness of your cultural and individual style patterns. Organizational development professionals can help you access these. The more of this work you have done, the less you will be at the effect of unconscious reactions. The sentence "I just don't understand why I react the way I do in certain situations; it certainly wasn't my intention" will begin to disappear from your conversations. Knowing yourself is a first essential step to being able to make conscious choices about how you respond to diverse situations. It is also an essential skill for creating an environment that supports dialogue. Many of us have developed ways of leading based on the modelling of authority figures we've grown up with that are not congruent with dialogue and collaboration. Before we can bring our styles into alignment with new ways of talking and working with others, we must first be aware of the incongruence within ourselves.

Two powerful by-products of building your own self-awareness are an appreciation of its complexity and challenge, and compassion for others who are struggling along the path. You will begin to be able to see how to be helpful to others, when to encourage, and when to be patient.

✷ Strategy 2 ✷

CREATE A SPACE WHERE IT IS SAFE FOR PEOPLE TO SPEAK ABOUT WHAT IS IMPORTANT AND MEANINGFUL.

"I make it safe for people to say what is. I use meetings where I ask people to tell me what is wrong. Now, it is not easy to get them to do it. But if I can get one person . . . to stand up in a meeting and say 'you know, we've really heard all this before and we don't believe you' and I look at him and say 'Good!'"

—R. A. Harrison, Jr., VP CIGNA HealthCare

Developing trust is one of the greatest challenges facing you as a leader. Typical conversational patterns in organizations are built on competition, fear of authority, and survival of the most politically astute. There is no magic formula for building trust. But an unswerving dedication to listening, curiosity, suspension of judgment, and nondefensiveness will see you a long way down the road.

A primary ingredient is your ability to speak *your* truth about difficult issues and listen to others do the same. Again, it is your example in applying Strategy #1 that is crucial. Here we outline the elements we have found absolutely necessary. Many of them are based on the skills and guides you read about in Part II.

Speak from a Place of Respect and Honor for the Other Person

This theme is so essential to dialogue that it is one of the guides in Part II. Respect doesn't mean you have to like the person. But it does require that you be willing to listen, to "re-look," and reconsider what the person has to say. It requires that you look beyond your personal dislikes and judgments and accept the challenge of learning from everyone you meet. Respect is about honoring a person's being and valuing his/her right to life and expression. If someone offers us respect, we know we are safe with that person. If I do not respect you, I may harm you without a second thought.

Some people say that they cannot respect someone they don't like or trust. You might take a moment to ask what your thoughts and feelings are about this—it is important. Can you offer everyone in your group respect, whether you like them or think they are competent or hold the same values? If not, you will find this a difficult behavior to model. Unless you can speak to all people with respect and honor, everyone will know that open expression is not safe.

If you can't feel respect for someone you don't like, consider this: Shift your focus from the other person to you. Make it your goal to leave each interaction with that person feeling good about your behavior. Did you speak in a way that left you liking yourself? If you can answer yes, there's a good chance that you will have spoken in a way that was respectful of the other.

Your Truth is Your Truth, Nothing More and Nothing Less

What you perceive, your observations, feelings, interpretations, are all *your* truth. Your truth is important. Yet it is not The Truth. When you speak your truth with this understanding, your words do not require that the listener agree with you or change in any way. They will be words that others can listen to because they will be spoken without blame or judgment. It is not the other's fault that you feel a certain way. His ideas are not stupid or bad. They are not the same as yours. You are not any more right than he is. Your perception and the thinking behind it are yours. When you accept responsibility for your thinking, you can speak without pushing your truth at the other person and minimize defensive responses. Chances are, people will listen more closely to what you say if you first acknowledge that it is your perception and may not be shared by anyone else.

TRY THIS: SPEAKING YOUR TRUTH AS A TRUTH

Begin to pay attention to the words you use, to how you offer feedback or an alternate perspective. Do you leave room for other people's perceptions and feelings, particularly when they are different than yours, without needing for one of you to be right and the other wrong?

1.   When you give someone feedback, do you say "When you say _____ *it makes me feel* _____"? Try shifting to "When you say _____I feel _____ and this is what I'm thinking and assuming." Lift the responsibility from the other person.

2.   When you offer a differing perspective, do you find yourself saying something like: "No. No. That's not it. What happened was . . . ."? Try prefacing your differing perspective with "I think I hear you. Let me check my understanding. Okay. My experience was different. Here's what I observed and the interpretations I made."

When You Have a Different Perspective, Be Willing to Listen to the Other Person First

The payoff here is huge. However, it requires great self-control. Once we feel we have been really listened to and heard, it is difficult to not return the favor. What follows is a description of a technique called "shifting gears." It is adapted from Carl Zaiss[2] and Tom Gordon and is a powerful tool for working with potentially conflictual situations. Here's the scenario. Imagine yourself as Harry. Put yourself in his shoes. Feel his feelings. Imagine yourself responding as he does.

Harry and John are managers of different departments within a corporation. They are in a meeting together. Harry wants to bring out a recurring problem with reactor shutdown procedures. Everyone present is involved in some way, and he thinks there will be value from talking together. But he's hesitant because he thinks John may get defensive. He starts with the following statement. *Notice how he owns his own perceptions, rather than stating them as fact.*

Harry says, "I'd like to bring up some information about the last reactor shutdown. I realize that what I'm about to say is purely my interpretation of events and others may see it differently, but I'd like to get it out in the open so we can tackle it together. When we were going over the data yesterday, I thought I might have seen a pattern indicating inadequate or incorrect maintenance procedures. Now, I know this might be tough to hear, but it could be just as dicey for all of us if we don't talk about it."

John bristles and begins shaking his head. "Damn, Harry, you know we're doing the best we can . . . the pressure lately has been horrendous . . . we've got some new guys on the crew . . . and besides everyone is just looking to blame us so they don't have to look too closely at their own departments! Get off my back, will you?"

At this point Harry's natural tendency is to reiterate his point. After all, if John didn't listen the first time, maybe if he says it again, with more emphasis, he'll get it across. Of course, what actually happens is that John gets more defensive; the whole thing escalates. It is scenarios like this that discourage us from speaking about difficult issues. And any possibility of dialogue dissolves. What can Harry do that may help get things back on track? He can "shift gears." Here's how.

Rather than continuing full speed ahead, Harry shifts into neutral and begins to listen to John. He might say something like, "Hmm, I can see you're under a lot of pressure. I didn't know that you felt others might be scapegoating you or about all the new recruits. Tell us more about what's going on."

John, who has been getting ready for Harry's next attack, is a little surprised. He may actually have a chance to get listened to here. So, he begins to talk. If Harry can suspend his own defensive response and open the door to listen to John's perspective, chances are very good that before long John will also be able to listen to Harry and the whole group will be able to engage in dialogue around a potentially volatile issue important to them all.

It's really as simple as "I'll listen to you if you listen to me." The hard part is suspending your need to be heard and listening first. Simple, powerful, challenging. Try it out. Use the image of actually shifting gears. It helps! When the other person gets defensive, feel yourself downshift into neutral.

Develop Your Willingness to Not Know, to Not Have the Answers

> It's the third time you've met in as many days; the problem has become an emergency. The president says he is open to hear all ideas, but every time someone says something that he either doesn't understand or disagrees with, he shuts the person down. You can't leave, but you wish you could.

Leaders who are unwilling to "not know" are often caught in the grip of two assumptions: 1) they are supposed to do the talking, and 2) they are expected to have the answers. Take a moment to reflect on the impact of these assumptions. Recall a time when you showed up at the meeting with The Answer. How did this influence the way you listened? Did you listen from a place of respect and openness to differing views?

When you have all the answers, there is no room for anyone else. If others are only present to validate and agree with you, you will never create a safe place where people feel that their ideas and creativity are valued. One VP of marketing takes this approach. "I tell people I don't have the answers. I say this to very large groups of people. I tell them that I think most of the answers rest with them. My job is to figure out how to help them surface and implement the answers."

There is a saying that nature abhors a vacuum. Your willingness to not have the answers, and even if you've got one, to not jump forward with it, creates a vacuum. People will engage it; they will move in and give you the benefit of their vision and thinking. The key is for you to maintain the opening by practicing your inquiry and listening skills and encouraging others to do the same. Ask open-ended questions. Resist the urge to speak. Employ the 80/20 rule: listen 80 percent of the time and speak 20 percent of the time.

Some leaders and managers we've worked with actually fear that if they stop talking, start listening, and encourage questions, particularly ones that may challenge their assumptions and solutions, they will be viewed as losing control. However, most of the people in their groups didn't hold this view at all. They know who is going to make the final decision, even if things get a little rowdy during the process. What they do want is a framework that supports getting all the ideas out on the table and encourages people to listen rather than move into debate. This is what will get them to the solution that incorporates all the knowledge and creativity in the room. Show the way by example. Ask questions. Suspend judgment and help others remember to do the same.

Learn to Use Vulnerability as a Strength

Vulnerable can be a bad word in a competitive culture. It is too often associated with weakness. But being in situations where you need the help and support of others in your group can be a golden opportunity to build safety and trust. Here's one example offered by a manager whose job consists primarily of troubleshooting one hot spot after another.

"Two of the men I work with were arguing and arguing. We were getting no place. Soon I was going to have to step in and make the decision but I knew that wouldn't solve anything...they would still not like each other, or me, or any decision I made. I took a risk. I said to one of them. 'Look, Steve, I'm feeling pretty vulnerable right now because I really don't know what is going on between the two of you, and you are not working this out, and it is putting me into a place where I really don't know what the best answer is. But I have to explain this whole situation to the owner. I'm not feeling very good about it. What's going to happen here?' Now Steve, who is one of the most egotistical people I know, turns to me and says, 'Karl, you know what, let me call Bob (the other side of the argument) and see if we can't work this out.' They got together, they worked out the problem, they both compromised a little, and then they came back to me and told me what they were going to do. It never would have happened if I had just driven straight ahead and made the decision. And the decision they came up with was pretty damn good."
—KP Seevers, Regional VP Service, NUPAK

A willingness to admit not knowing what to do and asking for help shows that you are human. Every one of us has been there. If you can risk being vulnerable, you can create opportunities for others to come up with their own solutions. Your willingness to be vulnerable becomes a strength that helps others share responsibility with you and build their own confidence and self-reliance. You are modeling a most important aspect of collaboration—that vulnerability is not bad: it can create strength within a group.

TRY THIS: REFLECTIONS AND EXERCISES IN "NOT KNOWING"

- Do a little self-assessment. How willing are you to not know? Do you go into every meeting with an answer that it is your job to advocate? When you don't know, do you come up with something anyway? What is your response when you don't understand something someone has proposed? Do you say you don't get it and ask for help? Or do you become argumentative and debate the proposal?

- Try going into your next meeting without any preconceived answers or, if you can't do that, try putting your answers on a side burner temporarily and seeing how many other different ideas you can gather.

- See if you can shift the balance of listening to speaking just ten percent in favor of listening. Notice what kind of response you get.

- Experiment with being the last to offer an opinion.

Safety is Highly Dependent on Confidentiality

In your one-on-one relationships, confidentiality is important. We tell some people some things and not others. You may use many criteria in your assessment of what you say to which people. One common one is whether you trust people to keep what you say to themselves. If you tell someone something and he does not keep it confidential, then when you tell him, you know you are potentially telling any number of unknown people.

Agreement on confidentiality is just as essential to creating an environment of trust and openness within a group. What is confidential and what are the boundaries in terms of expressing what takes place or is said within the group? There is nothing as destructive to trust and safety as taking a risk to tell your truth and finding that there was no shared meaning and agreement around confidentiality. If the risk was predicated on assumed agreements, the sense of betrayal will undermine openness, and future dialogues will become shallow and of little or no value.

Most of us take for granted that there is shared meaning around what confidentiality is and what the essential elements are. Yet, few groups are not surprised at people's different perspectives when they open the topic up for conversation. It is important to talk with others, to find out what is important, and to come to some initial agreements, and then, later, to revisit and update those agreements.

TRY THIS: AN INQUIRY INTO CONFIDENTIALITY

Create a time for the team to talk about what confidentiality means to each member and what actions are important to honoring confidentiality. Ask each person to be specific. For example, if you want to share an insight or learning from a conversation at a meeting, what is appropriate? Do you give the names of all involved? When would this be okay? When wouldn't it be? What about sharing a story that someone else told during the conversation? You'll be surprised by the diversity of opinions and needs. At the close, see if you can come up with a few guides that the whole group agrees will help promote safety and that they can commit to following. It is important that people know the minimum they can expect. They can then take responsibility for their own safety and the nature of their contributions.

Safety is a Shared Responsibility

Ultimately the safety in any group is the responsibility of all members—
yet the leader will always need to set the example, demonstrating all the
behaviors we have spoken about, acting with awareness of her power
and position and its impact on others.

Each person must be encouraged and allowed to monitor his own
internal "safety gauge" and act accordingly. There is no room for lapses
in attention, or for thinking that someone else is going to take care of
your interests. If it does not feel safe to share particular information,
take responsibility for your own safety and do not take that action, no
matter what the group wants. This will be a powerful model for everyone in the group. Additionally, it is everyone's responsibility to recognize that groups of people can bring powerful pressure to bear on
individuals encouraging them to participate in ways that may not feel
safe. Groups can exert this pressure without ever saying a word. You
all have a responsibility to one another to be aware of this phenomenon
and to call attention to it if you think it is occurring. Groups build safety
and trust over time. You may feel as though the going is slow in the
beginning, but there is no safe substitute for allowing the group to
develop at its own pace.

A Closing Thought

The Constitution of the United States of America starts "We the
People," in recognition of the power of collective thought and passion
to forge reality. The First Amendment guarantees the "right of free
speech," as an essential and irrevocable right of all people. Deep in
our memories we know the importance and power of speaking our
truths. Your work as a leader is to create environments where it is safe
and highly valued to speak up and contribute different views.

TRY THIS: SMALL ACTIONS THAT SPEAK LOUDLY
Actions speak much louder than words. Here are some things that
you can do that will help create an environment of safety that

honors all those present. They may seem small, but they will have significant impact.

o   However you greet people to welcome them, extend the same welcome to every person, whether they are your favorite, someone you've just met, the quiet one, etc. Let everyone know you are glad they are there.

o   Take an attitude of service towards those in your group. We know a manager who makes a point of serving people coffee, soft drinks, or water as they come in. He actually gets the drinks. Don't expect others to do something for you because you are the leader. In fact, do it for them.

o   Try being the last one to sit down at the table. Don't place your things to reserve your spot. Take the seat that is left after everyone else is seated. Accepting a place among your group signals them that you are not special or above them.

o   Come with a clear purpose for the meeting but without expectations for the specifics of how people will participate to formulate the outcome.

o   Make direct eye contact with everyone and let your gaze send the message "Welcome. Glad you are here and contributing your ideas."

o   Dress down a little. This is not a power meeting. It's a collaborative endeavor. People need to feel loose, informal. The energy is like that of a breeze through a willow tree or water flowing. Stiff and formal will not encourage participation and a feeling of safety.

o   When you just want to jump in and make a statement, ask yourself if it's absolutely necessary and if not, bite your tongue, count to ten (at least), and continue shifting the balance to listening.

o   Practice suspension of judgment in every single conversation.

o   Ask a question instead of giving an answer.

o   Look through the Appendix and experiment with some of the activities. Two in particular may be useful: 1) the talking stick, and 2) the inquiry and reflection circle. Both help create space for those who are speaking to do so without fear that they will be interrupted by someone else. Many people have commented that the second one is particularly useful since people seem to go deeper into what is meaningful to them about a particular issue because they know that not only will they not be interrupted, but that there will be no rebuttal or evaluation following what they say.

○   Listen to each person as you might listen to a person you consider to possess wisdom that will be helpful to you in some way.

⁂ Strategy 3 ⁂

SHIFT TOWARDS SHARED RESPONSIBILITY.

Place the responsibility for solving problems and responding to challenges where it is the most effective rather than the most controlled. At some point, all leaders come to realize that it isn't the knowledge they bring so much as their skill in helping people share in the responsibility and use the information that is valuable.

When people "go up the ladder for answers" because of past experience and conditioning, responsibility becomes concentrated at the top of an organization or group. This often limits vision and creativity because the number and diversity of perspectives are dramatically decreased. You can begin to shift this balance by returning issues and problems to those who bring them to you. Employing this strategy encourages people to re-engage their thinking capabilities and apply them to information that often only they possess. In organizations where we hear cries of "people just don't care anymore," this strategy is an important step on the path to re-engaging people in their work.

The shift towards shared responsibility is essential for collective thinking and learning. It is the key to decentralized decision making that maintains aligned action. When people share in responsibility, they know they make a difference, they participate more creatively, and they have a higher degree of investment in the outcome. In short, they care.

When there are multiple stakeholders, it is important to find a way for everyone to interact with one another's ideas. This can be difficult if they are spread out across time zones. Consider utilizing teleconferencing or an E-mail list to engage the conversation. But do everything you can to get people interacting. Otherwise you will only get the benefit of them interacting one-on-one with you and the flow of responsibility will move primarily in your direction rather than being shared.

As leader, your role is particularly important in this strategy. You will need to make the initial move in shifting the responsibility. Then set an example by identifying and suspending assumptions, asking questions, and listening. You may also need to offer the benefit of your knowledge of the whole system. Your objective is to help unlock the best of everyone's thinking to craft a solution that works to address the problem in the context of the overall organization. You are successful when the group is successful and vice versa. With each success, you demonstrate the power of conversation and collaboration to engage collective intelligence and produce aligned action and results.

TRY THIS: FOSTERING SHARED RESPONSIBILITY AND COLLECTIVE LEARNING

o   Create ways for all members of the group/team to share responsibility for functions that make meetings successful. Consult the team to find out what they think the crucial functions are and then rotate these from meeting to meeting.

o   Whenever anyone brings to the group an issue that involves an important decision, create the time for at least one round where each person is given the opportunity to speak about the issue without questions or response. If people have questions, they can write them down so they don't forget. This creates a pattern of everyone sharing responsibility for providing pertinent information and applying their thinking to issues.

○   Make a point of doing postmortems at the end of meeting, where everyone says what they observed as supporting the group in its work and what was missing or could be improved for the team to be even more effective. Then make sure to create an action plan with the group to address the results of this reflective inquiry.

○   Ask team members for recommendations on how responsibility needs to be distributed for any given project/task. Go with the recommendations. If you see some reason not to, be sure to reveal the thinking and questions behind your concern or alternative proposal.

Sharing Information

It is very difficult for people to accept shared responsibility without open access to information, yet information can be one of the most tightly guarded of possessions. What stops us from sharing information? It is the belief that information is power. In the competitive model, those with the most information will prevail over those who have less. *In a collaborative model, only those who have access to information can contribute effectively.* When information is withheld, the consequences can range from poor decisions to outright lack of support and sabotage. Here is a case in point, a not uncommon occurrence, taken from an interview with an executive-level VP.

"Trust is a big thing. One of our Senior VPs recently gave a speech that left many of us thinking: 'This is an astute businessman. How can he come to this conclusion?' It had gotten to the point where I was having difficulty dealing with him. Last week I met him for lunch. When I asked him about the 'earnings versus margin issue,' he told me he's been fighting with the CFO since the day he took the job. He knows we need to focus on earnings to have growth. When I hear this I think, 'What a shame' because two months ago when he was out to talk about the right business strategy for California, he never said 'Guys, I've got a problem. The CFO is going for margin. I know we need earnings, but I need your help in figuring out how to tackle this.' Instead he stood up there, created a whole scenario, and even though he never said margin we all knew what his hidden agenda was. There was such a complete lack of trust that he really did end up failing because nobody was behind him; we were even looking for ways to make him fail."

By sharing information, leaders can enroll people as partners in determining what to do. Not giving people the full picture can lead to having no partners and to creating adversaries. The growing move towards "open-book management" is based on experience that when we share information with people and give them the tools to use it, they become more effective and more engaged in their work. They also know a lot more about how their piece fits into and impacts the health of the whole organization, which in turn shows up in higher quality decisions and actions.

Individuals organize their lives around information. Groups and organizations build structure, make decisions, and take action based on information available to them. Information quite literally creates form. In *Leadership and the New Sciences*,[3] Meg Wheatley proposes encouraging the free flow of information as a way to circulate lifeblood to the furthermost reaches of the organizational body, enabling it to self-organize in ways that allow maintenance of a core identity and adaptation to a changing environment. Both are important for survival. Self-referencing maintains identity. Adaptation allows for evolution.

New information coming into a system stimulates creativity. Disturbances can stimulate new directions in evolution. This is true of biological organisms, development of high-tech products, and the creation of entire organizational structures. Taking advantage of such occurrences requires: 1) that information be available, and 2) a way of listening for these blips on the radar screen. Conversation is invaluable for both.

But, Not All People Want to Know What is Going On

Many people will be uncomfortable with shared responsibility and shared information. They will want you to tell them what to do. They come to work to work, to do the job, but they don't want responsibility, they've got enough of that at home. You may have room for some of these people in your group and organization. You'll have to make the call as to how many. But in areas where you want to encourage and benefit from collaboration and groups learning together, you'll need to help people develop a level of comfort with sharing information and responsibility. Use the questions at the end of this chapter. They will help all of you move through any discomfort you may feel.

TRY THIS: SHARING INFORMATION

○   If you are interested in developing the capability of your group or organization to intentionally work with information as a creative medium, consider sponsoring one or two open dialogue groups or town meetings that take place on a regular basis. Create a simple set of guidelines that will encourage the free sharing of information with the intention of: 1) asking questions that stimulate curiosity and reflection, and 2) listening for new thinking and connections that may be emerging.

○   To gain some clarity about your own assumptions relative to information, consider your responses to the following questions:

1. What is the function of information?
2. Who should have access to what information?
3. What criteria shape your decisions?
4. What beliefs would you have to hold in order to share information more widely?

All these questions would also be rich material for a group dialogue with your team.

○   Select one or two areas where sharing more information could increase people's understanding and ability to be creative partners with you. Or ask your team to help you select an area as a test project.

✻ Strategy 4 ✻

CREATE DIVERSITY AS A RESOURCE.

"I don't paint things. I only paint the difference between things."

—Henri Matisse

Diversity represents one of the most powerful paradoxes for us. We would not be able to live without it, and often it seems as though we won't be able to live with it. It is troublesome and difficult because we are more comfortable with sameness. We are socialized to look for our similarities. Yet it is our differences that provide us with our individuality and the unique perspectives and talents we bring to any collaborative effort.

Where is the *added* value in collaborating with someone who thinks and acts the same as you? A good friend, AnnaMay Sims, reminds groups that "There is no one just exactly like you in the whole world. If there were, one of you would be dispensable." You can program a robot to carry out your wishes. Creativity requires diversity.

Our planet is an incredible example of the importance of diversity. The evolution of the atmosphere and environment that support such an array of life-forms is an anomaly in our solar system. Our breathable atmosphere exists as a metabolic by-product of microorganisms that began giving off oxygen over 3 billion years ago. We digest food courtesy of other microorganisms that had to go into hiding in oxygen-free environments, like our intestines, in order to survive when the oxygen producers hit the scene. We could trace this for a long while, but you get the idea. Our continued existence depends on a diversity of life that surrounds and quite literally inhabits us. And still we have an innate distrust of diversity. Until we create immediate experiences that demonstrate to us that diversity is an asset, we will find it difficult to act from this belief. Much of your work as a leader in addressing this area is to help create such experiences.

Differentiation in Teams

Differentiation is required for teams to operate at full potential. It is how you get to know one another's strengths and weaknesses and learn how to create a collective resource that is greater than the sum of your parts. The ability to move through the stages of differentiation is essential for us to tap into our full human potential. Very few groups move beyond the first stage.

We briefly describe the process of differentiation so you can reflect on where you see your group and on how dialogue might be useful in moving further. You will notice some correlation with the stages of group development that we summarized at the close of Part II. In this model, difference is first developed and then integrated into a whole. The whole and individual parts are interconnected, standing side by side, neither collapsing into the other.

Stage One

Initially, group members look for ways they can interact that build on what they perceive to be their similarities. They ignore, deny, and/or avoid dealing with differences among themselves. There may be a lot of pretending to agree or just not rocking the boat. This corresponds to the forming, or inclusionary, stage mentioned in Part II. People are finding their initial places within the group. Dialogue can accelerate this process. Using advocacy and inquiry with the intention of learning more about how all members think about any issue can break the ice and move the conversation into more open, deeper waters fairly quickly.

Stage Two

After a while, the group is unable to deny their differences. These often appear as different work habits and communication styles that have a direct impact on how well people work together toward accomplishing their goals. The group may become chaotic, conflictual, and highly uncomfortable. Terms for this stage are chaos, control, or storming. Most groups don't have the skills to deal with the diversity and resultant conflict that surfaces. They are unable to move on to the next stage of differentiation and higher levels of performance. Practicing dialogue can help the group to suspend judgment, remain in inquiry, listen openly, and begin building a shared understanding of the diverse experiential backgrounds in the group. As people share their ladders of inference with one another, they gain the deeper understanding necessary for honoring diversity and integrating it into a powerful resource.

Stage Three

Openness and trust grow. Members transcend their need to be right and begin to think collectively and create in collaborative ways. Diversity is experienced as a resource rather than as a problem to work through. The group builds shared understanding. This does not mean that everyone comes to agreement on the same point of view. It means that members have learned now to hold an awareness of all the points of view present. Now they can begin to create new approaches and solutions that incorporate the strengths of their diversity. The whole team becomes greater than the sum of its individual members. Shared leadership becomes possible because the group knows itself well enough for anyone to step forward in ways that best assist the whole team. The team has become a hologram: Each member contributes a unique aspect and is capable of reflecting or representing the whole team in his/her speaking and actions. The group has become fully differentiated and integrated, while maintaining its diversity. Other names for this stage are: openness, affection, norming-to-performing, or emptying-to-community. In this stage, an ongoing practice of dialogue will support the group in sustaining a high level of openness, learning, and performance.

Differentiation and In-and-Out Dynamics

As groups differentiate, people often cluster in subgroups. Being with others who are similar feels more comfortable, safer. Power differences create issues of inclusion and exclusion. Some people have control, others don't. Usually, those with the control are the in-crowd and everyone else is out and trying their best to get in.

In-and-out dynamics create separation, tension, and mistrust. Whenever people feel they are second-class citizens because of religion, race, sexual orientation, gender, cultural heritage, personal style, or lifestyle, collaboration and partnership are the furthest things from anyone's mind. Dialogue provides a way for the group to talk about these difficult and important realities, to build the awareness needed for people to begin to take actions that promote respect for the differences present. When people feel accepted and honored for who they are and the contributions their differences bring, collaboration becomes a possibility. Until then, it will be only words.

TRY THIS: EXPLORING DIFFERENTIATION

○ Ask your group what diversity issues it would be useful to explore. A fairly safe place to start and one that can immediately yield value in terms of work productivity is personal styles. There are some simple instruments you can use with minimal outside guidance. One is the Firo B, which looks at communication styles. Another one is the Meyers Briggs Type Indicator. There are many more.[4] The results are always useful. For help deciding which one to use, ask an organizational development consultant in your organization. Conversations around personal styles are great practice fields for suspension of judgment, identification of assumptions, listening, and inquiry.

○ A diversity issue that comes up in many groups has to do with pacing. Some people are more extroverted, move faster, and can end up dominating the conversation. Others like to contribute but process information internally and look for openings to speak. Often they have trouble finding one. If you are working with creating guidelines customized for your group, set aside enough time to allow for the conversation to go to some level of detail and depth around statements such as "respect one another," "no one dominates," "everyone contributes." See if you can help the group bring to light *specifically* what these mean to everyone present and what actions will be needed on everyone's part to make them a reality.

- If there is a high degree of cultural, ethnic, and/or racial diversity in your group, it may be valuable to create the space to get to know more about one another and how people's differences influence their participation in the group. You may want to ask someone experienced in facilitating such conversations to help you get started, and to help build a foundation for further conversations.

Strategy 5

REFRAME DISAGREEMENT AND CONFLICT AS AN OPPORTUNITY.

We live in a predominantly conflict-adverse culture. Conflict is bad. We wouldn't "touch that one with a ten-foot pole," because we don't want to end up in a big controversy. Yet, where people are working together to accomplish tasks within very constrained time limits, personal differences create fertile ground for conflict. Ignoring conflict does not make it go away; conflict driven underground often surfaces as sabotage or explodes unexpectedly. Conflict, like diversity, can be reframed as a resource for those teams that understand how to explore it with the intention of learning from it.

Conflict will always be present where there is diversity. In the most highly functional and healthiest of groups it exists out in the open because people are not afraid to enter into disagreement, initiate inquiry, listen to one another, and learn. They are confident that they can discover the shared meaning that honors their divergent views by working together. Unfortunately it is more common for groups to avoid diversity. When people with different styles and cultural backgrounds try to work together without developing an understanding of their respective worldviews, conflict often results. People may feel dishonored, unable to express themselves and be heard. Since most people do not possess the skills to work with conflict in a constructive way, they often resort to avoidance behaviors such as denial or forming cliques. Dialogue is invaluable in helping a group create value from its diversity and diminish the occurrence of conflict.

However, even in groups experienced in dialogue, there will be times when conflict erupts and threatens the ability to move forward. Usually, this happens when people are highly invested in an issue and emotions are running high. For example, a team is in disagreement over how to invest the training and development moneys available to them for the year. Highly charged issues tend to fragment and polarize groups. Polarization makes it difficult to see the larger picture that encompasses and can make sense of all the divergent positions. Judgment and advocacy predominate. Dialogue helps us suspend judgment and introduce more inquiry and listening into the conversation. Our objective is to open the door for innovative alternatives to emerge. When things heat up, it becomes even more important to refocus on an intention to step up one level, to expand the view. From this vantage point, conflict can become raw material for learning and creativity. In addition to practicing all the skills of dialogue, here are two more principles that are especially useful at such times.

○ *Focus on roles, not individual people.* A role can be one side of a controversial issue. Using the example of the team that was in conflict over how to spend training and development moneys, one role was the position "to spend the moneys on an off-site retreat" and the other was "to support only programs that take place on-site, in the actual working environment." Roles might also be functional job roles such as sales and service that often end up on opposite sides of a customer-service issue because they have different views and needs. The key to remember is this: By maintaining a focus on the roles rather than on specific individuals, we make it safer for people to talk about what is important, what is really at the core of the issue. When we personalize conflict, it becomes dangerous to speak openly. Most of us shut down when we feel we are at risk of being trapped in, held forever to any single thing we may say; conversation becomes guarded, and it is almost impossible to get out in the light of day what is important.

○ *Use polarities to gain clarity, flesh out a larger picture, and discover alternatives.* Most of reality exists in the gray zone. However, when we feel strongly about issues, we often think and act as if everything were a clear-cut polarity, black and white, plus or minus. If your group gets caught up in this polarization, civil war can erupt. To use this tendency to advantage, the first step is to identify the polarities or opposites that are magnetizing everyone's energy. For example: Off-site training is more impactful because we get away from the day-to-day demands and can focus on our learning. And, on-site training is more valuable precisely because it enables us to work on real day-to-day issues and bring the skills into the environment where we are expected to use them. Once the polarities are clear, it is important that all involved be encouraged to experiment with speaking from both roles or positions. It is like a pros and cons debate, except it is transformed when each person takes both sides. Paying attention to suspending judgments and assumptions and a willingness to listen to the opposing polarities are the keys to transforming the debate, taking the high road to a fuller picture. The results are enhanced understanding and stronger relationships among team members and a powerful experience of how creative alternative ways of working with an issue can emerge from what has in the past been a circling and stalemated conversation.

Using dialogue and the skills that support it to approach conflict as an opportunity to learn and helping others do the same can be the beginning of a fundamental change in group culture. Aversion to conflict gives way to a capability for fuller and more open conversation. Undiscussables and differences can start to inform and enhance the group's thinking and decision making, rather than undermine it.

TRY THIS: WORKING WITH CONFLICTING POLARITIES

You can apply the principles we just covered to work with a personal dilemma or issue that you are in conflict about with another person by creating an experience for yourself. These same steps may also be used to help a team member work with a conflict. First, you each work through the issue on your own and then bring your insights and learnings to a group dialogue.

1. Identify the roles or positions that are in conflict. Flesh out each side until it is clear to you.

2. Begin writing a conversation, moving back and forth, from side to side. Speak first from the side you most identify with. Then move to the other side and imagine what you would say. Really allow yourself to explore how you would feel from both positions. Challenge yourself to see how many views you can come up with for both sides.

3. Each time you notice yourself reacting with a judgment of one side or the other, practice suspending it and continue to listen.

4. After a while, your energy may start to diminish or you may notice that you don't feel as strongly as you did. Stop and reflect on what you have learned from expressing both sides. What aspects of the issues did each position pay attention to that the other side may not have noticed or thought was important?

When you encounter conflict that is chronic and entrenched, we suggest you seek the support of an experienced organizational development practitioner who can take a neutral position and help guide an exploration of the situation. Unless you have developed a high degree of shared leadership in your group, any attempt by you to facilitate such a process may feel unsafe to the group and will not help you build and maintain a high level of trust.

Strategy 6

CREATE A VISION/MISSION STATEMENT THAT WORKS FOR PEOPLE.

"As we act together in the world, our organization's identity grows and evolves. It helps periodically to question what we have become . . . . Do we each organize our work from the same shared sense of what is significant? Such an inquiry helps us return to the energy and passion of that space of early vision."

—Meg Wheatley, *A Simpler Way.*

"You discover core ideology by looking inside. It has to be authentic. You can't fake it."

—James C. Collins and Jerry I. Porras, *"Building Your Company's Vision"*

At their best, mission statements and visions guide and fuel collaboration. Useful visions are beacons, references points, that allow people to navigate through unfamiliar waters and make appropriate decisions. They create a degree of dynamic tension between where an organization is and what it sees itself in the process of becoming. Like a rubber band stretched between two poles, the vision is anchored out front to create a pull that motivates and inspires. If the rubber band is stretched too thin, it simply breaks, leaving behind disillusionment and frustration. Not very inspiring. If the beacon is not strong and clear, it may even confuse the navigators, resulting in poor decisions and leaving the organization aground on some unseen reef.

Crafting effective visions/missions is a natural application for dialogue. Visions and missions that work are built on shared meaning. They grow out of ongoing conversations about what people consider important, about what they want to be, the work they consider worth doing, and how they see themselves accomplishing it. Visions and missions are not static. They are not finished when they have been inscribed on plaques, coffee cups, and T-shirts. Those that work for more than a week at a time are living, evolving conversations that are constantly calibrating the tension in that rubber band and moving energy into the system.

Living, breathing visions involve all the people who will be responsible for making them come true. Those who have not had the opportunity to discover their place within the vision of the organization are unlikely to contribute their full talents and energies. Visions literally help us see where we are going. If they are not clear to each of us, we don't know which direction to go, which choices to make. Visions built on the clarity of shared understanding are powerful. They are at the core of all aligned action. Those shrouded in fog produce disorientation, uncoordinated action, and stress.

Below are some ideas about different approaches you might take to applying the principles and skills of dialogue to add substance to your vision/mission process and make it useful and powerful.

TRY THIS: MEANINGFUL VISIONS

Consider your position and role relative to your company's visioning efforts. If the vision in your organization is developed by the top leaders and then rolled down, and your role is:

Mid-level leader/manager, try the following:
When you receive the vision and are asked to create action plans to drive towards implementation, gather all those you work directly with who will be affected by the vision. Before the meeting ask everyone to consider the vision from their personal point of view. Ask them to be prepared to express to the group how it will affect their role and job personally. Ask them also to consider

any questions they have regarding the vision, what is inspirational about it, and what else they would like to see the vision express. Giving out the questions for reflection prior to the meeting reduces the anxiety and allows the conversation to drop to a deeper level of meaning. The questions should tap into each individual's underlying values and help the group learn more about how each shares in the underlying values of the vision. They should also help each participant see how they all personally connect into the whole and one another through their respective roles.

When the group comes together, address the following questions. Remind the group that the meeting isn't about trying to come to any decision. It is to explore the meaning of the vision for the group and to see if there are concerns that should be addressed. If issues arise that need to be acted upon, this will be done at a later time.

1. What inspires you about the vision?
2. How does the vision fall short for you?
3. How does the vision affect your specific role?
4. What questions does the vision leave you with?

Allow everyone a chance to speak to the whole group. (You might start and model with your own responses to the questions.) Depending on the size of the group and the time available, you could open the conversation up for general responses.

Upper-level leader/manager, try the following:

Add time to the front end of your next visioning process for a facilitated dialogue. If you typically gather together your management team and go off-site for a few days, add one day or at least a half day. During this extra period, ask a facilitator familiar with dialogue to help your team engage in an open-ended conversation that will allow an inquiry into the challenges and opportunities posed by the process. Let everyone know ahead of time that this will happen so that they have ample time for reflection. You may want to summarize key learnings and post these on the wall before the formal visioning process begins.

During the visioning process itself, direct attention to exploring the assumptions, beliefs, and values behind the various components of the vision.

At the end of the visioning process, provide some open-ended time for reflecting on the process itself. Ask the team members what they liked about the visioning process and what they think could have made it more productive. Record your reflections for future visioning meetings. Also consider if there are any new challenges and/or opportunities to pay attention to as a result of the visioning process itself.

A member of a team, try the following:
Ask your peers and team leader if they would be willing to spend some time to explore alignment with the organization's vision and how the ways you work together either do or don't support and align with that vision. If issues arise that need to be addressed, explain that these can be considered at a later time and passed on to the appropriate person in charge.

Some questions that may be useful:

1. What is your understanding of the vision and the values it represents?
2. How well do the underlying values agree with what is important to you personally?
3. How does your job and the charter of the team fit with your understanding of the vision?
4. What suggestions do you have for the way the team operates to improve overall alignment with the vision?

At the close of the session, ask for a summary of the key learnings. See if there is interest in continuing this conversation at a later time. If there is, bring the key learnings as a departure point for the next session.

An individual, try the following:
Write down your reflections on:

1. What you perceive as the underlying values behind the vision of the organization.

2. Your commitment to these values and how aligned they are with your personal value system.

3. Changes you could make in your work to increase alignment with the vision of the organization and with your own personal value system.

✳ Strategy 7 ✳

REFRAME PROBLEM SOLVING AND DECISION MAKING FOR MAXIMUM APPROPRIATE INVOLVEMENT AND DOUBLE-LOOP LEARNING.

"If decision making were a choice between alternatives, it would come easily. Rather, decision making is the formulation and the selection of alternatives."

—Kenneth Burke

Until we begin to move further upstream to the thinking, beliefs, and values that underlie the actions that create the results, we will continue to solve symptoms rather than problems. Nightmares of reappearing problems that consume our time, energy, and resources will continue.

People come together in organizations primarily to solve problems and make decisions. Bringing the power of dialogue and collaboration to these processes will have a positive impact on effectiveness at all levels—individual, group, and organizational.

The primary key to more informed decisions and effective solutions lies in a group's ability to think together. The practice of dialogue supports this capability. Individuals gain the advantage of seeing an issue through multiple lenses. They are able to attain a vantage point built upon a composite of one another's perceptions, transcend the level at which the problem was created, and imagine alternatives that allow them to break free from repeating cycles. They are able to uncover assumptions or values that may be creating unintended results and blocking forward movement.

Below we speak briefly about seven specific areas where incorporation of dialogue and its skills will pay off in terms of alignment, effectiveness, motivation, and morale. Consider them as you think at a macro level about the decision-making and problem-solving processes currently in use in your team/department/division/organization and again at a more specific level as you prepare to engage with your colleagues around specific issues and challenges.

Clarify the Decision-Making Process Up Front

We have seen very few groups where decision-making processes are explicitly defined. Mostly they are implicit and assumed. Lack of clarity around decision making, who will input it and how, the way the final decision will be made, and by whom is a significant source of frustration and lack of trust in teams. People are unsure how to participate and often are disgruntled because their expectations are not met.

As a leader, it is important that you get clear on the decision-making process you are using.[5] This requires that you ask yourself some hard questions about where you stand on the issue, how much involvement you want others to have, and how open you are to being influenced. Once you are clear, talk with your group about it. Tell them how you would like them to participate in the overall process.

An open inquiry into the decision-making process of a group can in and of itself be a useful step in building a basis for collaboration. The decision-making process may not change, but once clarified, greater levels of collaboration may be possible. Some of the most valuable conversations are not about changing how things are decided but about being able to talk openly about it and come to terms with what is so and what is needed for maximum effectiveness.

TRY THIS: CLARIFYING THE DECISION-MAKING PROCESS

Open a conversation to consider:

1. How are decisions currently made in your group?
2. What are the assumptions about the reason for using this process?

3. Does the process change based on the context?

4. What questions do people have about the most effective way for them to participate and contribute to the process?

5. What could improve the process?

You may want to announce the conversation beforehand, so that everyone has time to reflect. Before beginning, ask the group if there are any guides or skills that they think would be useful to pay attention to during the conversation. Ask people to give their reflections, one at a time. After everyone has had a chance to speak at least once, open the conversation up. When you close, ask for key learnings and questions to take forward. You may wish to use these for another conversation or as guides for other meetings.

Getting Emergent Issues on the Table Early

Often, issues and problems become crises because they were not recognized earlier. Incorporating brief periods of dialogue in regularly scheduled meetings provides a way to bring emergent problems forward so they do not grow to crisis proportions. When dialogue precedes your agenda-based meetings, you may discover important information emerging that has a bearing on topics you are preparing to consider. Having accessed this information will increase the quality of further deliberations and decisions.

Determine Relative Priorities

Only when groups can see issues in relationship to one another and within the larger territory they inhabit can effective prioritization be done. Dialogue encourages the development of a more complete picture that takes into account the dynamics of relationships as well as the nature of specific parts. For example, the interrelationships between sales, service, and manufacturing are crucial to effectively resolving the all too frequent problems that emerge from pressures to increase sales, the demands this increase places on manufacturing to deliver, and overloads in service that often result in loss of customers.

Understanding the nuances of how these patterns are playing out in a particular company is necessary if the steps to resolution are to be effectively prioritized and implemented.

Develop Shared Understanding of a Problem or an Issue

How many times have you been part of solving the wrong problem? You did great work, but the problem you chose to go after proved to have minimal impact on the larger issue. People come to problem-solving sessions highly charged and ready to get to the problem fast and get it taken care of. This often results in shortcuts.

We make assumptions that we are all talking about the same thing. We don't bother to inquire into assumptions and the thinking behind our conclusions. The time we save is often lost twofold later due to misunderstandings or solutions that do not address the highest leverage points in the process.

Generate and Examine Alternate Solutions

Someone suggests a solution that sounds good and away we go! Too often the first solutions that pop out are single loop alternatives and do not result in significant learning and long-term resolution. We can learn from history, save time and money, by pausing to ask about the thinking and values behind the strategies and solutions being suggested. What about considering how the solutions will impact related loops within a system? Will a solution simply shift the burden to another department or process loop, possibly even creating new stresses?

Create Aligned Implementation

During the implementation phase of a project, people may no longer be in close communication with one another, yet they must still make aligned decisions. Success requires a high degree of shared understanding. In addition, thinking through the details of implementation can surface information that may even change the solution chosen. The conversation suggested on the following page can be useful in both the solution and implementation stages.

TRY THIS:

The next time you consider a recommended solution for a complex problem, and before making the final decision, gather those who are key players in the implementation and ask them to do the following:

1. Describe fully what their role will be in the implementation.

2. Speak about the key challenges for success of the operation from their perspective.

3. Detail what they need from the group for success.

After each person has spoken, open up the conversation for inquiries about one another's roles and how the proposed solution will work. Make sure you leave a few minutes at the end to collect key reflections and open action items and questions to bring forward. Outline any next steps needed.

Develop Early-Warning Feedback

We often miss important feedback because the situation hasn't reached crisis proportions and can't compete with hot task items on the agenda. Again, incorporating short dialogue periods in ongoing meetings will help detect emergent and subtle, yet important, feedback.

✹ Strategy 8 ✹

BUILD A RELATIONSHIP WITH AN ORGANIZATIONAL
DEVELOPMENT COACH.

And who will support the leader? That's you.

There is an increasing emphasis on you, the leader, learning to conduct your own meetings and work with groups as well as one-on-one. This is a great opportunity to model new behaviors and shared leadership. It is also essential that you arrange for any support and coaching you need. Many upper-level executives we work with have established an ongoing relationship with an organizational development (OD) coach they respect and trust. Where dialogue is concerned, your coach can play an invaluable role for you and the group by observing and providing feedback designed to help you derive the greatest benefits from integrating the skills in the most useful ways.

If possible, we suggest that you interview and work with more than one person until you find someone that you are "comfortable being uncomfortable with;" you will get the most out of the relationship if you choose someone who will help you stretch beyond your comfort zone.

One distinguishing characteristic of a skillful dialogue group is its capacity for self-facilitation. While it is not within the scope of this book to go into a full discussion of how groups become self-facilitating, we do want to bring the topic of facilitation to your attention as leader. Self-facilitated meetings are not the norm. Most of us show up for meetings, group conversation, and events expecting them to be facilitated. Some are more structured. Some have more free space and flexibility. But no matter what the design, there will always be one or more persons who have been designated as official facilitator(s). To that person(s) falls the responsibility for process design, helping with skill development, making sure that everyone is able to participate, dealing with any conflicts or chaos that may arise, and in general keeping order and moving the group towards whatever desired outcomes it has set for itself.

As you introduce dialogue and its skills into your work environment, it will initially be useful, even essential, for you to work with your OD coach or someone who possesses a solid foundation in dialogue to help you and your co-workers. This person will take a more active role in facilitating the conversation by 1) helping frame times, 2) creating an appropriate and safe environment for the conversation, 3) coaching people to become more skilled at inquiry and advocacy that invites curiosity rather than defensiveness, 4) pointing out assumptions and patterns in the conversation, 5) asking questions that help people to reflect on both the content and process, integrate what they are hearing, and move to new levels of understanding.

The exact role and degree of participation of the facilitator will depend on the group, people's skill levels, the issue at hand, and your growing facility with the process. How this will unfold should be determined in conversations between the two of you prior to and even during meetings and dialogue sessions that you convene.

As you build your relationship with your coach and/or facilitator, it is important for you both to remember that dialogue is ultimately most powerful as a self-facilitating process. If your goal is, in fact, to develop shared leadership, self-facilitation, and the ability for collective thinking and learning, you must keep this uppermost in your mind. It is much too easy for groups to learn skills and continue to maintain a dependence on the facilitator. And it is too easy for facilitators to unconsciously promote this dependence because it means their presence and skills are needed and valued. Until the official facilitator either becomes a participant or moves on to help other groups, it will be difficult for responsibility to be fully shared by group members. Groups that develop the capacity for self-facilitation and shared leadership are a special breed and are awesome in their creativity and ability to move to aligned action.

✖ Strategy 9 ✖

THINK FIRST, ACT SECOND, REFLECT CONTINUOUSLY.

In a culture where "ready, aim, fire" is a way of life, introducing dialogue can create many and powerful changes in the way people think and act. A healthy respect for the work you are undertaking, your expectations, and the challenges you may meet along the way is essential to the successful implementation of all the strategies outlined. Know yourself, know your group, know your organization. And remember that dialogue can create conversations capable of transforming all three.

This strategy is about gauging how ready you and your group are to work with dialogue. By thinking through some important points you, your group, and your organization will gain the most from its practice. In real life, this strategy frames all the others. We place it last because, having read the others, you now have a more complete picture of what is involved in bringing the value of dialogue to your work environment.

In the first pages of this chapter, we called your attention to the shift in power dynamics that occurs when dialogue is practiced and groups move toward collaborative partnership and shared leadership. We return now for a closer look at this sensitive and yet very important phenomenon.

Power dynamics are a sensitive issue. When power arrangements are structured and stable, there is a certain degree of safety simply because we know the rules. We have lived most of our lives within the confines of fixed notions of who is in charge and who isn't. This can make moving towards collaborative partnership and shared leadership tricky. In addition, dialogue encourages a degree of openness and authenticity that is somewhat uncommon in most organizations today. While the shift in power dynamics takes place over time, greater openness begins almost immediately. Below are some areas for you, as leader, and for your group to consider. If you and the team are not ready for the kinds of changes we describe, dialogue may either simply fail or lead to a kind of boomerang effect, where you get a taste of a good thing and then end up back in the same old rut, only more dissatisfied than before. We hope that neither of these will be the case and that the information below will help you do some preventive scouting of the territory.

Things for You as Leader to Consider

Team dynamics can shift quickly You need to be prepared so that you can respond in ways that support collaboration and the development of the skills and behaviors you want to encourage, rather than find yourself reacting out of a position of defensiveness.

Power Shifts

One of the biggest changes has to do with responsibility for leadership. You need to be comfortable with how you envision this shift because your behavior will set the tone and boundaries for the group. For example, you may need to clearly set and/or redefine limits and be comfortable with communicating them. Dialogue is not necessarily about moving all decisions to a consensus model, but it is about making processes, like decision making, explicit.

Letting Go of the Need to Be in Control

At times in dialogue you may find yourself wanting to exert your authority to move things along or redirect the conversation, but stepping in may not encourage openness or collaboration. You may need to suspend your desire to speak and provide the opening for others to step forward and assume shared leadership. If you are always jumping into the conversation with judgments and decisions, your walk will say "business as usual," even though your talk may be "encourage participation." Some coaching from a consultant familiar with dialogue and with your personal style can be very useful.

Defensiveness

Because open communications within a team may bring up material that was off-limits and undiscussable in the past, you will need to develop a plan for handling the personal defensiveness that you are sure to feel as such issues arise. These may include vulnerable areas that team members previously carefully avoided. You may come in for criticism of past decisions, your style, ways of managing or working, etc. If you become defensive and reactive, the team will go back to business as usual and will not continue to risk openness. In the beginning stages of building trust, defensive behavior by a leader always stops the dialogic process cold. There are no exceptions.

Being More Accessible

One leader in a public service agency reported: "I can no longer hide behind my role as leader. People question me about my assumptions.

And they seek me out more often, not to make decisions, but to find out my thinking on issues."

○   How comfortable are you in general with disclosure and openness? Would you be willing to speak with your team about your issues, fears, and personal challenges as a leader?

○   What do shared responsibility and leadership mean to you? What specific changes would you be willing to see in terms of shared leadership? What are the boundaries?

Using Your Own Discomfort as a Learning Tool

By now you have a fairly detailed picture of the challenges this work may present and have probably identified a number of places where you may expect to feel discomfort. You may even have begun planning how you will stay on track and move forward. When we work with groups, we generally set up a coaching partnership with the leader to provide support in working through rough spots, which we call "learning edges." Learning edges are times when you literally stand poised on an edge, where you can turn back to familiar patterns or you can step through your discomfort and create new possibilities. The questions below offer a way to use reflective inquiry to catalyze new insights into your own thinking and discover what will aid you in effectively moving forward. In Part IV, chapter 8 outlines common learning edges that groups experience as they continue a practice of dialogue. The questions below can be applied to those collective learning edges as well.

TRY THIS: USING REFLECTIVE INQUIRY TO MOVE THROUGH LEARNING EDGES
You become aware that you are uncomfortable. Notice what is triggering this response in you. What is going on? What is the situation? What specifically are you uncomfortable with? Once you've got this clear in your mind, ask yourself the following questions:

1. In response to my discomfort, what behavior or action am I either engaging in or wanting to engage in? Do I want to leave? Check out? Judge the group or a person as wrong? Stop listening? Become argumentative?

2. What creative action can I take to expand my ability to remain present and open a door for my own learning?

3. What shift in thinking would I need to make to support this action? How would I have to think differently in order to shift my perspective enough to create an opening for new learning?

Things for the Group/Team to Consider

Some of the best indicators of group readiness are current practices. Are you as a team already integrating some of the principles of dialogue? Have you begun to explore some of the "Try this" suggestions in this and other chapters? The more questions given below that you can answer in the positive, the more advantage you will be likely to gain from dialogue.

QUESTIONS FOR THE GROUP TO CONSIDER _____

O Have you participated in team-building experiences together?

O On a scale of 1 to10, would you rate the openness of communication at 6 or higher?

O If you have worked with some of the "Try this" suggestions in other parts of the book, did you get value from them?

O On a scale of 1 to 10, would you rate your willingness to experiment with processes that ask you to change your norms of behavior at 7 or higher?

O Do you engage in reflection on your process, asking: What is working for us and why? How could we improve our next meeting/conversation? Do you follow through on these reflections?

O Are you willing to address and work with interpersonal issues as they arise? Do you have agreed-upon processes for doing this?

○   Do you periodically take the time to consider structural or process changes that would improve your work together?

○   Do you talk periodically at some depth about what your shared purpose is and how each of you individually fit into it?

○   Do you take the time to get to know one another? Are you curious about how each of you thinks and sees issues?

○   Are there ways in which you currently share in leadership?

○   On a scale of 1 to 10, would you rate your degree of comfort with "not knowing" and being willing to stick with a process in order to learn at 7 or higher?

In addition to the above survey, you can gain information about a group's readiness by convening a meeting where you all speak about dialogue, what it has to offer, and what people think about it. Provide an overview of the process and explain what type of commitment you believe to be required. Then ask everyone for their observations, opinions, and questions. It is often useful to do this in partnership with a consultant or facilitator trained in dialogue. The group will need to hear from you, as leader, about the value you place on open communication, partnership and shared leadership. The consultant can answer any questions that might arise about skill-building for dialogue.

Things for You to Consider Relative to Organizational Readiness

We've outlined strategies to support bringing dialogue into an organization. Here we ask you to think about whether you expect the organization to be neutral, to support, or to block you and your team in working with dialogue. An enthusiastic and willing group can make great strides forward, but it will still need to interface with others and with the larger organizational structure every day. If the culture is supportive, great. If it is unreceptive or hostile, this is not necessarily reason to cancel your plans for introducing dialogue. It is a call for you to devote some significant time to thinking and planning strategically how you will meet the challenges.

QUESTIONS TO CONSIDER RELATIVE TO THE ORGANIZATION⎯⎯⎯

o   What may occur when your group bounces up against other departments and teams that are not receptive to dialogue and its principles?

o   How will you integrate new members into the ongoing practice of dialogue? This one is crucial even in a supportive environment. What is the most efficient way for people to be brought up to speed on issues, skills, and guides? Including and orienting people quickly will increase both their desire and ability to contribute meaningfully. Any plan you create needs to provide realistic approaches that will work within your specific work environment.

o   What are the prevailing values in the organizational culture? How aligned with the values of collaborative partnership and dialogue are they?

Encouraging the Impulse to Engage in Dialogue

Trying out a new behavior for a day or two is quite different than making it a part of yourself and the culture of your group and organization. As you contemplate your strategy for integrating dialogue into your important conversations and fostering the creation of collaborative partnerships at work, it will be helpful to recall four essential elements: vision, planning, commitment, and practice.

o   **Vision**—Can you paint a detailed picture that has real meaning for you of the value you expect to gain from your work with dialogue? How do you see yourself and those around you communicating differently, and what advantages will this have? Be specific; tie your images to goals that are meaningful. The vision will provide you with a reason to do the work and a reference for making conscious choices about how to move from current reality towards more powerful conversation and results.

○ *Planning*—What structures and processes will support the work with dialogue? Which of the strategies outlined in this chapter will be the highest leverage for you? What small steps can you take to begin the work in a way that provides immediate value and encourages continuation? What is a realistic path that you and others can commit to and participate in?

○ *Commitment*—The philosopher Goethe said, "Until one is committed, there is hesitancy, the chance to draw back, always ineffectiveness. Concerning all acts of initiative (and creation), there is one elementary truth—the ignorance of which kills countless ideas and splendid plans: that the moment one definitely commits oneself, then Providence moves too." Talk does not demonstrate commitment. Commitment is expressed in action. Without attention to vision and planning, commitment is difficult to sustain.

○ *Practice*—Like any skill, dialogic attitudes and behaviors can only be developed and yield value through ongoing and continuous practice. Give some thought to ways you can create opportunities for yourself to engage in their use every day. These may be as simple (or profound) as a commitment to work with one specific skill each day in at least one conversation and then reflecting on your practice. Talk with your team/group about how all of you can intentionally create practice fields that will bring immediate value to your day-to-day activities.

3

FOSTERING DIALOGUE WITHIN

THE ORGANIZATION

"Organizational effectiveness [and learning] *is . . . increasingly
dependent on valid communication across subculture
boundaries. The ultimate reason for learning about the theory
and practice of dialogue is that it facilitates and creates
possibilities for valid communication."*

—Edgar H. Schein[6]

*"Organizations today face a degree of complexity
that requires intelligence beyond that of any individual.
Dialogue . . . holds promise as a means for promoting
collective thinking and communication."*

—William N. Isaacs[7]

Conversation is a centerpiece of culture; it communicates,
reflects, and reinforces the culture's norms. It is also a powerful doorway for transformation, offering a process for self-reflection and organizational learning. Dialogue allows organizations to apply Socrates'
prescription of "Know thyself" at the collective level.

In the last two chapters we considered the conversational values and
patterns present in most organizational cultures today and strategies
for working dialogically towards cultures based on collaborative partnership and shared leadership. But how realistic is it to think that you
can impact an entire organizational culture? And if you don't, how long

will the pockets of collaboration be able to survive? You can mandate behavioral changes in authoritarian, command-and-control cultures. People will behave in prescribed ways, but their behavior will be compliance behavior, in response to an external source of authority. Compliance will last only as long as force is applied. And force most often fuels resistance and reinforces the attitudes and beliefs that it seeks to change.

We voluntarily change our minds and our behavior in response to our own internalization of new values and thinking. This is much more likely to occur in an environment that supports exploration of new thinking and behaviors. So, if you are interested in fostering cultural change at the organizational level, you must ask yourself what actions will support the creation of such environments throughout the organization.

Organizational values, structures, and processes may need to evolve into forms more aligned with collaboration and shared leadership. Such changes can help reinforce new ways of thinking and behaving, but in order for the foundation of the culture to shift, it will require the continuous seeding and nurturing of new ideas and ways over time. The suggestions we highlight in this chapter are intended to plant seeds that will encourage and support the reawakening of the impulse to engage in dialogue. They are culled from the experience of many. The approaches are not new; in fact, they are common sense. Yet, in the midst of a "Just do it!" culture, common sense is often sacrificed to time.

Whether you are an executive leader or a change agent at any level of the organization, we hope these pages will help you till the ground, plant and nurture the seed, and eventually reap the fruits of dialogue within your organization. These suggestions will be most effective if implemented as part of a well-thought-through large-systems change process, yet by themselves they will bring value to those they touch.

Be the Change You Wish to See

We know we've already said this, but it is important enough to say over and over again. You and your group are the primary showcase and argument for bringing dialogue and its skills forward on a larger scale.

You can literally lead the organization by your example. In 1992 and 1993 we worked with the Commuter Management Services (CMS) Department of Orange County Transportation Authority. They described their situation: "The most critical issue we face is how to organize and become a functional group quickly in order to get on with the business of achieving the very aggressive performance goals that have been established for us." They participated in a two-and-one-half-day introductory program and continued their practice monthly as a group and informally among individual members. CMS was able to grapple with a number of thorny issues in the following months as well as manage to exceed their aggressive goals and objectives. Group members reported that "People want to know what we are doing. They want to know 'what is in our water.' Everyone is so energized and working together . . . collectively, as a team, there isn't much we can't do." Their success stimulated high levels of curiosity and interest.

Start Small

Choose a few high-leverage places to start. Begin a few pilot groups. If there is an interest in organizational learning, consider creating a learning community to explore the learning process. Or, select a few upcoming meetings where you feel dialogue could create some immediate value. Examples might be planning the process for integrating a new company recently acquired in a merger, working effectively with a diverse international workforce, or thinking about the implications and consequences of a move into a new market. The idea is to choose an opportunity where the ability to consider multiple and diverse perspectives and inquire into the thinking behind them will enable people to craft a better plan, to make a better decision. Take the path of least resistance where the highest probability of creating value can be had with the fewest impediments. Once you get a track record, it will be easier to enroll people in taking on more difficult challenges.

Handpick a Group to Get Things Started

If you choose to go with a pilot group, select the people carefully. Consider your objective. Is this a first exploration to learn what works within your environment? If so, choose a group that reflects the people you hope to work with as you move forward, but balance it a little on the side of supporters to help you get started. A sponsor at a high level will be an advantage, but you don't want the group under a high-powered microscope just yet. If you are ready to create a group to help build support for a more expanded rollout, then go for a group with high visibility and influence in the organization. Examples might be an executive group within a division composed of a cross section of people from finance, marketing, production, and design; a special council specifically chartered to deal with an important issue such as diversity or moving into a new international market segment; or a research group with a charter to explore the value of dialogue. Any group you choose will need to have some charter or purpose that is considered worthy by the organization in order to justify the investment of resources required by a commitment to engage in dialogue over a significant period of time. If the pilot is just one more task piled on an already full plate with no priority status, it will almost certainly land on the floor in short order. Charters that have been used are: learning communities centered around the development and transfer of capabilities for organizational learning, high-level strategic visioning and planning, and ethical decision making in an international marketplace. If possible, invite people who possess the following characteristics: 1) They want to be involved for the sake of their own development and that of the organization; 2) They already demonstrate dialogic skills in their interactions; and 3) They have some capacity for working with paradox and honoring diversity. Include both men and women who are respected by others in their peer groups and the organization at large.

Enroll Leadership

If the leadership is not "bought-in" and willing to work the program with you, there will be little hope for success. Grassroots movements do happen, but sooner or later they always run headlong into the power structure. The kind of revolution in culture dialogue encourages those at the top to support it. In a competitive culture this is a highly unusual request. Whether you are working with one group or with a larger program, the leader is crucial. If a leader does not understand the implications of dialogue for her own position, it is likely that sooner or later she will pull the rug out from under the entire exploration. We spoke in chapter 2 about the way dialogue changes the relationship between the leader and the group and the need to reflect carefully on this before jumping in with both feet. It is no different at the organizational level. If the leadership is not interested or supportive, and you want to start a grassroots movement with the intention of increasing effectiveness and satisfaction within your group, we encourage you to do so. But be very clear about the boundaries and what your expectations are because you are unlikely to gain support in the larger organization, at least initially.

Dialogue Makes a Lousy Mandatory Process

It does not make sense and is too much work to try to force people to go where they don't want to go, particularly when you are talking about a process grounded in open communication and building trust. Mandating dialogue is a surefire way to undermine its effectiveness and have people end up talking about it as just another fad with no real usefulness to their organization. There have been scenarios where individuals gave in to the pressure to participate, opened up, and then found themselves in deep water and unable to swim. Not pushing will help you avoid such potentially damaging situations.

Acknowledge Current Reality

Few of us believe in rose gardens without thorns. Anyone proclaiming that they have the latest and greatest solution to our problems, assuring us that it will make a big difference immediately, is going to be met with resistance. No organization is going to change overnight, nor are most people. And everyone knows it. While we might wish there were a magic wand that someone could bring in and effortlessly change things for the better, deep in our gut we know that that is not how it works. We know that we are the ones who have to do the work of change and that it takes commitment and courage. So, if you want to bring us something new, something that will require an investment of time and energy, then it had better produce some immediate results that help us move day to day. The primary motivator will always be "What is in it for me/us?" In creating a strategy for dialogue in your organization, it is key that you keep in mind the need to meet people where they are, acknowledge current reality, and create a plan that will make the integration of dialogue into day-to-day applications worthwhile. Each problem you solve together, each small change you make in the direction of your own learning, increased effectiveness, and satisfaction, will make life a little bit better and strengthen your motivation to continue.

One final note on meeting people where they are. None of us enjoys being put in the position of being wrong. Approaching others with a proposal for improvement that carries the implication that what they've been doing is wrong or not worthwhile will only create resistance. We live in a culture that survives on being right. So, the ability to identify and build on the pluses that already exist is crucial to encouraging people's willingness to participate in something new. Once you've established communication that honors everyone involved, you can begin to open a few more windows and doors.

Eat the Elephant One Bite at a Time

Dialogue represents a significant shift in the way we communicate with one another. Trying to move too fast can provoke a response not unlike indigestion—you may even get "thrown up." Injecting dialogue in too many places at once or taking on a project that the group/organization isn't ready for will be counterproductive. Keep your focus on identifying opportunities where it would be of value for people to talk more openly about what is important. Then be ready to support whatever next steps emerge. Dialogue is based on inviting people to move to deeper levels of conversation, to expand their thinking and skills. You can't push people to listen more deeply or to be more curious. Think strategically about what small steps will create opportunities for people to derive value and you will build sufficient momentum to eat the whole elephant over time.

Use Off-Site Programs to Get Things Started

Dialogue represents a change in the way we communicate at a cultural level, where the beliefs, thinking, and values that shape our behavior reside. It can be very useful to take people out of their usual organizational environment, which consumes their energy and attention, and give them the reflective space to devote their energies to learning and practicing something different. Off-site, retreatlike settings provide the opportunity for a more focused and in-depth experience. Rooms with natural lighting; lots of blank wall space for group reflections, inspirational quotes, free-form expression; a sound system to add different musical themes; grounds where you can wander among trees, over grass, sit in secluded spots, swim, climb, relax in a hot tub, stare out across an expanse of water or land; food that feels nurturing, that grounds you but doesn't drag you down. All these are helpful.[8] Such settings create an environment that is like a tuning fork for slowing down and being able to focus on skills such as reflection, listening, and inquiry into and observation of our thinking process. Providing the opportunity to go deeply into an experience creates a touchstone in people's memories that can be invaluable to them when they find themselves back in the work environment attempting to integrate new skills.

Off-site programs can backfire. They can be powerful. That is their purpose. However, if no plans are made for the integration of learnings and the practice of new skills before leaving to return to work, the whole experience can backfire. Creating a powerful experience that energizes people and then sending them back into an environment that consumes their energy is a recipe for disillusionment and frustration. Any program needs to include significant time for participants to work out a plan for integration that makes sense for them. But even this will not be sufficient if there is no support for the new skills being a priority back at work. If you are the leader of such a group, you need to give some serious thought to how willing you are to rearrange priorities to encourage the integration of new skills. If people come back with just one more thing to do that takes up time without yielding added value, we all know what will happen.

Create a Distinctive Physical Space for Dialogue

The idea is to remind one another that dialogue is not the run-of-the-mill way we always talk with one another. If dialogue becomes a buzz-word within your organization and people begin to say "Let's dialogue" whenever they mean "Let's talk," the distinction between discussion and dialogue will become blurred. The word will lose its power to focus your attention on the skills and guides involved and ultimately the process itself will be diluted. One way to maintain the distinction is to create a different physical environment where you engage in dialogue. One company we know has created a dialogue room. Groups convene there when they have determined that an issue deserves deeper inquiry and attention. Other groups have certain posters or charts that they put up on the walls whenever they enter into dialogue. Still others have a symbol that they place in the center of the group or a talking stick that is passed from one speaker to the next. (For more on talking sticks, see the Appendix.) It does not matter how you remind yourself of the distinguishing elements of dialogue, only that you do.

Do Things that Break the Norms

Actions speak volumes. Getting people outside of the nine dots in their thinking and doing helps create an environment in which experimenting and being just a little uncomfortable become expected, even looked forward to. Loosening up rigid patterns is what this is all about. Here are some examples given to us by the executives we spoke with.

> *Some examples.*
> ○ A VP of Sales and Marketing and a Chief Operating Officer instituted two different versions of coffee klatches with employ-ees. The VP created "bagels and coffee with Bob;" the COO, "lunches with Karen." Both invited people to sign up to join them for food and informal conversation. The result was that everyone discovered everyone was just plain people. Bob and Karen reported that most people didn't even talk about work, although it was not discouraged. They were more interested in

talking about what was going on in their lives or in asking questions to get to know more about one another and what everyone thought about different issues. Bob said, "What they really wanted was to be heard and seen." Karen concluded, "I became a person who was trying to be one of the team, and I learned a lot about how I could do a better job of that."

○ Dress is often used to create a more relaxed, fluid atmosphere. Dress-down and casual Fridays, and off-site programs where dressing for dinner means putting on jeans are examples. One group made it a rule that anytime they did creative brainstorming they would all take off an article of clothing or jewelry as a symbol of loosening up. There was one man who just couldn't do it for nine months. It was amazing how he loosened up and became just a little more flexible when the tie finally came off.

○ Start a meeting with an inspirational reading or a piece of poetry. Tell a mythical story or a fable.[9] Then ask people how the story applies to the situation, issue, or problem they have come together to address. Enroll others in creating different and interesting ways to start or conclude a meeting. The strategy is to use what is different to encourage people to engage new ways of perceiving and thinking about the same old issues. The purpose is to break through habitual patterns of behavior and thinking and get people expecting, even enjoying, thinking and acting outside the nine dots.

Celebrate People

We spend most of our time talking about what is wrong and what we can do better. It's hard not to fall into feeling that nothing is ever good enough, a steady diet of which is deenergizing and demoralizing. Give yourself and those you work with credit for the amazing accomplishment of working as hard as you all do, taking care of your families, coming up with the energy and creativity to face one challenge after another, and even managing to laugh and play occasionally. Acknowledge the courage it takes to assume responsibility and create new ways of working together when many would rather you just did it the way it was always done. Talk to one another about what energizes you and makes it worthwhile to give as much as you do. Then create an agreement to focus attention on at least one of these requirements for each person over a specified period of time.

Be Smart

Use your own homegrown common sense. Think before you act. Inquire into your thinking before deciding. Think through the context, the people, the highest leverage moves, and then prepare and act. Find out who the stakeholders are, both those who will support you and those who would like to shoot you down, and find out what could be in it for them. Ask people like you and unlike you to think with you.

Caution! Care Required

A final note. Dialogue can produce profound changes in the way people talk with one another and think about important issues. It will make whatever is present more visible. Dialogue can also be subversive to the status quo, to how things have always been done. By its very nature, dialogue encourages people to be curious about the thinking behind conclusions and actions, revealing well-thought-through and incoherent decisions alike. It will tap into people's creativity and the power of collective thinking and learning. People will experience higher levels of trust, the discomfort of new behaviors and skills, the excitement of unexpected insights. In the balance, most groups that open this door want to continue. Yet, even with a desire to continue, the practice of dialogue often falls by the wayside usually because leadership or the overall infrastructure and culture of the organization do not support it. Here are some examples: 1) There is a change in leadership and the new leadership doesn't get what the big deal is and decides the time used could be applied somewhere else. 2) The reward system of the culture only recognizes individual contribution and encourages high levels of competition, fire fighting and individual heroics. 3) A leader thinks it's a good idea, opens the door, and then when the power dynamics begin to shift, pulls the rug out from under the group in order to maintain control.

Getting a taste of the power of dialogue and then having it taken away can be frustrating and deenergizing. You could compare it to driving a turbocharged car for a week and then climbing back into a Volkswagen beetle, but it's worse because what has been lost is more important than a fast ride; it is the possibility of a better quality work life. We cannot stress enough the importance of giving significant thought to both the value and the challenge of dialogue before moving forward. A smaller scale, well-thought-through approach may yield much more value in the long run than a full-steam-ahead just do it! approach.

IN REAL LIFE

What truly matters in our lives is measured through conversation.
Our dialogue with customers, employees, peers,
and our own hearts is the most powerful source
of data about where we stand.

—Peter Block
Stewardship

We've devoted two entire chapters to outlining strategies for bringing dialogue to work. We close with some examples of contexts and applications where people are already applying these strategies. These brief descriptions are the result of our own experience and that of others who are involved in finding ways to bring the value of dialogue into real life settings every day. While there are as many applications as there are contexts, we've organized the more common ones in line with some of the strategies offered here, and added a few additional eclectic ones.

We recognize that some of you may want to know more about a particular application. It is beyond the scope of this book to provide detailed descriptions. We hope these highlights will stimulate your own thinking as you look for possible starting places within your organization.

Leadership Development (Strategies 1 and 2)

At Abbott Northwestern (part of Allina) the principles of dialogue have been introduced throughout this health-care organization over a period of more than two years to enable meaningful conversations across job and departmental functions. Dialogue has been instrumental in bringing patients and families together to talk about the care experience, and clarify and arrive at a shared understanding of what is important. Dialogue is integrated into personal mastery programs for nurses to develop personal awareness, self-knowledge, understanding of others, and a capacity to create shared understanding and vision around the practice and work of nursing.

A nonprofit occupational medical health provider has found dialogue to be a core element in creating meaningful conversations among physicians, nurses, health educators, administrators, and support staff. Their goal was to overcome the fragmentation that had evolved among them over the 31 years of the foundation's existence. Over the course of a year, the group moved from anger, fear, resentment, and frustration to openly talking with one another about the importance of community, truth, trust, difference, and teamwork. A result of this work has been the creation of a culture where community, creativity, innovation, and mutual trust are the prevailing spirits in the workplace. People both internal and external to the foundation have been openly astounded at the work accomplished.

A Fortune 100 Company has incorporated dialogue into their year-long leadership development program for upper-level managers nominated as future senior executives. The intention of the program is to develop and expand awareness and skills for leading the organization into the twenty-first century. Dialogue is recognized as a key skill in the arena of interpersonal relationships and for integrating individual, team, and organizational values and strategies.

Creating Diversity as a Resource (Strategy 4)

Fetzer Institute's "Diversity Dialogues" have been exploring what is happening in the field of diversity across the country. Participants are from a wide range of disciplines: organizational development, training and development, human resources, freelance consultants, entrepreneurs with an emphasis in diversity, educators (from public and higher education), corporate people responsible for diversity within organizations, people who work within corporations and communities in the area of healing racism, university professors, physicians, psychologists. The dialogues are focused on what is going on, what is working, and what is needed to make a difference.

Levi Strauss & Co. incorporated dialogue into two of its core programs, "Diversity" and "Valuing Diversity and Ethics." Dialogue was introduced on the first day and then used throughout the program as a vehicle to deepen conversations among participants and help them consider challenging issues. The intention is to increase awareness and encourage behaviors consistent with viewing diversity as an essential business resource. As we write, these programs are being redesigned. Dialogue will remain a core aspect of the new offering.

Digital Equipment Corporation was one of the first corporations to become widely recognized as a leading pioneer of diversity work. In the early 1980s, they began working with dialogue in a Core Group Model that was part of their "Valuing Differences" program. Core Groups focused on helping participants learn how to strip away stereotypes, inquire into different assumptions, and build relationships with people they regard as different.

Reframing Conflict as an Opportunity (Strategy 5)

Dade County Highway Department. A quality management improvement initiative was in jeopardy because of strife between union and staff members. A series of dialogues between 35 staff and union personnel were successful in building the shared understanding needed for the program to continue.

The Public Conversation Project is well known for its work in creating dialogues to enable meaningful conversation around the very controversial issue of abortion.

GS Technologies used dialogue to help management and labor representatives explore intractable differences that had persisted over a 35-to-40-year period. This work was part of a Kellogg Foundation grant with Bill Isaacs acting as Director for The Dialogue Project, in affiliation with the Organizational Learning Center of MIT.[10]

Clarifying Core Values and Crafting a Shared Purpose and Vision (Strategy 6)

Hewlett Packard Labs. Dialogic principles and inquiry were integrated into the design of a full-day gathering convened on Earth Day 1997. More than 800 employees and others linked via satellite in Brussels and Japan participated in a Celebration of Creativity: The Conversation Continued. The purpose was to deepen conversation and understanding of what it means to be "HP for the World." What are the responsibilities? The possibilities? How can employees incorporate learning from this collective conversation into their day-to-day work?

Dade County Land Use Conference. Two hundred fifty participants from various citizen and constituency groups gathered to talk about and develop a vision around land use in the county. Three groups of 70 people each engaged in dialogue for 2 hours around issues and questions, with a large-group reflection at the end. County board members reported that this was the "first time we've talked about issues without yelling at each other." Citizens reported feeling that they "finally understood the issues and felt much better educated." The dialogues were followed by speakers and panels and small-group work on developing goals for land use.

Fetzer Institute asked that all staff and board members participate in dialogue training. Dialogue was subsequently used at retreats for clarification of values, purpose, and vision with the entire staff of the organization. Dialogue is often incorporated into day-to-day meetings.

People take more time to inquire into one another's assumptions in both interpersonal interactions as well as when assessing areas such as program development. A "diversity group" has formed and uses dialogue to help open conversations into areas that can be uncomfortable to speak about. An ongoing dialogue group meets monthly.

Santa Rosa Junior College, Fullerton City College, and Pasadena City College. One- and two-day dialogue sessions helped create shared visions and strategic plans that addressed the challenges of implementing shared governance (a process in which administration, faculty, and students collaborate in decision making).

Strategic Planning and Problem Solving (Strategy 7)

Telecommunications company. A senior management team, made up of the CEO and VPs, meets every two weeks in the evening at the CEO's home to explore issues of strategic importance to the organization. Their intentions are to learn more about one another, build trust and their ability to challenge one another, inquire together to explore more deeply the strategic issues facing the business, and dissolve barriers between cross-functional departments.

Hewlett Packard. Five executive teams within the Medical Group used dialogue to look at strategic issues, to release the need for immediate decision making and deepen their ability to inquire and listen together. At a manufacturing division, an engineering group participated in dialogue to develop common definitions, enable more effective exchange of points of view, streamline decision making and planning processes, and build a cohesive plan that could be supported by all involved.

3-Com Corporation. An executive engineering team worked with dialogue over a period of a year to help arrive at a shared understanding of their work and how they might bring more value to their division and the overall organization through their collaboration.

Orange County Transportation Authority. Commuter Management Services employed dialogue in monthly sessions to talk about important issues, particularly ones that crossed departmental boundaries and required aligned coordination. Individuals continuously used the skills they learned in their daily interactions to prevent and resolve problems.

Cultural Change, Organizational Transformation

City Government in Columbus, Ohio. One leader applies what he has learned in dialogue to how he works with his group. By building dialogic guides and principles into all their meetings, reminding people about assumptions, listening, and suspending judgment, they have reinvigorated their capacity and desire to work together. Individuals are creating new possibilities where none were visible before. For example, one woman with no official position initiated and led an entire effort to create a neighborhood park.

A *pharmaceutical department within a large hospital* is introducing dialogic skills to facilitate a structural change from supervisory roles to team leaders. The rationale is that if the change is to be successful, people will need to explore different mental models and develop their capabilities for collaborative work processes.

Learning

Toronto Institute for Studies in Education. Dialogue "fishbowls" are used to work with oppositional issues such as authoritarian versus facilitative leadership. The dialogues are convened for a set period of time, followed by a large-group reflection. Students are learning how to work with paradox more effectively.

LOCI (Learning Organizations Community Inc.), Ohio. Two groups have been established and have met over a period of more than three years. One group is composed of executives in different types of businesses who gather to work with the question "If we are going to talk together, what kinds of learnings can we provide one another that would benefit our businesses and communities?" The second group is composed of internal consultants, middle managers, and organizational change people who meet monthly for a few hours. Their intention is to meet with no stated agenda and explore learning together in a noncompetitive way.

Corporate Collaborative Learning, Europe. A group of small- to medium-sized organizations are using dialogue to explore how they might create a collaborative partnership/alliance without being owned by one another.

And More . . .

Outpatient group work. At Lovelace Health Systems in New Mexico, dialogue is used as part of an outpatient program for people who have completed an intensive inpatient program. The follow-up program runs for 10 to 12 weeks, meeting twice a week for 3 hours at a time. The participants have been introduced to assumption identification, suspension of judgment, listening, inquiry and reflection, and storytelling. The therapist for the group says, "This population has a high tendency to rush to judgment. Learning that they don't need to judge so quickly or dramatically is probably one of the most helpful skills and insights for them. The process also helps them understand that they don't need to be the expert and know everything."

Prison dialogues in England. Prision inmates meet regularly in dialogue.

Refuge dialogues. These programs are designed as retreats to introduce people to dialogue and use the practice as a way of slowing down and engaging in a reflective inquiry on what holds meaning for them in their life and work. They are envisioned as renewal and learning experiences.

Acknowledgments. We want to thank the following people for the continuing work they are doing with dialogue in various settings that is reflected in the material in this chapter: Juanita Brown, Sarita Chawla, Elizabeth Fadell, Peter Garrett, Christine Glidden, Maggie Herzog, David Isaacs, William Isaacs, Gary Jackson, Ronita Johnson, Chris Kloth, Mary Koloroutis, Wendy Lombard, Christoph Mandl, Denis Nixon, Teresa Ruelas, Doug Ross, Joan Saries, Peggy Sebera, Justin Sherman, Toni Wilson, Barbara Walker, and Barbara Waugh.

While we could have included the work of many others, we needed to stop somewhere and go to print.

IV

THE
TRANSFORMATIONAL
POWER
OF
DIALOGUE

"At the deepest level it [dialogue] is about the development and transformative power of the collective mind."

—David Peat
Infinite Potential

"The real voyage of discovery consists not of finding new lands but of seeing the territory with new eyes."

—Marcel Proust

"Thus, the task is not so much to see what no one yet has seen, but to think what nobody yet has thought about that which everybody sees."

—Schopenhauer

"A change of meaning is a change of being."

—*David Bohm*

What you are about to read is a sampling of stories and reflections about experiences associated with the ongoing practice of dialogue. If even one meaningful conversation can change the way a group sees a problem or thinks about a new product, think how transforming it would be if such conversations became the rule rather than the exception. All the experiences you will read about here have one thing in common: they are accompanied by what we call *shifts of mind.* These *shifts of mind* represent new ways of thinking and perceiving, which in turn lead to changes in action and results. We say these experiences produce changes in meaning (thinking) and, therefore, in being (action). This is what we mean when we say dialogue is transformational.

Dialogue becomes transformational conversation when, through its practice, people tap into another level of awareness, creating a shift in their thinking, actions, and relationships with others. For example, conversations between a Chief Operating Officer (COO) and employees of a large health-care organization revealed that communicating by memo was creating more distance between upper management and employees, rather than eliminating it. The COO learned about consequences of her written communications and the employees learned about the actual intentions behind them. Both came away with a new understanding that changed their assumptions about one another and altered the ways they interacted from that moment on. Such conversations can form the foundation for cultural change when people begin to intentionally inquire into the assumptions that underlie structures and processes within an organization.

Some transformational conversations are accompanied by blinding flashes of insight and excitement. Some pass quietly through, their impact recognized as you begin to notice changes in yourself and the way you respond to what is happening around you. Perhaps the way you experience a particular relationship changes, or your reactions to a person or situation, or you see connections or possibilities where before there were none. Such changes of perception are all signs that a transformational shift has occurred.

Our intention here is to provide you with specific glimpses of how the ongoing practice of dialogue can give you new eyes to see the same old territories differently, opening the door for new ways of thinking about and creating collaborative partnerships and shared leadership. Each chapter is self-contained. Each is different. They can be read in any order. What follows is a brief description of ways the chapters interweave the themes of collaborative partnership, shared leadership, and shared meaning.

Collaborative Partnership

Every chapter in this section is about an awareness, an attitude, or a capability that contributes to the creation and maintenance of such partnerships. For example, though synchronicity is not a requirement for partnership, it is a product of interdependent relationships that interweave within the unbroken web David Bohm called a holographic unified field. Awareness of interconnection and interdependence is essential to the creation of successful collaborative partnerships. The ability to leverage diversity is a powerful resource for collaboration. The capacity to work with holding the tension of paradoxes, including those surrounding what we call "fuzzy agreements," is crucial to developing environments where polarities can generate creative alternatives rather than conflict and fragmentation. Working with shadow material and with undiscussables is necessary for building trust and creating alignment. Collective energy fields can either trap us in competitive and conflictual relationships or support us in developing collaborative ones. Can the on-line medium be a vehicle to support us in developing collaborative partnerships? We'll give you our thoughts. And, last, we consider times of group discomfort, frustration, and doubt and the essential discipline needed to persevere.

Shared Leadership

All collaborative partnerships share leadership responsibilities differently. Chapters on collective energy fields, shadow, holding paradox and diversity all deal with elements that can either support or hinder the development of your capacity for shared leadership. Collective energy fields that reinforce competitive relationships and behaviors make it difficult to move towards shared leadership. Undiscussables around power and control can be powerful shadows undermining your efforts. Building awareness in these areas will help you make useful strategic choices in the journey towards shared leadership.

Shared Meaning

It is not possible to develop true shared meaning that is representative of all participants and points of view without focusing attention on how we relate to diversity, paradox, and undiscussable shadow material.

A word of acknowledgment and gratitude. The experiences that inspired these pages come from work done by many groups of diverse composition and size. Some were composed of people attending public seminar programs; others are work groups within organizations. Some engaged in multiple dialogues over a period of three to five days. Some have met on a regular basis over years. The participants come from all walks of life and professional backgrounds. We are grateful to them for all they have taught us about the transformational power of dialogue to open our eyes to the many interrelated dimensions of the organizational territories we inhabit.

The Opening of Eyes

After R.S. Thomas

That day I saw beneath dark clouds
the passing light over the water
and I heard the voice of the world speak out,
I knew then, as I had before
life is no passing memory of what has been
nor the remaining pages in a great book
waiting to be read.

It is the opening of eyes long closed.
It is the vision of far off things
seen for the silence they hold.
It is the heart after years
of secret conversing
speaking out loud in the clear air.

It is Moses in the desert
fallen to his knees before the lit bush.
It is the man throwing away his shoes
as if to enter heaven
and finding himself astonished,
opened at last,
fallen in love with solid ground.

David Whyte[1]

1

SYNCHRONICITY AND DIALOGUE

"There exists a type of phenomenon, even more mysterious than telepathy or precognition, which has puzzled man since the dawn of mythology; the seemingless accidental meeting of two unrelated causal chains in a coincidental event, which appears both highly improbable and highly significant."

—Arthur Koestler

Synchronicity is often referred to as coincidence. Yet, when studied, the frequency of synchronous occurrences defies all we know about probability of random (coincidental) events. Synchronicity implies a more continuous fabric to reality; the same continuity that underlies quantum physics, the holographic universe of David Bohm, the morphogenic fields of Rupert Sheldrake, the self-organizing systems of Prigogine, and the *unus mundus* (one world) of Carl Jung.[2] What all these authors point to is an unbroken continuity between everything that exists. While complex processes may be comprised of multiple levels and parts, they all belong to a greater whole.

Synchronicity is an external manifestation of an internal connectedness. It is a symptom of a perceptual change that is rooted in the deep relatedness of all life. When we develop an awareness of the whole within which all parts and interrelationships sit, synchronous events become commonplace occurrences. While synchronous events are fascinating and useful, it is in the change in awareness, the focus on relatedness and the whole system that produces them, that the far-reaching value lies. Collaborative partnerships and shared leadership depend on the development of this focus. Dialogue encourages this *shift of mind*. In dialogue we listen for connections, for relationship. We release the need for any particular outcome and ask questions that seek a new and yet unseen level of understanding. We expand our listening to perceive connections and wavelengths that we might have previously filtered out. It is no surprise that our awareness of and availability to synchronicity increases.

Experiences of Being in Collective Synchronicity

The core experience that leads to the perception of "symptomatic" synchronous events is described beautifully in a poem by Eric Oksendahl, a participant in one of our programs.

Trust
What faith, so marvelous,
wells up within this frame?
What fabric woven between
our being heart to heart?
"Inside or outside?" you ask.
"Both" we reply.
And now we sit together.

A profound message is reflected in the subtle yet powerful shift in language Eric uses. He writes of "a fabric woven between *our being*," not our beings. Here, in the simple change of a word, from plural to singular, is the core awareness of ourselves as one, as a collective entity.

Exactly what the step-by-step dynamics are that produce this shift, we don't know. What is clear from experience with many groups is that when people come together in dialogue, make a commitment to an intention of listening and learning with one another, and focus their attention on what is important to them this shift often occurs. What follows are descriptions that illustrate some of the synchronistic "signposts" that groups encounter as they move into this shift of awareness.

"Someone Will Speak for Me."

When groups first begin to practice dialogue, the conversation is most often a collection of individual views of reality. Each person wants to be heard and contribute his particular, unique slant on whatever is being talked about. You say something and I can't wait to agree and describe my version of it. I don't necessarily have a different perspective, but I have another, and to me, better way of saying it. So I do. Sometimes a conversation can sound like a "report-out" with 16 variations on a single story line.

Why do we feel this need to repeat what has been said? Here are some commonly held assumptions that may contribute. "Participation equals speaking. By participating I will belong to the group, become a bona fide member. If I sit quietly, I won't be known, I'll become invisible. No one else sees this just the way I do; if I don't say something, they won't really fully understand this idea." All these can motivate and create a repetitious, and eventually boring, conversation.

As time passes and people begin to have some confidence that they are seen and acknowledged as contributing members, it becomes possible to focus attention on the emerging collective meaning and how each can most effectively contribute to this. The metaphor of cooking a pot of soup together is useful. No one knows exactly what kind of soup it will be in the end; it's an evolving creation. Each person tastes the soup as he listens. Each asks what ingredients she might want to add. The answer may be "none at this time" or "a little bit more of what Joe just put in" or "some spice no one else has put in so far." The group is continuously tasting the soup, asking, and listening. Each time the blend is new. And to this soup of the moment, each contribution is added.

The soup metaphor illustrates, and can actually evoke, two shifts. First, the group may experience a slowing in the pace of the dialogue as people begin to taste, savor, and reflect on possible additions, and refocus their attention towards the group as a collaborative cooking partnership. People learn that it is unnecessary, even undesirable, to repeat oneself; everyone may believe pepper is good in soup, but if everyone adds it . . . help! Imagine a collection of creative, individualistic chefs, each making his own recipe in the same pot, without paying attention to one another. I doubt I would want to eat the result. Is it any wonder some conversations can give you indigestion?

The second shift can be startling. As the pace slows and listening increases, people often begin to report curious experiences such as the following: "I was sitting and I suddenly had this flash of a question that might bring us some new insights, but before I could find an entry into the conversation, Amy asked the same question. Then it happened again with someone else. Today, I've been experimenting with just waiting and listening and seeing who else will speak what's on my in mind into the circle."

Discovering the Unified Field through Art

We sometimes start a dialogue with what we call collective art. The details of this activity were described in chapter 5 of Part II.

Collective art always provides surprises. Here are some frequent occurrences. First, every piece is totally different, depending on what was initially placed on the page. There is an experience of creating a "strange attractor" that the collective additions then organize around. There are also striking similarities; patterns that show up over and over again. Carl Jung would no doubt say that we are looking at collective archetypes percolating up from the collective unconscious onto the paper. We call them images of shared meaning. They create an experience of connecting into a collective field.

Another happening can be a bit more personal and startling. People will have in mind something they want to draw on their initial sheet of paper, but they don't know how, or they may have a feeling and not know what the appropriate symbol is to express it. When their paper returns to them, the symbol is on it! And no one has spoken a word. This is a powerful personal experience of connectedness. Still others find the group has transformed their piece into something unexpected, which takes on a particular significance for them as they reflect on it. People report being surprised, unsettled, and ultimately astounded by the messages of meaning these occurrences bring them. Synchronicity is speaking through the medium of art.

A Few Closing Reflections on Synchronicity and Transformation

The experiences we've described for you here all point to the line in Eric's poem, "fabric woven between our being," to a collective, unified field through which we communicate. What explanation is there for these experiences? Are there really some levels where we are connected that we just don't normally tune into? Are these occurrences part of the "fabric woven between our being"? Is this what telepathy is about? Are we all participating in a collective mind that we are seldom aware of? Whatever the explanation, these occurrences create a *shift of mind* to a perception of ourselves as parts within a holographic and synchronous universe.

What does all this mean for you in day-to-day life? People report becoming more attuned to synchronous events, or sightings, that provide additional information and insights or bring their attention to aspects of an issue they may not have considered. You may find yourself more relaxed as you begin to experience that a collective intelligence is at work and realize you don't have to provide all the perspectives. This will flow over into your capacity for effective collaboration as you begin to let it sink in that you neither need to, nor can, do it all, that others have valuable aspects of the picture to add. You will begin to shift your focus to listening for collective shared meaning and in doing so will actually be playing a role in helping it to emerge. In short, you will find yourself and your group more engaged in the behaviors of shared leadership and collaborative partnership.

Following are some ways you might experiment with increasing your awareness of synchronicity and its usefulness in providing you with additional information that you otherwise might not have considered.

TRY THESE: TUNING IN TO SYNCHRONICITY (MOST WILL WORK FOR INDIVIDUALS AND GROUPS)

○ Collect stories and speak to others about synchronous events they have experienced. This will focus your attention on and develop your receptivity to synchronicity.

○ Practice being open to suggestions and offerings from unexpected sources. See where they take you, what new connections emerge.

○ Make a practice of noticing symbols that seem to repeat or appear in unusual numbers. Suppose you observe that you are noticing an inordinate number of fish images on car bumpers and in windows, fish in aquariums, fish trophies, fish everywhere. Ask yourself "What does this symbol mean to me? Why am I seeing fish everywhere?" There are also books that tell you what certain archetypal symbols mean in dreams. They are useful, but always ask yourself for a personal meaning first before consulting the "official" guide.

○ Focus on an issue, a problem, or a question and then create the intention of noticing synchronous occurrences that will aid you in your exploration.

○ Many people maintain that we can develop our listening for synchronous events and signals through practices used through the centuries for divination, such as the I Ching, the Tarot, and the Runes. There are many such systems. They do not purport to give answers to specific questions so much as to suggest ways of looking that may have been passed by or not considered. If you would like to explore any of them, they can be obtained at many bookstores. Start with a question or an issue that you are seeking further insight into. "Consult" whatever medium you have chosen by asking for additional vantage points from which you may build a more complete picture. The idea is to inquire and expand your view rather than narrow it down to a single perspective or answer.

2

COLLECTIVE ENERGY FIELDS

*"Biologist Rupert Sheldrake proposes that
subtle fields provide a resonant infrastructure
within which material reality becomes manifest . . .
the field of morphic resonance . . .
contains our collective thinking, feeling, sensing."*[3]

Groups create vortices, or fields of energy, which become distinct and palpable. This happens as any group defines the nature of its relationships, the foundational assumptions of its culture, and reinforces them over time. It is not the presence of such fields that is uncommon, rather the conscious recognition and implications of their existence for both group effectiveness and learning. Because such fields influence people's behaviors, in both constructive and destructive ways, being aware of them and how to work with them is a powerful asset for individuals and groups. The reflections below are one person's description of experiences with such a field.

Beth watched her thoughts and feelings—changing, fluxing, as one after another in the circle gave voice. As she listened to each person, she found herself feeling "I am home." Some days later she wrote these reflections on the weekend.

"There is something here among us. It did not appear suddenly. It has emerged, unfolded, taken shape and substance over these two and one-half years we have met. With each coming together, it has grown more sure until now it waits to greet us as we all come in the door, and move up the stairs to "our" living room; space in a rented home we have made our own. We enter, one-by-one by -two or -three. We sit and begin. No, that is part of what is different. We don't begin; we continue. The thread, the tapestry we weave together has become a continuity, even through the months we live our different lives. And, every six months when we enter our circle, we continue.

Our dialogue spans all our days, across time and distance. And each time we sit again in our living room I am curious and awed. Whatever each person brings is added to, kneaded, rolled around, set to leaven, and returned, a more complete and hearty loaf of bread. It is as if we meet, bake bread together, and eat at each other's tables. When we leave we are more fully ourselves than when we arrived."

—*Pajaro Dialogue Journalings, 1995*

Members of groups that meet with some regularity over time often speak of similar experiences. Some people use words like "stepping into an already present field of energy" or liken the experience to some friendships—when you meet after years, it's as if you had never been apart. It is almost as if the interaction never really adjourns, the connection does not dissolve, rather they continue in some form in between physical gatherings. A physicist might describe this as an energy field that exists in time and space that we step into whenever we gather, be it every six months or every other week at noon.

If Beth's reflections didn't ring any bells for you, it might help if you relate this to the realm of personal relationships. Think of a relationship with someone you've known for quite some time such as a spouse, a partner, or a long-term colleague. Usually there are certain ways that you interrelate, familiar topics of conversation, places you like to sit relative to each other in the room, ways you tend to divide up tasks. These patterns, which become set and reinforced over time, are all part of your collective energy field. As soon as you get together, you step into the field. In most relationships these fields are comfortable and supportive and even exciting. On the other hand, you can probably think of relationships where every time you see the person it seems that the two of you always fall into the same arguments or other uncomfortable behaviors. Some couples, business partners, even teams, would truly like to change their patterns and yet find it extremely difficult. It is as if the field they have created awaits and overwhelms them each time they are together. It is not uncommon for partnerships to split up in order to get away from the collective field they have created. "I just couldn't make the changes that were needed while I was in the relationship" is an often heard statement from people who both have the desire and willingness to change but just can't seem to do so.

Getting Out of the "Whirlpool"

An ability to notice collective energy fields can be useful in helping generate new solutions to repeating problems that involve two or more people or groups. Most such patterns are the outgrowth of underlying assumptions and behaviors that have reinforcing loops built into them. Many systems thinking diagrams are examples of such interdependent loops. Dialogue helps surface these, making it possible to depict the relationships and see where changes might be made that will create alternative results and begin to dissolve the troublesome energy field.

Moving towards Cultures of Collaborative Partnership and Shared Leadership

Collective energy fields do have a life and mind of their own. If the field that two people create together is strong, just think how much more powerful are fields created by larger groups such as an organization, where thousands of people may be interacting based on a common set of mental assumptions and models.

People often say that creating an organizational culture based on trust and partnership is very hard because the system will not allow it. We used to respond with some variation of "Well, okay, but we are the system. All we have to do is decide to make the changes." Over time we have begun to realize that while there are no doubt many ways in which we contribute to the system, it is also a powerful collective field that has been sufficiently defined and reinforced to influence us when we step into it. This is one of the very messy things about living in a world of relationship and interdependence. What you create interacts with you and to some degree creates you as well, in ways you may not even be aware of. There are no one-way relationships.

So, when people talk helplessly about a system such as an organization, we understand. What we are also beginning to understand is that we *can* change the nature of the field, but it is definitely going to be a *we* endeavor. Even an incredibly strong leader, in the highest position, will not be able to shift the field alone. She may strongly influence it. She may plant the seeds for a shift. She may create a new infrastructure. But it is only the collective that can fundamentally shift the shared sets of assumptions that have been lived with over time and have become integrated in all of us. *Only group mind can shift group culture.* Leaders can serve as catalysts and holders of the flame, but they cannot singly craft collective reality. *We*, the people, craft culture.

Intentionally creating collective energy fields within organizations is one way to collectively begin to shift culture. You begin by shifting your patterns of relating and working together to ones that support collaboration and partnership, by practicing dialogic skills and guides (see Part II) in your day-to-day interactions and activities (see Part III). When you make this commitment, the energy configurations will begin to shift simultaneously. This is exciting. Yet, it is also true that it is very difficult to do this work if you have little or no awareness of how collective fields function, of how they can either hinder or support your efforts. Practicing dialogue can help you develop this capability to work intentionally with shifting patterns and cultures.

Responsibility and Creating New Possibilities

When you first begin to experience how groups create energy fields supported by patterns of behavior, you will also begin to grapple with the link between creation and responsibility. This can be uncomfortable. Many people approach this issue and step back, approach and step back, over and over again. Perhaps it is frightening to consider taking on responsibility for what is in our world today. Many of us feel overwhelmed. We feel we can't do all that is needed. The field or system immobilizes us and we resign ourselves to continue doing what we've always done, and to getting the same or similar results. This "all or nothing" thinking can put a stranglehold on us.

Overwhelmed is one possible view. But, history is full of stories of pioneering groups of people who intentionally began the work of creating new fields to support new ways of working and living together and the huge shifts that have resulted. Who knows what energy fields grew within East Germany that culminated in the fall of the Berlin Wall? Small groups of people are taking responsibility and reclaiming their power to create new possibilities all over the world today, in organizations and communities. In the laboratory division of one Fortune 100 company, groups that self-organized after a one-day division-wide event to celebrate creativity have continued to meet and create activities that impact the entire culture of the division. At a foundation, ongoing diversity dialogues are generating increased awareness of and attention to issues that previously went unrecognized. Like catalysts of a chemical chain reaction, a little goes a long way. In the words of Margaret Meade, "Never doubt the power of small groups of committed people to change the world. Indeed, nothing else ever has."

Below are two cases to help you consider how you might benefit from an awareness of patterned energy fields in your day-to-day activities and relationships.

TRY THIS: TWO CASES FOR REFLECTION

Case One. Where in your professional or personal life are you a member of a group that has created a collective energy field that supports you in your ability to be effective in your work? How could you be more intentional about reinforcing this energy field? Now consider one such collective field that blocks you from being as creative and effective as you know you can be. What might you intentionally do to help shift this field? What behaviors and patterns can you identify to focus some attention on? And finally, consider yet another field, one that you would like to create that would add aliveness and energy to your work and home. How can you intentionally work towards its creation?

Case Two. Consider a team where there is dissatisfaction about how roles are distributed and tasks are getting performed. The original role distribution may have happened in many ways. Some people may have had preferences for what they wanted to do and made them known. Others remained quiet. Roles may have been distributed based on assumptions about what different people were good at. One person may have had the power to hand out roles based on what he did and did not want to do himself. Over time this group developed its own pattern of getting things done, but it seems everything was always a struggle, some people doing more than others, with no one satisfied. The team created a new plan and started over more than once. Nothing seemed to work; things seem to end up being handled in much the same way as before.

You have a good friend who is a member of this team and has asked you for some help, a little personal coaching. Where would you start? What questions would you ask? What elements do you think might have contributed to this collective field of patterns? What questions might you ask team members to think about in order to help the group move forward? Where does responsibility of each team member and the group as a whole come into this picture?

3

HOLDING PARADOX

*"Living with paradox is not comfortable or easy.
It can be like walking in a dark wood on a moonless night.
It is an eerie and, at times, frightening experience.
All sense of direction is lost . . . . Come the dawn, however,
and your path is clear . . . . So will our world look different
and less frightening if we can bring light to the paradoxes."*

—Charles Handy
The Age of Paradox

*"One must have apocalypse in one eye and the other
millennium in the other, and as you look out through
that double vision, the third eye develops and sees the
resolution of tragedy and conflict and the rest of it."*

—William Irwin Thompson

What perspective can I imagine that could hold and relate
these seemingly irreconcilable polarities? The ability to hold paradox, i.e., work with divergent views, without choosing sides is crucial
to conflict resolution, to discerning ethical decisions in contexts where
values may be at odds, and to building true win/win alternatives. A
highly developed ability to work with paradox and ambiguity is essential to creating and sustaining collaborative partnerships that tap into
the power of diverse people and worldviews. To hold paradox requires a

shift of mind from either/or to both/and thinking. Dialogue is a practice field that encourages this *shift of mind*. In dialogue, paradox becomes an opportunity for movement towards new alternatives rather than a dilemma that immobilizes and separates us.

How does this *shift of mind* occur? Here's one example from an Introduction to Dialogue workshop. It concerns the potential conflict all groups face around pace.

Quite suddenly, we were a group divided. It only took a few words. One woman was frustrated with the pace and made a comment about needing to slow down and ground our conversation in more of a feeling level. Of course, her comment was immediately considered a judgment of everyone who had spoken to that point, particularly the woman who had spoken just before her.

As soon as the words were spoken, the entire group shifted into a conversation of "What should we do?" and explanations of what everyone thought everyone else was feeling/thinking. You could feel the separation between the two women and the tensions in the group as people felt around for answers, for a way out. Perhaps a talking stick. Some decision as to which way to go. Yes, that would do the trick.

The group was smack in the middle of a conflict and a paradox. People's needs were different. Everyone wanted to create a space for conversation that could include a diversity of personal styles, but the drive to move into evaluation and choice was strong. Everyone knew in their gut that such a choice always makes one person right and another wrong but were convinced choice was the only solution.

We gently suggested that they not try to fall back on guidelines as a way out, that they see if they could stay present to what each was perceiving and take full responsibility for their perceptions without placing blame or interpreting others' realities. The intention was to listen and suspend the need to move to any decision. Listen and let go. Listen and let go. And then, the miracle happened. There was a shift and no longer did anyone need to make anyone else right or wrong. No need to do anything, fix anything, explain anything. Just listening. And in the listening, the separation dissolved. When they released the need to choose, to decide, they found themselves able to sit within the whole of the group, with no need to emphasize one style over another. *The two distinct perspectives did not disappear but the feelings of separation and tension did.*

You've probably all witnessed how this kind of conflict gets started. Someone makes a comment, any number of people take it personally, and defenses are activated. And quite suddenly there you are, stuck and yet also on the threshold of possibility. At such times the key questions are "Can the group resist the urge to make a decision, to organize its way out of the discomfort?" and "Can you sit with what seems irreconcilable paradox or polarity without taking sides?" That afternoon the answers were "yes."

When you find yourself able to hold paradox in this way, it can often feel like a miracle has occurred. What is the shift in focus that will allow you to honor any two polarities of a paradox simultaneously? When the collision in the group described first occurred, everyone's attention was focused on the individual perspectives, on the differentiated opinions and positions, and on deciding how to resolve them or choose between them. When they made the choice to not choose, to simply stay present and be with what was going on, the shift occurred. There is something about the acceptance and willingness to sit with paradox that allows for integration.

This is a powerful transformation. Paradox ceases to be a dilemma to be resolved and becomes a catalyst for you to expand your perceptions, to validate and integrate more of what is present into an inclusive whole. Interrelationships between previously disconnected perspectives become visible. Looking from the new vantage point, you can see beyond the level of thinking where the dilemma originates. From this more inclusive level you know that *whether you feel connected or separate and at odds is a matter of where you place your attention.* Will you focus on separation and polarity or on the whole that encompasses the paradox? You decide.

The implications of learning to hold paradox for creating and sustaining collaborative partnerships should be obvious. Collaboration requires the ability to seriously entertain the question "What if we start by assuming the truth of all perspectives?" Development of shared leadership and meaning both require the full participation of all parties present. This means finding alternative vantage points that can honor and leverage diverse perspectives. Without an ability to hold paradox and suspend judgment, this is unlikely to happen.

One of the greatest challenges to forming collaborative partnerships is people's personal differences in style, which are a product of our life experiences and assumptions. One classic example is the person who likes to plan ahead and work the plan and the other who likes to be more spontaneous and is often energized by pushing against a deadline. Learning to embrace these differences without judging either one wrong allows both parties to explore moving beyond defensiveness and jointly discover some third alternative that will serve them in the context of the partnership.

Another somewhat more complex example might be the apparent paradox presented by the question of whether to focus energy on individual excellence or on teamwork. Most reward systems focus on individual performance. When things get tough, this encourages choices that will benefit the individual but may not support the partnership. On the other hand, reward systems geared to team performance can demoralize high performers if they feel they must "carry" others with them. How do we motivate individual performance in the context of partnership or teamwork in the context of diverse individual excellence? There is no simple answer. Only by engaging both ends without choosing one over the other will organizations discover how to create forms that integrate and leverage both. The ability to talk at depth about the assumptions, history, and challenges involved is essential.

Because our perceptions of reality are so intimately connected with either/or thinking, it is very difficult for us to even begin to think about and find words to describe the awareness where paradox is embraced. But that does not mean it is not real or possible. It simply requires a willingness to hang in there and refocus attention on the whole system and the relatedness of the diverse aspects involved.

Bringing It Home

How can you begin to explore your own thinking around holding paradox and bring more flexibility into your daily activities? Here are some suggestions for reflection and for experimenting with bringing this shift to your interactions.

TRY THIS: STRENGTHENING YOUR CAPACITY TO HOLD PARADOX

Think of a meeting where an important decision was on the table and you were either involved in or witness to an escalation of tensions between two strong and opposing positions. What were your assumptions about how resolution could happen? What were your assumptions about what would happen if no decision or choice between the two were made? Among those present, how many people "took sides"? How many do you think remained neutral? What do you think might have happened if the conversation could have taken place in an environment where everyone knew there would be no final decisions and no evaluation of which position was right or wrong? What would happen if everyone were asked to consider the question "What perspective can I imagine that could hold and relate both of these very different positions?"

The next time you are in a similar situation, try asking the above question either aloud for the group to consider, or internally as a way to help yourself focus your attention on the whole that creates relationship and possibility. Imagine yourself able to hold both aspects of the paradox without needing to choose. See how long you can do this before you just have to evaluate, choose, and move to action. Notice what happens. Keep working on it and witnessing the shifts within your own awareness and your relationships.

4

FUZZY LOGIC, POLARITIES, AND

FUZZY AGREEMENTS

*"So far as the laws of mathematics refer to reality,
they are not certain. And so far as they are certain,
they do not refer to reality."*

—Albert Einstein

*"The most savage controversies are those about matters
as to which there is no good evidence either way."*

—Bertrand Russell

Fuzzy logic is the latest revolution in thinking about polarities. A very basic description would be this: We think we live in a binary, either/or world. An apple either is an apple or it is not. But when does it make a transition from a seed to an apple? The idea is that binary, either/or thinking is only true at the extreme ends of any continuum (at seed or apple). Everything in between is some combination or composite, in transition from one form to another. What if our ability to perceive is just as fluid but we have trapped it within the limiting dimensions of either/or? What if our inability to hold paradox and recognize it as a continuum with two polarities at either extreme has limited our ability to see all the realities in between? How does this affect our ability to create shared visions, meet diverse expectations, and reach useful agreements? The following story illustrates one group's experience with fuzzy agreements and the shift in awareness and relationship that it brought with it.

"What time does the meeting start?" The group had revisited the topic many times. Always it was the same. Some people preferred to start later, some earlier, one was adamant about ending early. We always came to the same agreement: we would start early and end early. There was just this one fly in the ointment: few of us showed up on time; most were anywhere from 15 to 45 minutes late.

Why is it we kept revisiting and remaking our agreement and yet we just couldn't commit to it? It seems it should be simple, yet the reality is that it has not. We asked ourselves why. First we dealt with all the surface stuff—traffic; long distances some were driving; different perceptions about rigidity and personal styles relative to time; how this was after all not a work session, it was more informal. One woman said it reminded her of a program she attended where eight people were given the task of deciding when breaks and mealtimes would be. After more than an hour, they were so frustrated they just wanted the session leader to decide.

In our dialogue group where there was a level playing field and no structure of authority to fall back on, the task of finding shared understanding rapidly brought to the foreground the dynamics of creating collective agreements. "What time does the meeting start?" became a series of questions. Who is the perceived leader and what influence does this have on the agreements reached? What about personal freedom? Would we have to change our preferences in order to fit in, to belong to this group? Do we keep the group agreement regardless of whether it is to our liking, putting our desire to belong as highest priority? Or do we do our own thing, putting the expression of our individuality as first priority? Are norms and agreements born of the assumption that belonging and individuality cannot be simultaneous and equal priorities? These questions were further complicated by all the unconscious baggage we all brought around authority, rules we had learned about keeping commitments, our judgments of others who behave differently, and so on.

We rapidly got to the point where we wondered if it was even reasonable to expect that an agreement about meeting time would ever endure and be honored. If, as it appeared, everyone was thinking differently about commitments and time and it was actually impossible to predict when a meeting would start, why bother to even agree to a set time?

We came to the notion of fuzzy logic and fuzzy agreements. We saw the agreement like a lighted beacon, helping us aim in a direction rather than as fixed and immutable. We realized our group aim would always be off by "so much per person." There would always be divergence. We did come to a decision. It was no different than the one before the conversation took place. We would still designate an early start time and end early. But because we now understood much more about the thinking and feeling behind people's behaviors, we were also much more able to flex with the differences. The behaviors didn't necessarily change, but the degree of unrest that they created decreased noticeably. Now we could refocus the energy that had been diverted into confusion and frustration around this issue on our dialogues.

The above conversation went on for over two hours. A first response to this might be disbelief and dismay at the time taken to arrive at an agreement that seems no different than the one we started with. No wonder rules are so common. They are based on a fundamental assumption that without rules people are incapable of aligned action, that without policies and procedures (a longer name for rules) people will not know how to act, or will act in many different ways and chaos will reign. Most rules and policies are not formulated collaboratively; it takes too long to create the shared meaning needed. Top-down authority directives are seen as both maintaining a greater degree of control and as more efficient. But if a group or an organization wants to tap the power of collaborative partnerships and shared leadership, unilateral agreements just don't cut it.

A primary purpose of agreements is to create alignment and coordinated action. The experts tell us how important it is to take the time for people to speak about their diverse perceptions so that in the end the agreement that is reached will include consideration of everyone's ideas. They tell us the chain is only as strong as the strongest agreement link in it, that agreements are like stakes in the ground, where we take our collective stands and where we will fall back to when the going gets tough.

What we don't often hear about is how agreements are not fixed, how the way in which they are implemented rarely goes by the letter of the law, how day-to-day activities and life change the playing field and make agreements obsolete to one degree or another. We rarely talk about how keeping to an agreement that no longer serves its original purpose can actually produce outcomes that are destructive to the system itself. We prefer not to address the resentment, rebellion, and sabotage that can result when agreements are not representative of all voices or are rigidly held in the face of significant changes in the environment that call for different action. We prefer to think of agreements as absolutes, as yes or no. Getting into the shades of gray and relativities that are actually the norm is uncomfortable.

Agreements are like Visions

They are living symbols of the relationships and shared understandings among groups of people. They perform two equally important and often seemingly paradoxical functions having to do with identity and fluid adaptation.

Creation of identity within the group, which provides for cohesion and self referencing. Here is where holding paradox enters again. Consider that agreements define identity. And that identity must be maintained within a range of flexibility in order for it to continue to exist. This is true of individuals and within organizations. The book *Built to Last* describes essentials for organizations that have endured the test of time. Of paramount importance was the continuous work of defining the core values and purpose of the organization and aligning decisions and actions with these. Agreements create identity and maintain it over time. They tell us what we can count on, what commitments we and others have made. They tell us who we are relative to one another: vendor and customer, husband and wife, parents and children, supervisor and subordinate, friend and friend. Our agreements with ourselves define how we see ourselves, our individual identities, and our purposes.

Continuous adaptation to the external environment. Individuals and organizations that survive and flourish in changing environments also recognize that the decisions and actions needed to carry core values and purpose into the world change as the environment changes and that failure to adapt means eventual death. So agreements must also have some fluidity, flexibility. "All or nothing" agreements have very short lifetimes. They are only viable at two extreme ends of a continuum, the "all" end and the "nothing" end. Everywhere in between, which is most places, they do not hold true.

Mathematicians would say that living agreements are fuzzy agreements, that they are all some combination of all and nothing. The strongest fuzzy agreements are those where the parties to them have an understanding of the diversity of assumptions that have combined to create them, of the boundaries and the degrees of flexibility.

Agreement making is a continuous process where each agreement reached is only a snapshot of what works in the moment. Your challenge, should you choose to accept it, is to hold the paradox of order and chaos, control and anarchy, from day to day, creating and maintaining a living flow of agreements and identity. Here are some questions and exercises you can use to reflect on agreements that are important to you and those you work with.

TRY THIS: DIGGING DEEPER INTO IMPORTANT AGREEMENTS

- ○ What agreements do you have with yourself that are essential to how you define yourself? Are there any additional ones you would like to consider? Any that might need updating?
- ○ Think about a team or group you are a leader or a member of at work. What agreements has the group come to in the past months that just don't seem to work, that you seem to be continuously returning to for conversation, or you just ignore

because it's not worth the hassle? On a sheet of paper, draw a line down the center from top to bottom. On the right side, write down what the conversation is about one such agreement. What is it that people say when you talk about this agreement? On the left side, write down what you think might be some of the unspoken conversation about the agreement. What do you think some of the concerns and questions are that people may not be raising, but that are influencing the way in which the agreement is acted on day to day?

○ If your group is willing, you might each do the above exercise and start a conversation by sharing what you have written. Each person would read without any comment from others. The purpose here is not to determine the rightness of any one opinion, but rather to gather information on the many ways different members see the issue. Once everyone has read their writing, the group can begin the conversation. The purpose is to understand more about the realities that influence the agreement. Again, it is not about right or wrong perspectives. It is about understanding more, so that whatever comes forth will be more aligned with and reflective of the collective reality. At the conclusion of the conversation, take about five to ten minutes to talk about what you have learned and how it will influence your actions as you move forward.

5

SHADOW AND DIALOGUE

*shadow . . . a comparative darkness within an
illuminated area caused by the interception of light;
a mirrored image as in "to see one's shadow in a pool;"
that which is disowned, disavowed, denied, hidden.*

—Funk and Wagnalls

In 1945 Carl Jung referred to shadow as "the thing a person has no wish to be" and cautioned "One does not become enlightened by imagining figures of light, but by making the darkness conscious. The latter procedure, however, is disagreeable and therefore not popular."[4] All individuals and groups have shadow aspects. We may be the last to see these shadows because they are those aspects of character or behavior we do not wish to identify with. Why shed light on them? Because out of sight is not out of action. Whether or not we are conscious of them, our shadows unrelentingly influence us from behind the scenes, often creating much havoc. Consider a few examples.

○ Shadow that remains unacknowledged and unspoken can lead to undesired results. Suppose a leader who places a high value on forthrightness and honesty as a result finds himself uneasy in conversations where subordinates are asking questions he feels uncomfortable answering. Because he does not want to be seen as anything other than forthright and honest, he may actually avoid such conversations altogether. Unwilling to come to grips with what he perceives as falling short of his high standards, his avoidance behavior (the shadow here) may create exactly the perception by employees that he does not want. Whether such a leader is acting intentionally or is unconscious of what is going on does not change the result.

○ Though we don't often think of shadow in terms of positive traits, there are times we may decide to disown even our strengths, like intelligence and creativity. I have a good friend who is a younger sister and always made less of herself in order not to provoke the jealousy and anger of her older sister and mother. Similarly, team members may hold back on valuable suggestions in meetings because they are afraid of provoking defensiveness or anger in someone higher up the ladder. Such a team's collective intelligence will never have a chance to develop.

○ Shadow can be evoked by strong focus on specific values. Imagine an organization whose vision and mission involves creating and supporting projects that will enhance wholeness and health through the integration of mind, body, and spirit. Physical, emotional, mental, and spiritual health are highly valued. There is a meditation room and a gym on the grounds. The food is mostly vegetarian and low-fat. Inclusion of everyone in all activities is encouraged. Heaven? Well, for some. But for others whose lifestyles may not fit the way this organization envisions its values in action, life can be quite uncomfortable. The focus on integration and wholeness can unknowingly create an unwillingness to acknowledge signs of unrest, exclusion, and separation because these are incongruent with peace, inclusion, and wholeness. The ungrateful and disruptive ones become the recipients of the organization's frustration and are blamed for the unrest that seems to keep recurring. The best of intentions and honorable values seem thwarted; there is conflict where there should be harmony.

Through the practice of dialogue, groups are able to become aware of and work with their shadows. In a practice field where judgment is suspended, disavowed parts of our thinking can be brought forward and integrated into the whole. We can talk about what we don't like without having to project it outside ourselves onto others. Our shadows, whether individual or collective, are part of our identity. Like our assumptions, shadows are always in operation, impacting our thinking, actions, and results. Shadow aspects do not go quietly into the night. It takes tremendous energy to keep shadow content in the dark, separate, unspoken, unacted on. Shadows are never inconsequential. The energy we put into concealing them invests them with importance. And we take them with us everywhere. Me and my shadow. We and our shadow.

By developing the capacity to integrate shadow, you and any group you are a member of will reduce the shadow's inhibiting or destructive potential and simultaneously release energy that has been tied up in concealing it. Acknowledgment and inclusion of our shadows is a source of energy and movement that opens the door for learning and new insights and paves the way for increased alignment and integrity in our actions. This *shift of mind* where shadow is reframed as discussable, even valuable, often occurs in dialogue, allowing shadow to become a contributing member rather than a recalcitrant outcast.

The Walk-Talk Gap

The remainder of this chapter is focused on one of the most prevalent shadows for both individuals and organizations. The walk-talk gap is the discontinuity between what we say we want to do or will do and what we actually do. It is a shadow because most of us are uncomfortable even thinking about this issue, much less talking about it openly. It is associated with integrity and credibility. We have all experienced the confusion and distrust this shadow can create in relationships.

Though we often resist it, inquiring into this gap is one of the most powerful learning activities available to groups and individuals. It is a potent and useful mirror. It readily shows us what we hold as real and important and the paradoxes and dilemmas of our value systems. Consider the following scenario from a "Redefining Leadership through Dialogue" program at a Fortune 100 company.

It was morning. We were engaged in an activity called "walk and talk" as a way to learn from data collected through a climate survey completed by all the leaders participating in the program. First they examined the information and identified themes that recurred, organizing them in matched pairs, with the "talk" in the right column and the "walk" in the left column. See Figure 1 below.

Figure 1

WALK (Theories in Use)[5]	TALK (Espoused Theories)[6]
People are expected to work 60–70 hour weeks to show their dedication	We want there to be balance in people's family and work lives
Leadership is almost without exception white/male/married/children/wife doesn't work	We value diversity as a resource and requirement for success

We acknowledged that there would certainly be matches between the "walk" and the "talk." However, for the purposes of this activity we would focus on the pairs where there was discrepancy.[7] After identifying the pairs, we asked that they choose one and continue to dig a little deeper. For each pair, they listed as many assumptions as they could that supported that "walk" or "talk." The beginning of one such list is shown in Figure 2 on the following page.

Notice how the assumptions on both sides are about values that we all hold to one degree or another—loyalty, commitment, character, family lifestyle, satisfaction and stability. Once the group was able to see that there were powerful reasons reinforcing and supporting each side, they began to consider how they all played out in the larger system. Now the really challenging work could begin, the work of holding the paradoxes involved and inquiring into the values and purposes they served, the work of asking what thinking and actions would increase alignment and coherence and decrease the double messages that were creating frustration, confusion, and resentment.

Figure 2

WALK (Theory in Use)	TALK (Espoused Theory)
Need to work 60–70 hr/wk	Family/work life balancce
Supporting Assumptions	**Supporting Assumptions**
People who have a commitment to their work will always go the extra mile	Balance is necessary for stability and performance over the long term
Times are tough and all loyal employees will do a little more	An unhappy home will result in distraction and poor judgment
Doing that little extra to complete the job is satisfying and builds character	Families are a cornerstone of our nation and our culture

The group concluded by identifying gaps that existed in their personal "walks" and "talks" in their day-to-day interactions within the organization.

It can be hard work to shed light on this kind of shadow. One reason we all prefer to keep the walk-talk gap in the realm of the undiscussable is the strong assumption within our culture that there is a right way and a wrong way to be. When we couple this with the value statement "to say one thing and do another is a wrong way to be" and with the knowledge that being wrong usually results in some form of exclusion from the community, it's no wonder we want to ignore and cover up any discrepancies between our walk and our talk. This dichotomy of right and wrong often results in strong denial behaviors. Too close a scrutiny might reveal incoherence between our thinking and actions. We might be judged bad, incompetent, dishonest, out of integrity, or a poor leader.

In some cases the pain of looking into the gap may be so great that it literally becomes impossible to see it at all. In medical history there are descriptions of a condition called hysterical blindness. In such cases the people are virtually blind, even though there is no physiological reason for it. Usually, they have suffered some trauma so profound and painful that they stop seeing as a way to avoid perceiving what will trigger the pain. If they can be helped to work through the pain, the blindness often disappears.

Chris Argyris speaks about how we create layers of defensive routines in attempts to cover up incoherences or gaps between our espoused theories (our talk) and our theories in action (our walk). What if some gaps represent such painful dilemmas for us, that we create cover-ups extreme enough to actually result in episodes of collective hysterical blindness, making the gaps virtually invisible, nonexistent? What we fail to recognize is that if we can look upon the gap without judgment or condemnation, the simple act of acknowledgment will begin the work of integration and result in more coherence and alignment. As David Bohm said, "Observed thought changes." Sometimes the most challenging part of the work is in the looking.

The gap is a powerful irony. It reveals our fragmentation, separation, and alienation. And yet at the same time within it also lies the possibility for wholeness and continuity between intention and action. The gap itself is proof of both our collective incoherence and dilemmas *and* the wholeness that has been fragmented. When you see a shattered cup on the floor, do you not also see the image of it whole? Otherwise, how could you recognize it as a fragmented cup?

The gap is a wound and an opportunity. When we are willing to walk into it, we find it is another door into collective awareness and new opportunities. As groups practice dialogue, they develop the skills needed to do this important work. They build capacity for inquiry, suspension of judgment, and deep listening and become able to look and see without beating themselves up. This is crucial. Inquiring into shadow requires looking with compassion, listening with an open heart, without the need for a final outcome or final answer to our dilemmas. Exploring this frontier calls for love in the greatest sense of the word, for a willingness to be in relationship with a reality that is not always easy to understand, and a capacity to step into the unknown and trust that together we can create a sustainable world.

Collective inquiry into the gaps in our organizational worlds, our families, and our global communities can redirect creative energies. Are we up to the task? Linda and I think so. We see people in organizations all over the world laboring at this work with commitment. Many have discovered the value that dialogue brings to deepening and sustaining their inquiries. Fred Kofman and Peter Senge remind us of some of the reasons why. "If members of a team [organization] cannot surface their hidden assumptions, opinions, and emotions, then they cannot build new shared views of the business issues . . . . [Often, when we] claim we want to learn, we normally mean that we want to acquire some new tool or understanding. When we see that to learn, we must be willing to abandon our old certainties, to put our old self at play, learning looks dangerous . . . . Only with the support, insight and fellowship of a community can we face the dangers of learning meaningful things." [8] Dialogue is a natural process for this work. It creates the environment for such conversations and learning by focusing our attention on relationship, listening, suspension of judgment, and a deep inquiry into our assumptions.

QUESTIONS FOR REFLECTION ───────────────────────────────

o   Where in your life do you experience a gap between your talk and your walk? Focus in on a particular relationship or project you work on with a team of people. Rather than judging yourself for your inconsistency or lack of integrity, ask yourself what information is here for you about the values that are important to you and the relative priorities they hold in your life.

o   Think about another team that your group may make comments about such as "I'm sure glad we're not like them." What characteristics of theirs disturb you? These are possible shadows for your group.

o   What are your most strongly held values? What behaviors would be inconsistent with these values?

───

6

DIFFERENCE AND DIALOGUE

"If you want to understand yourselves,
[find a way to] *be yourselves and you will."*

—Franklin Greenwald

"Each of us is the strongest one in his own skin.
Characteristics should take off their hats to one another,
instead of spitting in each other's faces."

—Bertolt Brecht

Without diversity, our day-to-day existences would be devoid of color, lacking the variety of perspectives that combine in ever more complex patterns of continuous creativity. And, diversity may also prove to be the Achilles heel of our species. If we can gain the ability to hold our diversity within a collective awareness of relationship and wholeness, it can become a resource for unlimited creativity. Dialogue creates a space where we can bring the separation between us into a field of listening and suspended judgment that can heal the rifts. May it be so in our lifetimes.

One of the most difficult things to speak honestly about is diversity. When I (Glenna) first wrote these reflections, I was pleased with what I had written. I thought I had put out some provocative thoughts and told a few powerful stories about learnings generated in dialogues where the focus was diversity. I sent the draft out to some good friends. Most told me how good and relevant the piece was. Then I called Pat and she told me a truth that made me sit down and start again. She said, "It ran hot and cold for me. You are saying some important things here. And yet, I didn't get the feeling that you were going as deep as I know you can go, as I've seen you go. I wondered what it is you really want to tell us." Her words brought me up short. I took a deep breath and began to ask questions. As we spoke, I began to recognize a feeling moving through my body. It was fear. My friend Pat was so right. I had said some very important things and told a story or two. And most of you would never know I had copped out. But Pat knew. I had stayed on safe ground and that made the writing less than it could have been if I was willing to risk a little more. I am convinced my conversation with Pat was a mini-representation of the challenges that demand our attention and the fears that stop us.

It is fear that makes talking about diversity so difficult. Fear that I will say something that will offend you or reveal my ignorance or prejudices. Fear that you will think less of me after I speak. Political correctness may have originated with a desire to respect difference, but it is a double-edged sword that also keeps us from talking with one another in our real voices. And what we need more than anything when it comes to diversity work is the ability to simply begin to talk together honestly. We need to be able to lay our fears on the table, to put out what we think and feel and what we've been taught about those who are different from us. We need to be and feel heard, to be willing to listen without feeling that we must change to conform to another's way of thinking and being. Until we can create a place for such conversations to occur, I doubt we will be able to create new ways of being together that honor us all.

How is it that our diversity has become a wedge driven between us when within it rest our gifts and our hope for wholeness? *Diverse* is defined by Funk and Wagnall as "differing essentially; to be unlike in a basic, intrinsic and indispensable way." Diversity is about identity.

When our diversity is not valued, we are not valued. When I perceive your diversity as a threat to me, it becomes unlikely I will be able to value it. If you and I have differing styles of dress, for example — big deal! I may not like yours. So what? But let's suppose we're working on a project and one of us is going to have to change or go against a value that is important to us. Then, we are going to have a problem. Our diversity becomes a separator and source of conflict any time what I hold to be true and necessary clashes with what you hold as true and necessary in a way that feels dangerous to either one of us. The bottom line is "I'm not going to let you mess with who I am." When we approach differences like religion, sexual preference, and race, the fear indicators can easily begin jumping off the scale.

Diversity is a huge dilemma and question for our species. All of us want to be honored for our diversity, our individual identities. We want to believe that all our diverse perspectives are necessary to the health of our whole, our community. At the same time, all of us want to be right about how we see the world. A friend put it this way: "I am my norm. I am the measure against which I assess everyone and everything around me."

So how do we learn to embrace our diversity as both a source of discomfort and a resource, simultaneously? How do we embrace the paradox? I use the word *embrace* because I don't believe it's about getting rid of the discomfort but rather learning to stay with the relationship, without having to leave or fight. It's about suspending our need to be right, creating an opening for new possibilities, and noticing what emerges.

Ultimately it comes down to you and me. In a world where conformity, fitting in, being alike and being liked are keys to belonging, difference is frightening. If you and I are afraid of those parts of ourselves that are too different, that may get us labeled inappropriate or worse. If we have not been able to accept our own diversity, our strengths and weaknesses, our brilliance and our shadows, how will we be able to stand unafraid and welcome one another's differences with excitement and curiosity?

When we can talk about what happens inside us as we become aware that someone is different from us because of race, gender, sexual orientation, cultural background, personal styles, or religion and how this influences our relationships, we will begin to heal our wounds of separation. With this healing, our conversations about diversity as a resource, even a necessity, will become more than superficial and empty words.

"If you want to understand yourself, be yourself and you will." If we want to understand ourselves collectively, in all our diversity, we need to be able to be ourselves in the presence of one another. A good start would be creating opportunities for conversation about what is important and meaningful to us. I believe dialogue offers us this opportunity. Perhaps more important, it offers an opening into the awareness of ourselves as relational beings from which it is possible to experience our differences as the absolute necessities for our wholeness. The differences that underlie the "isms" can be either separators or unique gifts that allow us to be a rich and alive whole. It all depends on whether we look through our fear of or our love for one another.

What does all this have to do with organizations? Everything. Meg Wheatley and Myron Kellner-Rogers call organizations "irreducible." An organization's life energy, its vision and the decisions and actions that give it shape and form, all reside in the collective thinking, feeling, and acting of the people who are the organization. To make the statement "diversity is a resource" a reality, it must become a reality within each individual.

In most organizations, respect for difference is mandated and behavioral compliance is enough. Compliance is a surface phenomenon; if it looks like you're complying, then you're doing what you need to do. Compliance may get and keep a few jobs for people and prevent people from publicly demeaning each other and I personally think these "results" are preferable to the alternative. But compliance makes me uncomfortable because it is based on fear. "You behave, or else." Most disturbing, compliance tends to reinforce the very thinking and behavioral patterns it seeks to eliminate.

Compliance creates resistance. It says in effect "Who you are is not okay. We know we can't control your thoughts and feelings, but if you want to belong here, during these hours, you will at least change your behavior." Compliance drives into hiding what is not acceptable and thus creates separation within the individual and the organization. It creates a dichotomy of the way we act in public and what we really believe and can get away with behind closed doors. Compliance creates covert manipulation of the system. Worst of all, it makes the open, authentic conversation of dialogue an even greater risk.

A dilemma? A huge one. There are no easy answers. To move beyond compliance requires creating possibilities for new awareness, new ways of thinking and feeling to emerge. Because this often occurs in groups practicing dialogue, many diversity professionals bring the process to groups they work with. They have experienced dialogue as one way to create a space for the kind of conversation that is needed; a "clearing in the forest"[9] where people can enter and meet, where fires may be built without burning down the surrounding trees, where there is space to move, to speak and be heard, and to listen for the emergence of new possibilities.

The story below is about one group's experience of being together in just such a clearing and the learnings that emerged for some.

A *story*. This story is about transformation. It is a disturbing and a powerful story. It is the story of a group of people gathered to create a field of inquiry, to explore authentic conversation and collective learning.

Our group was predominantly white, with a small number of people of color. It was morning, and our facilitators had just suggested a process. An African-American woman had reservations about the process and whether it was appropriate for her to participate in it. She stated her concern. Another person responded with a different opinion. An exchange followed. It was not long before the conversation became centered around race and the inability of some of us to begin to understand the experience of others, in this case the inability of a white man to know the experiential context that shapes the reality of an African-American woman.

There were feelings of anger, of not being seen, on both sides. The entire group became involved. But the conversation was not about race; rather, it was about what process we would follow. It was not that no one had anything to say relative to the conversation around race and context. There was plenty to say, but it was too uncomfortable. It was undiscussable. So the energy of the disturbance manifested itself in a discussion about the process. The conversation continued. Some interaction occurred among different individuals. The details are blurred. The morning ended.

Later that evening, a smaller group continued the conversation from the morning. The going was tough. It is so hard for people to talk about race. I think white people often feel that they have two options, ignorant or guilty. Not much comfort there. And people of color don't have it any better. They get to be angry and/or educators. Either way, we all end up in pain. And the question becomes: Can we hang in there? Can we stay in relationship and create an opening beyond the pain? It's not fun. It's the hardest work I know. The African-American women left exhausted and with real questions about whether to return to the large group the next morning.

They did. It was as if the work of the evening expanded and continued in the morning. We all got an up-close and personal and extremely painful look at the context within which many African-Americans live. The stories were told with great compassion. Only great compassion could have held the pain and rage in those stories in a way that did not lash out and attack. Only great compassion could have provided the space for all of us present to open our hearts, hear, and feel one another's pain and create an opening for new possibilities.

I am always awed by such experiences. And yet I am also saddened by the cost to some of the participants. The cost of laying open the pain, over and over again, for the sake of educating others. The cost of an experience where the only way you are known is through your color and the pain associated with it. The cost of having your greater individuality relegated to a backseat because, first and foremost, people will respond to the color of your skin.

And I suspect the cost may be deeper on a collective level. It seems likely that any time we relate to a person based on a single characteristic we cut ourselves off from her unique gifts and perceptions. Correspondingly, any time a stereotype we hold about a group or a culture blinds us to the diversity within the culture, we lose.

This is the violence of stereotypes, when one characteristic becomes seen as the whole. When diversity becomes singularity. When individuals become invisible, then relationships become reservoirs of resentment, anger, and pain. We all suffer.

Once again I had witnessed a group of people in deep conversation create a crucible for our learning about compassion, love, pain, and courage, about the impact of stereotypes on relationship, about our ability to dissolve stereotypes and create the possibility for open and listening relationships where previously there was only deafness and separation.

While this story speaks to us of the power of dialogue in exploring diversity, it only hints at an even more essential relationship between the two:

> *Diversity is an absolute necessity for the power of dialogue*
> *itself to unfold. Dialogue gains depth and the opportunity*
> *for learning from the diversity within it while simultaneously*
> *providing a way for that diversity to be honored.*

Without differentiation there is only homogeneity and sameness. Differentiation is an absolute necessity for creativity. Attachment to the rightness single differences creates separation and polarization. When we can honor one another's differences and allow ourselves to move into fluid conversation with one another, we will discover the true power of diversity and open a new era.

7

ON-LINE CONVERSATIONS

*"Conversations are the way knowledge workers [people] discover
what they know, share it with their colleagues, and in the process
create new knowledge for the organization. The panoply of
modern information and communication technologies . . . can
help knowledge workers in this process. But all depends on the
quality of the conversations that such technologies support."*

—Alan Webber
Harvard Business Review

*"If on-line technologies do no more than increase the quantity of
conversation that we already have, without changing the quality,
they may indeed prove a disservice to humanity."*

—Community of Inquiry and Practice Seminar participant

The Internet may represent the greatest transformation in how we
communicate since the telephone. Over the last few years, many
people have approached us about the possibilities of dialogues, even
trainings, on-line. There already exist a growing number of on-line conversations that characterize themselves as dialogues. What they all seem
to have in common is the desire of their members to engage in conversation with other people who possess similar interests. Here the com-
monality stops. These on-line groups focus on many topics from
community building to the practices of a learning organization. The

guidelines they use for the conversation vary widely, from structured discussion, to simple emphasis on listening and inquiry, to a Bohmian[10] group, to a form known as Insight Dialogue[11] that incorporates meditative practices for focusing attention on the dialogue process. Just as with face-to-face dialogue, there are as many different forms as there are practitioners.

In addition to these Internet groups, there is also growing interest in intranet conversations within the boundaries of organizations for purposes of disseminating information and facilitating learning. Some corporations have been holding conversations in cyberspace since the 70s.[12] Most are matter-of-fact exchanges of memos, questions, and answers. A few early projects went deeper. In 1981 Western Behavioral Sciences Institute launched an on-line School of Management and Strategic Studies for top-level executives.

Many companies have invested heavily in information technology, expecting the systems to increase productivity and help people collaborate. Knowledge-sharing communities of practice on their intranets use what is technically known as "threaded discussions." Though many such on-line conversations label themselves "dialogue," they are primarily characterized by advocacy rather than listening. Suggestions of slowing down and reflecting before responding are often met with surprise. In 1994 Arthur Andersen & Co. convened a global electronic dialogue for strategic visioning called "Creating Our Future." The technology and quality of information and knowledge received high ratings but little was said about the process of dialogue. Only now are companies realizing that on-line conversations need at least as much care and feeding as successful face-to-face interactions.

Mounting belief in the need to learn how to have powerful conversations in cyberspace along with rising levels of frustration with superficial interactions, connection overloads, and fragmented communities are pushing organizations up a steep learning curve. A number of professionals in this area are working to launch projects with the intention of furthering our knowledge about how the Internet and intranets can be used to support connections with customers, implement global teaming, and develop and appreciate intellectual capital.

There is no doubt that the potential power of the Internet is huge. Can this medium be used to encourage more meaningful conversation and the development of collaboration and partnership within an organization and between organizations? Can the *mind shifts* experienced by groups practicing face-to-face dialogue be facilitated via the on-line medium? We are excited and curious and cautious.

There are possibilities and limitations. Here is a potentially incredibly powerful way to develop new and more effective conversational practices, build shared meaning, and disseminate learnings. Yet, to those of us who have been practicing dialogue face-to-face over the years, it is clear that there are many challenges to meet and new levels of skill required to bring reflective inquiry, deep listening, and a focus on collective thinking and learning to the on-line medium. For groups to leverage this medium for transformational conversations, significant attention to exploring its benefits and potential pitfalls is needed. It was with the intention of investigating these, that in the summer of 1996 more than 50 people from around the world engaged in a five-month experiment. We called ourselves a Community of Inquiry and Practice (CIP). During those 5 months, we spent 12 weeks engaged in two dialogues, each structured a little bit differently in terms of how contributions were organized for viewing and response. These pages outline some of the questions we had going in, some of our experiences and learnings, and conclude with the questions we have carried forward.

Some Questions Starting Out

What occurs when people participate in an on-line group with people, most of whom, they have never met? How do cyberspace conversational practices compare with their face-to-face versions? What is it like to practice dialogue in this medium? How might the guides apply? What shifts in intention and attention might be needed to participate in this medium? What elements are important in a design that facilitates quality learning conversations? How can what we learn here be translated to face-to-face dialogue?

Experiential Highlights

We, One and All, Rapidly Found Ourselves Feeling Overwhelmed by the Amount of "Talking"

You might think that being on-line would decrease the sense of feeling overwhelmed by allowing you to deal with it on your own time line. Think again. While provisions had been made to create a number of different playing fields or ways in which we could choose to participate, an assumption most people appeared to operate from was that to be included and to belong to the community they would need to participate in everything. It was the "I don't want to get left out" worldview in all its glory. No doubt, you can imagine the volume of contributions!

What had initially been seen as a 3- to 5-hour-a-week commitment overnight turned into an 8 to 30+ hour a week engagement depending on your level of interest and availability! Three hours a week faded into the realm of nonparticipating. If you needed to participate in everything in order to feel included, you were in big trouble. It was clear that engaging in everything was simply not feasible. We had to ask ourselves some serious questions about our purpose for participating and how we could best define our involvement in order to fulfill that purpose.

Although On-Line Groups Allow People in Distant Locations to Communicate, They Do Not Guarantee that the Communication Will Result in Community or Collective Learning

One of the principles of dialogue that is inherently present in the on-line medium is the potential for including a wide range of diverse perspectives. But merely being included on a system that distributes everyone's input to everyone, does not in any way ensure that people will feel included and heard, nor that the diversity will be integrated into shared meaning by the collective.

Many of the common cues we rely on in face-to-face communication were not present here. If you know the people you are communicating with, you can envision how they may be looking, their facial expressions, etc. And yet, even this is an activity of imagination. You are making assumptions, not directly perceiving the person. Imagine the challenges of audio conferencing, where there is no visual input, multiplied. Professionals who coach people on audio conferencing often work on listening for the varied range of verbal tonalities, pace of speech, and pauses as cues for deepening understanding. In the on-line medium even these are missing. At the close of our five-month experiment, a participant wrote the following response to a learning inquiry question. "It is amazing to me how embodied phone calls now seem, compared to interactions on-line. I feel as if phone calls are to on-line what face-to-face conversations are to phone calls. An interesting shift in my perceptions."

One of the core principles of dialogue is to inquire into assumptions in order to understand more fully the thinking behind our positions, to see how we move from data to conclusions to actions. On-line, this discipline is even more important. So much data is missing on-line, we quite naturally fill in the missing pieces with our imagination. We actually create virtual realities, virtual relationships, as anyone who has participated in chat-rooms can attest. There is less data and much more interpretation. The ladder of inference becomes even more top heavy. We have many questions about developing practices that can prevent these virtual conversations from becoming flights into assumption and imagination. The danger is that rather than helping elucidate thinking and awareness of incoherences, we could actually end up with less clarity. Simply increasing the volume of information exchanged does not mean there is a corresponding increase in awareness and the ability to make conscious choices. That the intention of increasing awareness could actually result in just the opposite would be an example of the shadow[13] side of this form of communication.

On-line communication creates the possibility for even more speed in our communications and decision making. One eastern mystic said, "Speed is the source of all suffering." To simply increase the amount of information available without incorporating time for reflection will not necessarily lead to responsible decisions. As the volume of communication increases, so does the need for intentional reflection.

There Are Significant Challenges to the Way We Listen

We are accustomed to listening in a linear fashion; we listen to first one speaker, then the next. Usually the transitions and bridges between people's comments are obvious. We also listen for cues to additional meaning through our visual and auditory senses. We look at body language, and facial expression. We listen for tonal changes in voice. In on-line conversations, one person's offering may not follow another's and transitions may not be at all obvious. Voice tone and body language are not available. It is easy to find yourself focused intently on the words alone and lose subtle meaning. How can we as readers discover the meaning(s) that motivated the writer to place her words on the screen? How can we expect that what we write and send in will make any sense by the time it is uploaded and downloaded to others who are reading and responding in the same asynchronous, nonlinear manner? How do we begin to develop an ear for the collective themes that weave through the various contributions made to our collective memory in this non-linear medium? Listening for shared meaning in the "disembodied" on-line medium requires development of additional sensory abilities. The on-line medium may represent a significant opportunity for us to learn about listening on other wavelengths, tapping into synchronicity, and trusting that somehow our sustained collective attention and listening will eventually discern the meanings that we are weaving together.

In the course of the dialogues, a number of key ingredients for on-line listening became apparent:

O   time for reflection;

O   a personal practice of some sort (meditation, yoga, writing, other) that increased our ability to become quiet and centered and focus our attention at will;

O   a commitment to suspend our judgments and ask about one another's assumptions; and

O   large amounts of trust that if we persisted and stayed awake and observant we would become wiser both individually and collectively.

The need to generate and sustain focused attention is higher in on-line than in face-to-face conversations. Without a physical setting with visual and auditory cues to help, words on a screen easily become nothing more than luminescent letters strung into words, strung into sentences, strung into paragraphs, and so on, until one cannot remember what one just read, nor perceive any threads from start to finish. It is not that there is no substance to what is written. Yet, words on a computer screen actually feel less substantial, less real than words in a book that you hold in your hands. Only by concentrating your attention, with the intention that your awareness remain focused and open to receive the incoming message, can communication be completed. Without this ability, you look at the words and they bounce right off, ricocheting into space. There are many ways to develop this capacity.[14] The first step is recognizing its importance.

On-line conversations where we listen for shared meaning can be useful practice fields for tapping into fields of awareness that perceive whole systems and span time-space boundaries. Here is a story.

One day I was experiencing unusually strong feelings of being overwhelmed. I was about to log into the CIP conversation, download new contributions, and send something back in. I just couldn't imagine reading everything that people had written since the last time I had downloaded. But I wanted to participate. So, I decided to experiment. Instead of reading the new messages, I would get very quiet within myself, imagine that I could open a passageway, like a wavelength communication channel, between myself and the dialogue that was taking place in the group I was assigned to, and then sit and see if any words appeared for me to write. I was going to trust that somehow, some aspect of my awareness could tap into this conversation using some alternate sensory abilities and that whatever might appear for me to write would make sense when I sent it in. Sounds crazy? Well, I thought it was a little far out; but I also thought it was an interesting experiment. After I had sat for some minutes, I began to get some ideas, which I put down. I then logged on to download and sent in what I had written. Since I was already sitting there, I decided to just scan the entries I had just downloaded. To say I was surprised would be a gross understatement. The words I had written and sent in were almost a direct response to a question that a group member had posed three days before, but that I had not read!

This experience increased our curiosity even further about the non-linear qualities of conversation in general. How might a focus on linearity limit the diversity and richness of information that we allow to enter into a conversation? What practices might we develop that would encourage more multidimensionality in our conversations and lead to decisions based on a more comprehensive understanding of reality?[15] How could this capability benefit organizations of all sizes as they continue to enter an international marketplace of increasing diversity and complexity?

The above experience also reinforced the conviction that when we listen deeply for the collective meaning moving through a conversation and speak from this place, our contributions will prove to enhance the shared meaning. Although they may sometimes seem out of synch in the moment they are spoken, their place in the overall conversation will eventually become clear. Participants in face-to-face dialogues often do not speak when they are moved because they see no relevance in the moment, or because the last time they did speak the connection was not clear and they felt discounted. It is important both for individuals and for the group to suspend judgment about relevance and continue to listen in order to allow for the unfolding of these connections and the new levels of perception and understanding they bring.

The Intention of Those Who Create the On-Line Environment and the Guides Used Will Determine the Quality of the Conversation

Since the CIP experience we have participated in other on-line dialogue experiments. None of them even approached the level of quality that we encountered in the CIP. It is no surprise that suggestions to convene a dialogue on-line often meet with concerns about the inability to feel heard and acknowledged, the tendency for the collective conversation to get sidetracked into one-on-one conversations, or the fact that many conversations become increasingly more abstract.

We attribute much of the learning that was possible from CIP to the unrelenting commitment of Peter and Trudy Johnson-Lenz. They designed and maintained the environment in which we conversed. There were numerous intentional elements in the design that helped us craft meaningful conversation. For example, every time we logged on there were a series of portals that we passed through, designed to inspire and gently remind us of our purpose and the guides we had agreed to. These structures and the thoughtfulness behind them were as critical as the intention and commitment of the participants. The quality of the other on-line dialogues we have participated in has been almost directly related to the degree to which such aids were present. Without them, even experienced dialogue practitioners seem to lose their bearing. With them, even beginners can contribute meaningfully.

For the most part, the guides that we've listed in Part II also work on-line, though some may benefit from tweaking for the on-line medium. What requires attention is the development of additional guides that will address some of the peculiar challenges of this environment. Here are a few examples: 1) The length and number of messages, which is somewhat naturally handled by the presence of others in face-to-face dialogues, can become a daunting problem on-line. 2) Many people have a need to feel acknowledged for their contributions. In face-to-face circles, this can be accomplished with the use of nonverbals, alleviating the need for additional remarks. On-line this does not work. What are ways to acknowledge without interjecting significant verbiage? 3) How to help a group focus on listening for collective meaning among asynchronous entries that often produce the effect of many people speaking at once without any sequential order. Much work remains to be done and in fact is being developed even as we write.

In Summary

On-line conversations can be valuable practice fields that span space-time boundaries and provide individuals and groups with opportunities to inquire into and develop shared meaning around important and strategic issues. One value this medium brings that face-to-face conversation does not is the power of writing. If combined with skillful inquiry and reflection, the written medium can be a powerful tool for clarifying the thinking of both speaker and listener.

> *"Writing is thinking made tangible, thinking that can be*
> *examined because it is on the page and not in the head*
> *invisibly floating around. Writing is thinking that can be*
> *stopped and tinkered with. It is a way of holding thought*
> *still enough to examine its structure, its flaws. The road to*
> *clearer understanding of one's thoughts is traveled on paper.*
> *It is through an attempt to find words for ourselves in which to*
> *express related ideas that we often discover what we think."* [16]

On-line conversations provide a way to engage in an ongoing practice of dialogue, which in turn leads to many of the *shifts of mind* outlined in the other chapters in this section. There is no reason why these shifts cannot occur in on-line dialogues. The implications for organizations wanting to encourage the development of more meaningful conversations, even to the point of using these to shift the nature of their culture towards increased collaboration and partnership, are huge. The potential is vast, and so is the discipline and mindfulness required to deliver the value. On-line dialogue requires even higher levels of intention, particularly in the areas of attention and reflection, than face-to-face conversation. If we are willing to develop these capacities, on line technology represents unlimited potential for supporting the development of businesses and communities that will quite literally be able to think globally and act locally.

TRY THIS: LISTENING FOR COLLECTIVE MEANING ON-LINE
- ○ It can be difficult to focus on listening for collective meaning on-line. We tend to get focused on individual contributions. The next time you're engaged in such a conversation with multiple participants, try this. Take a deep breath, relax your body, and visualize yourself tapping into the stream of meaning moving among the words you've been reading.

What do you notice surfacing in your awareness? What themes or questions may be floating in the river of words and multiple contributions? This same technique can be very useful in listening for collective meaning in face-to-face conversations as well.

○   Often the contributions you read show up on your screen out of sequence relative to how they might have appeared in a synchronous conversation. This can lead to diverse branching relationships between contributions rather than a linear stream of thoughts. Imagine yourself asking what is the whole within which all these contributions rest and are integrated. In face-to-face conversation, practice letting go of the need for each person's contribution to follow a rational sequential pattern in the dialogue and see what is revealed to you when you focus on the whole field, rather than on linear streams moving through it. Whether with on-line or face-to-face conversations, this last practice is useful for learning to focus on the relationships between parts and wholes within a conversation, an issue, a system, or a relationship.

A FEW QUESTIONS GOING FORWARD ⎯⎯⎯⎯⎯⎯⎯⎯⎯⎯

○   How do we design on-line conversations in ways that help us focus our attention?

○   What additional skills might be needed for meaningful asynchronous conversation? What are the practices that will be useful in their development?

○   How do we proceed in ways that acknowledge that this technology is still unavailable to the vast majority of people in the world? This last question may be one of the most important for us to engage if we do not wish to create further separation through a medium that was designed to foster connection.

8

MOVING THROUGH
LEARNING EDGES

*"Your pain is the breaking of the shell that
encloses your understanding."*

—Kahlil Gibran,
The Prophet

"When you sit with a [good friend] *for two hours you
think it's only a minute. But when you sit on a hot stove
for a minute you think it's two hours. That's relativity."*

—Albert Einstein

When the Going Gets Tough,
the Tough Get Going

There's a saying athletes use when they get to a point where they feel
they can't go on—hitting the wall. A very graphic image. The wall is
the product of internal physical, mental, and emotional states accompanied by feelings of no energy, no will, overall exhaustion. When one
is at the wall, the only question is "Will I find a reason and the energy
to continue?" If the answer is yes, the athlete breaks through the wall

and often experiences a burst of energy, a second wind, that carries her onward. If the answer is no, she stops. She has discovered her limits, at least for the moment. All dialogue groups run into the wall, sooner or later. The wall can either stop you or you can use it as a learning edge.[17]

"Walls" come in a variety of shapes and sizes and are always accompanied by questions about the value of the process and feelings of frustration, anger, even sadness. They are times when the group will either find motivation to move forward to a new level of interaction and dialogue or will continue to cycle, and eventually disband. If you are a member of a dialogue group that meets over time, you will get to experience this phenomenon. When you do, it will be useful if you can recognize it for what it is. If you recognize it, you can use it to move to a deeper level. When you get stuck and frustrated, there are three keys to learning and moving beyond:

1.   the willingness to stick around;

2.   suspending judgment; and

3.   refocusing attention to engage at a different level.

Easier said than done? Yes, but not impossible. In this chapter we'll see how these apply to some of the common walls on the road to transformational conversations.

Abstraction Level Four and Climbing

A group can become stuck at any level of awareness. When one level predominates, the whole view becomes distorted. This can happen with emotional stories or at the conceptual level. These mono-level conversations usually result in comments such as "We're getting mired down in our reactions and emotions. Can we get on with it now?" or, "I'm tired of all this conceptual stuff. I can't follow and I'm getting bored." or, "This dialogue has only felt real once in the last hour and that was when Amy spoke about her daughter."

At this point most groups enter into one of the classic splits, better known as "the heads versus the hearts." Before long, everyone in the group will be judged. The heads will be judged by the hearts as unreal, dishonest, and inauthentic because they like to hang out at the conceptual level and don't frequently talk about feelings or tell personal stories. The hearts will be judged by the heads as unintelligent, limited, and overly emotional because they are more comfortable with people when they engage in personal stories and feelings and don't often look at reality from a conceptual framework. Both will be upset. Both will be calling the other unreal. Both perspectives hold some truth, but become inaccurate when extended to the whole.

Some conceptual people are uncomfortable with feelings and they may hang out up there as a refuge. But not all, by any means. And their conceptual perspective can make them great collective listeners, hearers of patterns, and synthesizers. To think that they have no heart because of this preference is at best inaccurate and at worst invalidating. The hearts, on the other hand, can sometimes get caught up in their feelings. But not all of them, and not all the time. Their openness to feelings means they may often help to bring what is powerful and important into the dialogue because often the powerful and important is inseparable from strong feeling. To think that they have no intelligence for the conceptual is at best mistaken and at worst, again, invalidating.

When this polarity rears its head, it is a strong wake-up call to pay attention to how one of our most popular judgments creates separation in the group. It is time to practice sitting with the polarities without choosing and to ask what each is listening for that the other is not. It is time to build a more integrated dialogue and fuller picture.

We're All over the Place and Going Nowhere Fast!

This can either be about listening to multiple individual perspectives without seeing any apparent connection at the collective level or it can be the result of disagreements and conflict beginning to emerge.

In the first case, there may be many topics or questions put into the circle without any apparent connecting theme. Until one appears, it can feel as though you are being pulled in many directions at once. When there are many themes put out in rapid succession, it may be that there is a lot that needs talking about, or it may be that none of the topics/questions proposed catches interest sufficiently to engage the group. In either case, it may be useful to notice that there is a lot of energy and then suggest a moment of silence to provide an opportunity for reflection and refocusing on listening for a connecting theme that could help hold and weave all the contributions.

Disagreements and conflict usually take awhile to emerge in a newly formed group. The desire to be included takes precedence over any need to express differences. But as time goes on, people will begin to take a few more risks. As soon as you begin to bring more of yourselves to the circle, the probability that you will bump into one another increases.

Because conflict can be very uncomfortable, there are many tactics for containing, isolating, and controlling it. Unfortunately, unless a group learns to work with the inevitable conflicts, sooner or later one of three things will happen. First, the group will dissolve. Second, conflict will be "disallowed." The group may stop talking about real and important issues, because to do so will eventually result in the possibility of conflict. Such groups die of "insignificant conversation disease." Third, the group will hang in there and learn how to engage conflict as a rich learning ground, hopefully using some of the suggestions in Part III, Strategy 5.

Let's Talk about "Them"

You find that the group is continually engaged in talking about either events or other people "out there." It is often easier to talk about the interactions we notice among others than it is to focus on our own dynamics. Talk about "them" may reflect an aspect of interaction within your own group that is difficult to speak about, a collective shadow. Eventually the group becomes bored because you are not talking about anything directly related to yourselves. At this point, the question is whether you will simply disband because nothing meaningful is happening or whether you will bring the conversation home. One way to do this is to notice that "we seem to be spending most of our time talking about events and people outside this group," and ask "I wonder how the issues and dynamics we are talking about may apply to our group?" Or "What is it we are learning from looking outward, and how do we see this reflected in our own interactions, and thinking?" The key is to listen to the conversation, notice what is being talked about, and then ask a question that will establish a connection or relationship between this conversation and the group itself.

Most groups become bored or disengaged because the dialogue is no longer grounded and relevant to the group. Attention has become focused elsewhere and with it the responsibility and the creative power of the group. The trick to moving beyond this learning edge is to refocus attention, reclaiming responsibility and the ability to create new possibilities.

I Didn't Sign up for a Therapy Group

Correctly or not, we often associate therapy groups with the recounting of emotion-packed personal stories and with trying to help someone find their way out of whatever trouble or distress they find themselves in. Dialogue invites feelings and stories; indeed, much of the richness and learning can come from these contributions. There are two ways this can become a wall for the group.

First, someone begins to use the dialogue as a sounding board for personal issues. If the group falls into the trap of helping with advice and counseling, the dialogue may begin to feel like small-group therapy (without the advantage of a trained therapist). All the energy becomes focused on one person. Some members become engaged in helping. Others become bored and check out. While the one person may feel energized, the group itself will eventually find itself deflated. In addition, the possibility of developing any collective meaning around an issue disappears.

A second phenomenon we call "personal stories run amok" looks like this. The group becomes engaged in telling personal stories around an issue. This, admittedly, can be the source of new information and rich learning, and for a while, it is energizing. As you listen to one another's stories, you may even begin to identify with one another and notice feelings of connection and a sense of community. What is often missing from this scenario is inquiry into what all these personal stories have to say about the group's collective experience, assumptions, and thinking. If your attention remains focused solely on the individual parts, the energy and learning available from a whole view are unlikely to emerge. Eventually, the individual level will no longer be engaging enough and the group will run out of steam.

Both the above scenarios, which are overly focused on the personal level, can result in complaints about not being engaged and wasting time. People will remind one another that they came to dialogue and to learn about issues that hold meaning for the whole group, not to spend time hearing individual and/or personal problems. Again, the key to moving through this learning edge is to recognize it, name it, and refocus the group's attention. Unlike the "Let's talk about them" wall, where attention was focused outside the group, the group is now talking about issues within its membership. The shift needed is to move some attention from the individual level to include the collective as well.

We're Not Doing Anything Productive

Sometimes groups new to dialogue find themselves using sessions to talk about issues as mundane as ordering pencils. When this happens, it's time to refocus attention on the purpose of dialogue: to inquire into issues that are real and important and develop your capacity for collective learning and thinking. If your group is talking about "pencils," then you have either forgotten the purpose of your dialogue sessions or you are avoiding talking about what may be an important and difficult issue. In either case, the first step is to notice what is happening and then inquire into what is needed for the group to refocus and reengage.

Life Is about Cycles and So Is Dialogue

All life moves through cycles. In spring, leaves burst forth, changing the view down the street almost overnight. Flowers bloom. In summer, growth continues and fruit ripens on the vine. And then comes fall.

The ebb begins. The trees prepare for winter. They begin to pull inside themselves. Leaves change colors and fall to the ground. Soon the trees are hibernating. It is winter. And then the thaw and the cycle begins all over again.

We think nothing of this cycle. In fact most of us would think it very odd if it didn't happen. Farmers may spend money trying to increase the fruit yield of an orange tree, but what would happen if they tried to get a tree to be in bloom continuously? In nature, interruption of this cycle most often results in death. Yet, when we encounter this natural flooding and ebbing in our own lives, we are distressed. We think we must be doing something wrong. Why are we tired? Why are we not producing at the same rate as last month? We expect it of ourselves and so do others. Is it any wonder burnout is one of the major causes of illness and turnover?

So, when your dialogue group cycles, when sometimes it is absolutely phenomenal, and you just can't believe what happened today and other times it is uninteresting and flat and it seems hard to get things going and to engage, remember that life moves in cycles and so does dialogue. "Learn by becoming more conscious of what is actually happening" [18] and ask what will best serve the group at this moment. It may be that there is a storm brewing and no one wants to talk about it and the ebb is a sort of flight. Or it may be that no one feels any passion or energy about the issue at hand and the questions "Why?" and "What would we find energizing?" need to be asked. Or, perhaps, today is simply a winter day and next week it will be spring.

All groups find themselves at learning edges sooner or later. Learning edges represent some of the greatest opportunities for groups if you are willing to work through them. Whenever you begin to question the process, one thing is certain. You are hearing a wake-up call, a call asking you to attend to what is going on both inside yourself and collectively in the group. Once you hear the wake-up call, it is time to remember and recommit to the three behaviors that will help you move beyond it. And, because these are group learning edges, the more people who are willing to work with you, the more success you will all have.

IN CLOSING

"The Institute for Research on Learning has found that knowledge creation is primarily a social rather than an individual process. People learn together in conversation as they work and practice together . . . ."

—Juanita Brown and David Isaacs[19]

"Keep in mind that Tao means how: how things happen. Learn to become more conscious of what is actually happening."

—John Heider
The Tao of Leadership

Dialogue is about conversation that is meaningful to people, that they can learn from. The learning we speak of is not about developing 20/20 hindsight, although this is undoubtedly useful. It is 20/20 vision in the present moment, awareness of how our thinking is influencing our decisions and actions in the very moments right up to and including when we make the choice or take the action; this is what interests us. It is about learning from history and applying this learning in the heat of the current crisis. It is about fundamental changes in the way we think that allow us to self-organize and interact with our world in innovative ways. This is the power of dialogue. Portia Nelson writes eloquently and concisely of the relationship between awareness and learning in the following poem.

Autobiography in Five Short Chapters

I.
I walk down the street.
There is a deep hole in the sidewalk.
I fall in.
I am lost.
I am helpless.
It isn't my fault.
It takes forever to find a way out.

II.
I walk down the same street.
There is a deep hole in the sidewalk.
I pretend I don't see it.
I fall in again.
I can't believe I am in the same place.
But it isn't my fault.
It still takes a long time to get out.

III.
I walk down the same street.
There is a deep hole in the sidewalk.
I see it is there.
I still fall in.
It is a habit.
My eyes are open
I know where I am.
It is my fault.
I get out immediately.

IV.
I walk down the same street
There is a deep hole in the sidewalk.
I walk around it.

V.
I walk down another street.

—Portia Nelson[20]

The ongoing practice and value of dialogue is about

- O   developing the ability to see the "deep hole in the sidewalk;"
- O   being able to see it in advance of falling into it;
- O   making the connection between accepting responsibility for falling into it and the speed with which you are able to get out;
- O   choosing to walk around the hole;
- O   being able to envision an alternate route; and
- O   choosing to walk down an alternate path.

For some, these learnings are the work of a lifetime. To develop these capabilities requires collaboration, partnership, and shared leadership. They do not occur simply because we wish them to. They are products of the vision, planning, practice, and ongoing commitment we spoke of in Part III.

As groups practice the skills and behaviors that support dialogue, they begin to notice shifts in their thinking and the choices they make. For some, the change occurs almost entirely at the level of interpersonal communications and shows up in more effective and satisfying working relationships that in turn allow for higher levels of creativity and productivity. Others find themselves able to see the thinking patterns that are operating within a group or an organization. This, in turn, opens the door for double loop learning and more coherent decisions that can shift the very culture and operational patterns of the organization. For all, the world will never look the same again.

All the *shifts of mind* described in this section open doors to increased personal and collective awareness and effectiveness. It is as if a turbocharger had been attached to the individual or group, with one very important difference. Turbochargers simply boost the power of an engine, they do nothing to inherently change its inner workings, to make it more efficient. Remove the turbocharger and the output goes back to previous levels. When conversation is transformational, it changes the thinking of the individual or group: the power of the turbocharger becomes integrated into the engine itself. One such conversation will have impact. Many can change an organization. When you and those you work with have integrated the learning from such conversations into your basic approach to relationships and collaboration, the resulting transformation and power available to you can never be taken from you because the source will lie within you.

A Reminder and a Prayer

Transformation is a natural outgrowth of the practice of dialogue and other forms of learning conversations. The experiences we've described were powerful and sometimes mysterious for those involved. They are also fragile and easily forgotten, particularly when you reenter a daily life based on competition and separation. Transformational experiences plant seeds. There may be drum rolls and brilliant flashes of light accompanying the planting of the seed—your first experiences with dialogue—but the fruits that tell us transformation has taken place are the result of ongoing attention. Planting is a beginning. It is the work of tending the garden, one day at a time, that allows the plants to mature and bear fruit. It is hard to overemphasize the importance of an ongoing practice of dialogue to the maturing of conversations that will bear the fruits of learning and transformation. May we all start each day with an intention to tend the garden so that we may reap the fruits in our lifetime and create a world that will sustain our children's children for many generations to come.

V

A DIALOGUE
ON
PARTNERSHIP

"What is it exactly that is different about dialogue? It sounds like any good conversation to me."

—Anonymous

"When groups learn to think together, individuals gain the advantage of collective learning."

—Glenna Gerard

✺

Our intention here is to provide you with a real-life example of dialogue. The following pages are an abstract of a two-hour dialogue convened to explore and inquire into partnership. The dialogue is followed by:

1. Excerpts from the group's reflections on content and process following the conversation.

2. A short epilogue, where a few people share reflections on how this dialogue impacted their actions in actual partnerships in the months that followed.

As you read through the transcript, you will notice that certain passages are italicized. This is not to emphasize content, but to highlight a particular aspect or skill that is present. In the margin to the side of the italicized words are notations that indicate what it is that we are pointing to: assumption identification, inquiry, inquiry into an assumption, listening for threads/themes, suspension of judgment, reflection (both on self and on group conversation), etc. We tried to do this in a way that would not distract from your reading, but would be a resource you could refer to. You may want to simply read through the entire conversation first and then focus on the margin notations on a second reading. The bullets indicate a change in speaker.

Acknowledgments: We would like to acknowledge and thank the people who participated in this dialogue for their time, energy, and creativity in creating this conversation and contributing their reflections on process and content. We do not name them here for the sake of privacy. In respect for confidentiality, even the few initials that appear in the transcript have been changed.

The Dialogue

○ I'll start with a little bit of history on how this conversation has evolved over the last few months until today. "T" and

Initializing inquiry

I have been *wondering "How do we expand our work through partnering with others?"* All our historical ideas about professional partnerships just didn't seem to hit the mark, to feel right. So, when I knew that many of us would be together in April I thought "Let's get together at the end of the conference." Then I got this idea to do some E-mail conversation before. We started the E-mail dialogue and it rapidly became clear that while the original question was about professional partnership, the E-mail dialogue was more in the spirit of "Okay, this may be about professional partnerships, but *let's get to the essence of partnership first*

Assumption

and then all this other stuff about how you do 'this and that' will all come out in the wash . . . . " That is the history of the conversation. I am here today *curious to inquire into "What*

Inquiry

are the stories about partnership? What are the questions? What are the things that we are discovering? What are the things that we still have no idea about?"

○ A little bit of background is that *I am a very private person*

Self-reflection & inquiry

and from my earliest history have had some significant personal betrayals. So I know that has something to do with how I come to these kinds of relationships or possibilities. Where I sit at the moment has to do with boundaries. Where can I place them and still be in relationship with people? So I'm sitting here thinking "I don't know how to do all this and still maintain some integrity that I need in order to continue."

Self-reflection & inquiry

○ My work is still unfolding. *My concern and question is that if I go into partnership, in some form or another, is it going to pull me away from where I need to be going?* I know I can get seduced because of community and I really like to work with people. So, I'm afraid of what in me lets me get off my own track. Another thing. I am working with three other people to see if we have a partnership. We're trying to see if we have common work together. *The two things we've been focusing on are "What gives you energy and where is your pain?" The notion being that your passion and energy come out of where your deepest pain is.* And you can't just do this kind of reflection once, you have to revisit it.

Inquiry

Assumption

○ Your words remind me of the importance of continuously asking *"Is the partnership continuing to support both of us in where our energy and our pain are and in addressing these?"* Because I think, as you said, it changes. Once you create or acknowledge that you have work to do together, *it is like a vision that constantly needs to be revisited. And for me that is a scary thing to do because the more I have invested in something, the more difficult or challenging it is for me to really inquire into, knowing that the possibility exists that it won't be meeting my needs and I might need to change it or leave it. So, it makes the inquiry difficult.*

Inquiry

Reflection

○ I'm in a partnership with three other women and what has been said really brought up a question for me that I keep going back to that feels like it wants to be said in the circle. It's the question of commitment. *It's about the feeling or assumption that when you commit to something you commit to it and that you don't walk away from it, even if it gets really hard.* Having a marriage that dissolved where I was committed and my partner wasn't, I think about what things have kept those three women together in that loose partnership. And one of the things we said to one another that finally helped us move through some really tough stuff was "We're not going to go away, no matter what. If I get mad at you, if I get angry at you, whatever happens, I commit to you to stay in there and say what I have to say, and see it through." *And yet a piece of me keeps thinking "Can*

Assumption

Inquiry   *we even say, as human beings 'I'm not going to go away'?"*
I mean I don't know how . . . nothing I've ever found is a
guarantee. I have a lot of confusion around this.

○   *What is real for me is some kind of tension between safety*
Reflection   *and being able to count on the relationship and then the*
level of excitement and stimulation in generative kinds of
collaboration. But one without the other is not for me satisfying or likely to stimulate commitment and creativity.

○   I'm glad you brought up the "C" word, commitment. I
have so many feelings coming into this. I'm really glad that
we are having this dialogue on partnership because as
some of you know from the E-mail, a woman, "J", and I,
started a legal partnership some years ago. Three years ago
we took on a third partner and last August this person
announced she was leaving. And it came out of the blue.
Boom! It's given me the opportunity to ask "What is this
about? What does it really mean for me?" *Continuity and*
Inquiry   *commitment and loss. I've tried to make some sense out of it*
by looking at partnership in other contexts, lover relation-
ships, friendships. What is the same? What is different? Why
can I be one way in one and yet in another I have different
feelings? What's adequate in one doesn't feel adequate in the
other. Why? We had a network organization, a hub of three
people and then many relationships with other consultants. And I didn't require the same kinds of things from
those other relationships that I wanted from those two
women. Even in the workplace, I had different levels of
partnership and interaction. And when "S" made that
announcement, I felt betrayed, I felt abandoned, but more
than anything I felt like I didn't get a chance to interact,
that the decision was made; there was no working through.
Even right now I don't even know why it happened. *And I*
Self-   *realize that so much of my frustration is never having the*
reflection   *opportunity to hear about or work it through. So the com-*
mitment I'm looking for is the commitment to communicate.

Assumption

○ As you were talking, I got really clear on something. You can create a partnership contract . . . we've been thinking of doing that but we never got around to it. Now I kind of understand why because I've always had this sense that these *legal instruments that we create around partnership are very fear based.* As if we have to treat our relationships like childlike ones rather than agreements between mature people coming together and consciously deciding they want to spend time and do something together. I realize nothing I sign could ever create a better partnership than what I have with "W." If I don't have trust with her around ability to clear personal issues as they come up, a contract won't create it. And also a sense of aliveness. I know it would be hard for me to be as creative if I didn't have "W" in my life. *This conversation is helping me see why certain relationships in my life work, versus ones where I thought I was making a commitment, where I was even ready to marry, that fell apart. It had nothing to do with the contract. It had to do with the fact that I hadn't really created that level of trust and ability to clear up personal issues.*

Reflection

Inquiry

○ I've been thinking, "well, commitment to what?" *I find it hard to think about commitment without saying "well commitment to what?"* One of the things your words brought up for me is the commitment to talk through whatever needs to be talked through going into partnership and coming out of partnership. It's been my experience that when that happens the violence isn't there anymore. The hurt and pain may be difficult, but it's not the same kind of pain that you have when people just walk away. This is important to me in partnering.

○ Those of you who know me know that I've been on a Buddhist spiritual path. Nowhere do you find the word commitment on this path. But that's how this culture sees it. Suppose I look at the mental model, say about marriage and commitment. "Well, I'm married. I'm committed. I'm still here. I'm still making this stuff work out in spite of my partner. I'm committed to this marriage." It can start sounding like that. Well, in my life when all of that fell apart, I figured out that what my husband needed from me more than anything was not that kind of commitment, the traditional commitment; what he needed from me more than anything else was to be present in the moment with deep listening, period. Period! But the only thing that drove us to that point was us looking at each other saying, "If we don't do this radically different, this definitely will not work." We had to be in that abyss to look beyond our illusions of commitment and really get to what was essential. And, it seems very counterintuitive to me, that the safest thing I can do is totally let go of making it work and just be with it. Hmmm . . .

○ I feel contrary . . . you know "yes, but . . . yes, but." Like, for example, we didn't have a contract and I wish we had. Because *it's not the contract that's important. It's the process* Assumptions *of creating the contract. We made tons of assumptions about what we heard each other say, about what we assumed was meant by the words.* And it's also true that we did change. Reflection *It's clear to me now that even what the words meant then were different than what the words mean now.* So, it's like we needed to continue to have the conversation. *If we had* Assumptions *hammered out a contract, our conversation would have had to have the integrity or truthfulness for ourselves.* There is a lot of pain right now . . . because we are working through the buyout agreement and it is . . . we're nowhere near close together. And I don't even know how we get close together. I'm really in the "I don't know what's going to happen" phase. So, I don't know.

○ A couple of things come to mind. In 15 years I can't think of a single piece of paper that any of us in the business have ever had between us. The other thing is the word *respect.*

And I guess I'm thinking RESPECT in capitals. Because what strikes me is respect for me, respect for you, respect for the issue, respect for the commitment, respect for the relationship, respect for the work.

○   I just formally ended a contract partnership. *Where we got*

Reflection   *in trouble was that we did not explore the differences because we felt our values were so alike.* And, those issues, especially in times of stress, family needs, wherever your business is financially, then the differences start playing out. The other thing that just occurred to me is that "X" and I were not always about heart-work. *So that is a lesson, an ahha,*

Inquiry &   *that just occurred for me in the moment, is that if you can*

assumption   *reach some clarity about what the work is, maybe that's something that can keep you together.* I know very little about "T" and "W" except about your mutual passion around the work that you do and for me it's heart-work.

Assumption   And *maybe if there is clarity and common ground there, you don't need contracts.* But . . . I don't know . . . *I want to say "Here's what you should do or here's what you shouldn't do" and I don't think there is any answer like that in the world.* It's just whatever emerges and the ability to communicate.

Suspension   *So I don't have an answer. It fails with contracts. It succeeds*

of judgment   *with contracts. It fails without them and it succeeds without them.*

○   I have a very deep curiosity about this heart-work because I'm working on a partnership with a friend of mine. And it feels very heartfelt. Yet, I have discovered over the last few months that *I need to hold my assessments much more*

Self-   *lightly because my emotional lens can distort to a level that*

reflection   *is just beyond belief!* So it makes me skittish because I think "*What is the tug with this person that has possibly got me*

Inquiry   *so off-center that I'm really not seeing some red light that I should see... and how would I know that?*" What would be the mirror that would show that? We're trying to be authentic with each other. This word authentic is driving me nuts! Because how the hell would I know if I'm being authentic? I mean I've got all these voices in here anyway. So which one do you want to choose? Do I have to get integrated before I can get authentic? That'll be tough! (laughter) And then the whole idea of trust . . . Trust the group? Are you kidding? I don't trust me! So what can I do? Back to this potential partnership. Soul-work is one thing, but he's got a financially demanding wife. I'm hearing this. I'm clicking into this, this wife he's got. So, you know, while "B" and I agree about what makes sense, his wife is another issue altogether. *So, when we consider partnership, just how* *big is a partnership? Just who all is in the partnership?* Because all this gets very personal. My husband doesn't like his wife. It does get complicated very fast.

Inquiry

○   I want to go back to what was said about heart-work. *A lot* *of the partnerships I fall into are those that I don't con-* *sciously make and yet they become formed. So, I ask myself* *"How do they get formed?"* And, it has to do with heart-work. So if we run into problems, it really helps me go beyond, to really want to work it out when you and I aren't getting along. At that point, the personal sits in the context of something else that we are both driven by, that we are honoring and we are respecting. Almost, like beyond individual values.

Self-reflection & inquiry

○   A couple of threads. First around heart-work versus working for money. I had an experience, trying to put a group of consultants together, where we were all doing executive coaching. We thought "What a great opportunity. We're all independents with 50-some years of executive coaching. Let's get together and go off and do executive coaching." It seemed like a great idea. And we spent many hours, years it seems...trying to figure out how to do it. And the only thing we ever accomplished was putting money into a bank account, getting a phone number, stationery, and a name. A name took us half a year. Other than that we never got any business, earned no money, and the whole time *the only common ground we had was money.* No one was in the partnership other than to make money. *We felt*

Reflection   *together we could make more money, and we never made a cent! We didn't have the shared vitality we're talking about.* And connected to this, I want to pick up on something around a nonverbal sensing; a sensing for trust, respect, and sense of aliveness. When I think about decisions I've made where those things weren't present in my body, where I didn't connect, but I did things because it made logical sense, but I didn't get this visceral connection of "I can create with this person. This person is open to me and can really hear me and I can listen" it's been disastrous.

Observation   *There is something for me in terms of trust and respect and aliveness that I think our bodies sense in relationship with others. It goes way beyond a contract, way beyond even a*

Inquiry   *conversation about a contract. What is this?*

○   I'm so pleased at the way thoughts come together. *I actu-*

Weaving   *ally have discovered that I am able to make money that way, the way you described, "L," and still stay in partnership, provided that I pay attention to where I am in the work, which is where I think "T" is coming from and what the work of discernment is about.* If I go into a room to do a leadership challenge workshop with a client who doesn't necessarily turn me on, with a partner who may not be coming from the same place that I am, I can go in a number of ways when all this stuff starts coming up for me. Sometimes I go down the path of thinking how crummy the client is and I go into all these different places, and all the while I get more and more ineffective. Then, if in the presence of all of that, I can sit down and ask for guidance, and say

Inquiry   *"What is this about? How can I be here?"* Because I am here in the service of something. If I'm here in this room, I need to try to be in the service of "that." Then I can stay and work with people who are not full partners, who are vastly different than me. I think it is about the work.

○   I'm more the systematic, synthesizer type of thinker. My passion is bringing together teams of people and balancing values and differences and creating a synergy that can propel the vision and the work. *I think the mind-set that we have* Assumptions *been in for a long time has been that "You are with one company or with one partnership and you make a contract and you have your duties and you make that work." And the lesson I'm learning is that is not the way this new world is working. Even in business, people are in different teams at one time and moving in and out of teams . . . and look at the power rangers on TV . . . kids are learning how to morph.* And we are kind of a lost generation in a sense because we weren't given those skills. We did not focus on how to use aspects of communication, dialogue, discussion, and debate. We didn't learn to be able to recognize what our value systems are and be able to tell people "these are my values." And what I think happens is that sometimes you think you have all the values covered. For example, sometimes we just think we are in universalism-particularism[1] ladder and say, "Okay, so we have a contract with each other. We're particularists . . . it's covered." But it doesn't cover the rest of the values. So I try to think in terms of the systematic way of putting it together. One cut. Is there the passion? Do we have the same passion for the work? Another cut. What are the levels of health? A healthy person is someone that you will be able to communicate with and work things out with. There are different cuts. You run it through filters. Then the work begins in terms of being able to balance the differences and create the synergy. And with the synergy you need a vision, a sense of belonging, a challenge, and fun—the four components of synergy. And I'm in and out of several different partnerships at one time and I've made different commitments to different partnerships in different ways.

○   Two things that have come up for me in the last several minutes are connected with boundaries and balance. Part of what I think about in entering partnership is *"Where is*

Inquiry   *my center and where are my edges?"* So, when I was thinking about going into organizations, *what concerns me is my ability to balance that sense of center and edge.* And if I get a sense that if I come in I'm not going to be able to balance, then I probably ought not to be in this partnership. If I know that about myself, then one of the things I need to do to start the partnership each time is to put that out. What is it we are agreeing defines the boundaries and the center of this relationship or this partnership?

○   About the edge and the center, *I find that in my life I have*

Self-   *a propensity to need to go to the edge and that sometimes I*
reflection   *go to the edge so far that I almost fall off.* I have taken myself to the edge of life-threatening kinds of experiences consistently in my life. So there is something that is real juicy for me in that process and I'm wondering if there isn't an easier way to go to the edge? (laughter) *It's really helpful*

Self-   *for me to remember in those moments when I'm dancing*
reflection   *at the edge of something to stop and remember about the center.* And do some of what you were saying, "S," about going back and asking for guidance. Remembering just to stop and breathe and let my shoulders drop and just go to a place of asking for guidance. And then I'm also reminded of something to do with the practice of aikido. In aikido I'm not only responsible for keeping myself safe but for keeping my opponent safe. And I can't do that unless I'm in my center. *And it is about keeping self and others safe.*

Inquiry   *And probably the biggest inquiry question of my life is "How in the heck do you do that?"*

Inquiry

○   I'd like to continue on the theme of boundaries. One of my recent discoveries is that some people can function very well in the world with fuzzy boundaries. I function very well in the world with clear boundaries. A couple years ago I started experimenting with hanging out with fuzzier boundaries and I've found that that can get me in trouble. So *it's one of those dilemmas of "How can I honor that which has gotten me through this world so far with being very clear on my boundaries and at the same time pushing that a little bit, going to the edge and trying to also have more permeable boundaries?" Because that is where I make contact . . . at the boundary, at the edge.* So if I want things to change and grow and develop, I've got to push that edge. But I'm going to go back to my partnership. "X" functioned very well in the world with fuzzy boundaries. And I didn't realize that when I was making a commitment I was doing it with my clear boundaries. And that was a lesson learned for me.

Reflections

○   *When you said fuzzy boundaries, I couldn't come up with an example of a boundary that would make me test that. For somebody it might appear fuzzy, but to another it is very clear. So it is not so much fuzzy as it's just difference of perception.*

Reflection
to group
& inquiry

○   I've been musing about boundaries and difference. *What I heard was not about clear, definite boundaries or fuzzy boundaries, but about what constitutes the definition of a particular boundary.* So I'm not sure that all of them are not clear, or perhaps all are fuzzy, but *what defines them is different for each person.* I think sometimes when we work with scales, like universalism-particularism or the judging/perceptive; extrovert/introvert (JPEI) scales of Myers-Briggs, we forget that those scales have been very particularly defined. And then we try to position people on them and they are never, I don't think, anywhere near

a fit, in reality. They are always gross approximations.
I wonder if the real work for those of us in partnerships and
Inquiry *relationships is to talk with each other about what actually*
constitutes how we define boundaries.

○ Can you give an example?

○ How do I think about work within a relationship within our
business partnership? About whether it might be done outside the partnership, or ancillary to the partnership, or over-
lapping the boundaries of the partnership? *There are so*
Assumptions *many different assumptions that come into my consideration*
of how I see that and where I would place the work, on
which side of an arbitrary boundary. And with each piece it
would be different. But I think what often happens is that
we come up with formulaic responses like "Well, we're
going to use this formula...and that's out...and this is in,"
but they never are quite right in many instances. So it is
really about *"What am I thinking about in this instance . . .*
Self- *where is it . . . where does it fit? Where do I think the bound-*
reflection *ary is today?" Because it might be different than it was a*
month ago. That's the kind of thing I'm talking about.

○ Part of *what that brought up for me was starting to under-*
Weaving *stand how two people who used to be part of our organiza-*
tion left. What this has helped me see is that for one of
them, when we came together there was a whole lot of
commitment to variety and not getting attached to any one
model or belief system. And at a particular point in time,
something jumped up for him that was so clear, that he
really could only do the work that way. So he got very clear
about a boundary within the partnership that was different
than what we had committed to together originally. It also
had to do then with testing our own boundaries as we tried
to figure out how to relate with that, and it became less and
less comfortable for all of us to manage that boundary
together.

○ *Partnerships . . . the ebb and flow of people that come and go*
Inquiry   *in our lives and how do you do that in an honorable way so*
that they can come back?

○ *Sitting here and listening to everyone I realize all this is my*
Weaving   *story, unfolding.* And one thing that is unfolding is a shift in
orientation to how I come into situations now. For me it
was a conscious shift from approaching the world from an
individual orientation to, and I can't even articulate this
very well because I think it's just starting...but making a
conscious decision to approach the world from a collective
orientation. And I don't even know what that means fully.
But the one thing that it means, that I've made it mean is
to choose to acknowledge the connection and come from
that space. So things like "building connection" don't
make sense to me anymore. Given this shift in orientation,
even the concept of boundary is shifting for me. *I have a*
desire for intimacy in all my relationships. And I have an
Assumption   *assumption that to get to that depth of intimacy on a con-*
scious level takes time. That it doesn't just happen immedi-
ately. That while the connection is there to be discovered, the
Self-   *discovery and the articulation take time. And maybe my*
reflection   *grasping is that I want the time to let it emerge.* And my frustration is that I don't feel that we give the time. It isn't just
in the moment. It's the collection of moments. There is
some flow or continuity. So I don't want people to leave.
I don't want people to quit. Because I'm just starting to
figure out what this means for me. So I can get very
graspy.

○ I want to talk about intimacy and I may want to talk about
"being there, showing up." *One of my hesitations* in com-
Self-   ing here was *"I'm just up to here with intimacy right now.*
reflection   *I don't want any more intimacy!"* (laughter) I want some
relationships that aren't intimate. I need a break! And
partly that's a function of where I am in my life because I'm
in this new relationship with a significant other that is

extremely intimate and intense and we even had to learn how to take breaks from that. *Where I spend my energy is*

Assumption

very important and intimacy takes a lot of energy and a lot of time. And a question I brought with me was "How can I

Inquiry

be present and fully engaged without it taking all my intimate energy?" The other thing that was sparked for me was about the issue that I have around *"being there, showing up, making a commitment to be there" I think there is a paradox about it.* And I'll just use the situation the last three days, with people coming and going. I made a commitment to myself to show up, on time, for the full thing, even though at moments I didn't want to be there. I would much rather have been in the hot tub or asleep. And I did that for myself and I did it for the group. Because I think it matters whether I'm there or not. And I also want people to be able to do what they need to do to take care of themselves. So when somebody says "I don't care if so and so left because it really doesn't matter" *it matters to me whether*

Holding
tension of
different
perspectives

you are there or not and it matters to me whether I'm there or not and it matters to me whether it matters to you or not that I'm there! So, I've come to try to learn how to hold both of those at the same time.

○   *Ever since this issue around leaving surfaced, I've had this*

Self-
reflection

unsettled sense. Because I'm in a very difficult family and I've set some boundaries for myself, and my family can't understand it. For them, the boundary says that forever and ever and ever I won't ever come home again. *And so, for*

Assumption

them, my not showing up for Christmas and Thanksgiving must feel like I'm saying that they are bad, and they can't even begin to hold that. So then they make me bad and I become the scapegoat. And it is a very painful role to be in. *I think, in an unhealthy way, what can happen in this*

Reflection

dilemma of comings and goings is that it can trap us into relationships that are no longer alive and we don't even know it and it's the guilt, shame, and . . . this is what I've

Inquiry

had to work through personally, all the ways I was forced to continue in the relationship that was causing me incredible pain. So I don't know. *"How do we hold relationship?"* If we hold it in the larger context, then when I don't show up for Christmas and Thanksgiving, it doesn't mean that I'm not part of the family. It means, right now, I have a rhythm that says I need to do my own inner work.

Reflection

Self-reflection

○ When you were talking about holding the relationship I was thinking about my husband, who is going to be my ex-husband. What I learned from him is that in his world, when he first went through the process of divorce, he saw it was the old ways of "You're leaving. This is betrayal. How dare you abandon me?" and it went on for a few days. But in the end it was *his love for me that was not about holding. It was about beholding.* He really beheld me and watched me and just loved me so much as to want me to grow and to be where I wanted to be and to respect the space and in doing that I left without feeling any guilt. *I felt honored.* I felt it was my "right" place. I don't know what his future relationships will be like and I don't know what mine will be. But we are in a family, he and I, because we behold each other and respect where we need to be because the love is so much bigger than he and I having to be in some little case together.

○ I have . . . compassion for you, "W", and the struggle with your family. And, I also recognize that the people who I have the most likeness to on the physical plane are my parents and the family in which I was born. Genetically, like it or not, we are the most similar of any other creatures on this earth. And that is fraught with all kinds of difficulty because there are some things about them that are abhorrent to me, and the connection is one that holds a place that is different than any other relationships in the world. And I really wish it weren't that way, because it would make my life a hell of a lot easier.

    ○   *This is really an edge. What is a genetic connection and*
Inquiry   *how, from a place where I want to live my life, do I hold that*
      connection? What is the meaning of that? What is the
      meaning of my birth to those two individuals who had me,
      who have caused me incredible pain in my life. I mean, do
      I choose to respect myself or do I choose to respect a rela-
      tionship that is painful?

    ○   *A question that keeps coming in listening is about respect.*
Inquiry   *And what does that mean? When you ask the question about*
      respecting yourself or respecting your parents and the rela-
Inquiry
about   *tionship with them I want to ask "Is there an assumption*
assumption   *that those two are mutually exclusive?" and "What is respect*
      in relationship?" The feeling here is that there is a place
      from which you honor the relationship with yourself when
      you do what you know you need to do, and you also honor
      your relationship with your parents, in the deepest way,
      when you do what you know you have to do to honor your-
      self in the relationship. And whether they can behold it,
      or you, has nothing to do with whether you are honoring
      the relationship. And I think that it is really only possible to
      say that when you sit in a larger context. It's not possible
      when we just sit inside ourselves, or inside the other per-
      son. So I wanted to thank you for your story because it
      reminds me once again of what I think *is one of the most*
      destructive and fragmenting either/or assumptions we have,
      that *if there is pain in the relationship when we do what we*
Assumption *need to to honor ourselves, that somehow we are not honor-*
      ing those we are in relationship with and it is our fault! And
      it lives in all of us, in relationships that are important to us
      and that have created pain in our life, and within which we
      have struggled to respect ourselves and another.

    ○   When I heard you describe the honoring, it sounded to me
      like the kind of honoring that would need to go on in every
      partnership. Like all these others. *And then it struck me*

Reflection   *that the partnership we have with our family is the one we can never leave, even if we want to, so it's like the ultimate training ground.* We pretend we can leave. I remember one time . . . I asked my parents to come into therapy with me and it just scared them. My father pulled me aside and said "Before we go into this I just want you to know that your mother will always be your mother and whatever you say can never be taken back." My father was a conflict avoider and I was in the fighter mode. I'm like "F--- you, go away, I'm going to do this no matter what!" But, you know one thing he was right about . . . my mother will always be my mother. It took me years to hear what he said to me. But I realized, I couldn't escape that one and it's been the practice field.

○   Just hearing you talk about that brings up so much stuff. Our parents may never behold us as we do and we have to let that go. I keep remembering back to the moment when my father and mother, on a visit, finally said to me "What is it that has caused you and your brother to have to do so much therapy? What is it that we did or did not do that created all this mess for you two? Because your brother won't tell us . . . we were hoping maybe you would." (laughter) And I took the bait. (more laughter) "I've been waiting for this chance all my life." An hour and 45 minutes later, with eyes swollen shut, I'm lying on the floor of my parents' living room. . . . They are sitting in their easy chairs sort of "uh!" and I'm lying on the floor, kicking and screaming, literally, physically kicking and screaming and shrieking and cursing at the top of my lungs, and my mother looks at me and says "Oh, for god's sake, S---!" (uproarious laughter) I finally got it! No more expectations! Let it go! This is what is!

○   *I just got a powerful learning about what family means.*
Reflection   *About how it's a contract, in a sense. And how we try and*

duplicate that by trying to get people to sign contracts and stay in our family; because we want to learn lessons and grow from them. And so these are the opportunities.

Inquiry   O   *The question that is up for me about this, then, is "Well then, what is the contract?" Because if you don't understand what the contract is in your initial practice field, you will repeat it. And you will make things personal that are not personal.* I'll use myself as an example. My main story line was "Those that love me leave me." And this started from early, from grandparents I loved that got mentally ill that I thought "If I could just say the right thing to them, I could bring them back." Having a friend who committed suicide in the ninth grade, two weeks after we broke up with each other. If I had just done the right thing. If I had just been the right enough something, my father could have got out of his head. Well, none of that leaving was about me. Those leavings were about them. So the story that has driven my behavior of trying to be enough was not even the right story! It wasn't about me! So what does that mean?

—the apparent end—

Reflections

It is our practice to follow all dialogue sessions with a period of reflection, where we collectively reflect on the process and content of the dialogue. We generally start with reflections on the process and then move to content. This prevents people from moving back into conversation around content. However, if you feel the desire to reverse these, simply ask individuals to limit themselves to their observations without engaging in further dialogue.

The purpose of reflecting on process is to enhance skill development by continuously looking at what is and is not supporting the group in dialogue. Process reflections are generally responses to questions such as:

o   What have we observed about how we have communicated with one another?

o   To what degree did we attend to suspension of judgment, assumption identification, inquiry, and reflection within the dialogue?

o   What areas would we like to focus attention on in the next dialogue?

When such reflection periods are maintained, each successive conversation becomes more powerful as people develop their inherent capabilities for dialogue.

When the conversation has been about an issue, a problem, or a question, the content reflection serves to collect the key learnings and understandings and identify any collective themes or threads of shared meaning that may be emerging. Content reflections are responses to questions such as:

o   What insights, learnings, and questions for further reflection will you take with you as we close this dialogue?

o   What collective themes or threads have you heard?

o   If there were one voice speaking here, what would it be saying?

These reflections can be carried forward to inform decision making and future actions.

Below are the reflections gathered after the above dialogue.

Process (How We Speak with One Another)

o   The environment felt safe for speaking about important issues and questions that are often difficult to talk about. Things that contributed to this were:

1.   a willingness to offer personal stories around the dilemmas and pains we have all experienced in partnership;

2.   acknowledgment that what someone else had said was valuable in helping me clarify my own thinking/feeling around an important issue;

3. a general attitude of curiosity versus evaluation or judgment about the differing perspectives offered; and

4. a high level of self-reflection, inquiry, and offerings that often built upon our diversity rather than juxtaposing them in discussion.

○ Sometimes the pace picked up to where it was difficult for some of us to reflect on what was being said and for others to enter the conversation without listening for a break to jump into. Occasionally someone would hold the tape recorder for a bit before starting to speak or after finishing as a way of introducing a pause and a call for attention to pace. The tape recorder seemed to operate like a talking stick.

○ There didn't seem to be expectations for any outcomes other than to learn from one another and delve deeper into issues and questions that were of personal and professional importance to us.

○ We had just come from a three-day conference together. I'm curious about how this previous experience may have set the stage for us to move into deeper conversation more quickly, than if we had just gathered on that morning.

○ There seemed to be a good deal of listening for and reflection on themes building on each other.

○ There was a high degree of self-reflective listening, focused on internal response to what was being said and on the connections between what others had said and one's own experience. Yet, there was little spoken reflection on collective meanings.

○ The sharing of different personal examples and stories really helped me ground the more conceptual pieces and gave me some very practical ideas to carry forward. One thing that stands out in these reflections is a noticing that little attention was being paid to listening for collective threads. One way to bring this into the next dialogue would be to agree to pause periodically and inquire about any collective shared meanings and patterns that people might be hearing.

Content (Themes, Insights, Learnings, Questions...)

Choosing Partnerships

- ○ When does partnership pull me away from or distract me from what I need to be doing?
- ○ How can I discern partnerships that are in alignment with my purpose?
- ○ Knowing oneself, one's styles, preferences, ways of working, areas of talent, and values, is essential to being able to discern and make choices around partnership.

Purpose

- ○ What purpose does this partnership serve? For each person involved? For the greater collective the partnership exists within? What is the work to which the partnership is in service?
- ○ Once you create the vision, it needs to be constantly revisited and reevaluated to see if it is meeting the needs of all involved. What change might be wanting to occur?

Commitment

- ○ What does commitment mean for each person in the partnership? What does commitment look like? Is it a guarantee to stay no matter how tough the going gets?
- ○ Commitment to what?
- ○ What is the relationship between commitment and continuity in a partnership?
- ○ What is the tension between the "safety" of mutual commitment and being able to rely on the partnership and the level of openness and freedom so important for creativity?

Boundaries

- ○ What are the boundaries for each person? How does each define them? What are the outer edges for each?
- ○ What is the distinction between clear and fuzzy boundaries for each?

○ Are there definite and clear boundaries that are required by the work and the partnership? On what do they depend? What might change them?

○ Continuous conversation is needed to stay current with boundaries as they flex and move within the partnership.

Communication

○ Ability to communicate openly and authentically with a partner is essential to discernment of the work, purpose, boundaries, and dealing with issues as they arise that may require changes in both how the partnership defines itself and how it operates.

○ Communication when leaving a partnership is as necessary as when entering to ensure that the relationship is left open for whatever may want to evolve in the future.

Contracts

○ Is the legal structure built on fear? Can it contribute clarity? When is legal control a substitute for communication?

○ Creating a contract together engages partners in conversations that lead to clarity around the essential aspects mentioned above. It is an opportunity to inquire into the underlying assumptions of all parties, and determine where shared meaning exists. It may be the creation, more than the existence, of the contract that is most useful.

Intimacy

○ What form(s) of intimacy is wanted and useful in a given partnership? What are the assumptions about what is required to create and maintain that intimacy?

Responsibility

○ Who is responsible for what?

○ How is each person responsible to him/herself, to the partner(s), and to the partnership itself?

○ How do partners determine what is "right action" within the partnership?

Trust and Respect

○   Trust requires a commitment to open communication to talk through whatever issues are deemed important.

○   The capability to trust oneself, to be able to discern what is appropriate within any given partnership is key to building trust within the relationship itself. If I cannot trust myself, then I surely will have trouble knowing how, when, or if I trust you.

○   Respect and a willingness to listen openly are needed to be able to identify our differences in perception, ways of working, even values, and discern what work we may want to do and be capable of doing together.

A Few Collective Themes

1.   Communication as an essential ingredient for discernment (clarity) in the partnership;

2.   Clarity as essential to effective collaboration and partnership; and

3.   Curiosity about the underlying functions of contracts and our assumptions about how these get met.

The depth and breadth of these reflections are indicative of a rich dialogue that has generated both insights and questions that have opened up new territory to investigate. The presence of so many questions in a reflection is characteristic of conversation where people are focused on digging into underlying thinking and want to see beyond current patterns and expand their perceptions and possibilities.

A Short Epilogue

Below are three sets of reflections on how the above dialogue was of value to people who participated in the days that followed. All the cases of partnerships described are business based. We believe the same benefits would apply to any partnership: family, community, etc.

○   The dialogue expanded my thinking around issues. I came in with one perspective and hearing others opened and expanded my view.

As a result, things were not as stressful. I could calm down, seeing the broader perspective. I was more capable of taking action I felt more confident in because I had explored a number of alternatives. Issues continue to surface with business partners, particularly around money. I find myself much better able to listen, be open, and respond more effectively. I have become less reactive. In crisis and conflict situations, when narrow-mindedness can escalate, dialogue helps me get out of narrow-mindedness. All kinds of problems get solved sooner because I can de-escalate the conflict.

O   Thanks for asking me to reflect on the dialogue and the days since. First I looked at what I did at the dialogue and what I've done since. In the dialogue, lightbulbs kept going off. I read what I had written more than once after I returned, and even reflected on the meaning for a month or so. I have done many, many things differently since the dialogue. The whole issue of boundaries in relationship is one that I have struggled with all my life. Since the dialogue, I have begun that exploration in earnest. I began setting boundaries that felt correct for me. Another piece emerged from a statement one of the women made about just being with her husband in those times when he wanted to kill himself, without having to make it work. I am learning to be me and be in partnerships without having to make it work. One final piece is about learning to be aware of what I do. Most of the time I just "do" without being aware. I am learning to notice more, without the need to fix, just notice. For example, what do I do when I am around a man that I find attractive, or a woman whose opinion of me matters to me? It is extremely instructive to just notice these things. To summarize one of Paula Underwood's teachings: I am learning that one has to circle between sensitivity to the data and perception that the data even exists. Only through this circling can one move to understanding and communication. One woman at the dialogue said "We have to be ravenous for differences." I am learning to be ravenous for my differences and working to do so with empathy and absence of judgment.

o   The April partnership dialogue helped crystallize for me the essential nature of a partnership that would be built to last. Traditional approaches would encourage you to craft legal documents, to externalize responsibility for the relationship, to formalize commitment. Experience has shown us how ineffective and painful this way has been [referring to stories shared in the dialogue]. And it occurred to me that this form of commitment is total folly. It is applying a structure to a relationship that is always in fact changing. A fluid relationship could never be held by a legal document [as the divorce rate indicates]. So, what is the lesson to be learned? That we cannot ask another person to commit to any specific form of partnership. The only thing we can look for in a partner is intent—an intent to always come from a place of loving kindness, an intent to be fully present with us in the moment, to share openly from the heart, to listen with deep curiosity, to foster continual growth, and to hold ambiguity with us. And if two partners come together with such an intent, one for the other, miracles can and do happen.

CLOSING THOUGHTS

T he time has come to say good-bye, at least for now. It is morning at the beach. I sit here with my coffee to one side and the paper to the other. The sun is just lighting the sky, and I am reflecting on what I want to say to you now as you leave this ongoing conversation with us, having read the book I introduced to you some hundreds of pages ago. Here's what comes to mind.

I want to remind you again of a key word in the title of this book, the word *rediscover*. When I was young and first heard about Columbus discovering the Americas, the history books made it sound like America might not even have existed until Columbus laid eyes on it. Of course this is not true. The land we now call the Americas was there all along. Just so, these pages have been written to remind us of the creative and transformational power of conversation that has always been present.

Writing, according to Socrates, is about remembering. It is a reminder to the reader who already knows those things that have been written. We write things down so that if we forget them we have a way of remembering. These pages are about helping all of us remember the power of conversation. They are about remembering a natural and deep impulse we all have for open authentic expression and deep listening, and about how the survival of our relationships and the quality of our lives and work often depend on such conversation.

Our world—at home, at work, in our communities—is at risk. There is alienation. There is lack of motivation. There is war between people and within people. People are tired, worn out, and uninspired. Meaning has all but disappeared from our lives. And all around us the search goes on, in our organizations, our movie theaters, our houses of worship, in all our relationships. We are looking for meaning that will inspire us, reignite our passion for life, show us new ways of working and living together that are more satisfying and sustainable. And all the while, meaning is right here among us. And we don't need fancy technologies or lots of money to begin to lift the veil that hides if from our view. All the raw materials we need are a little time, a good measure of desire, and the courage to remember that we craft meaning every time we gather with others in conversation. All that is required is that we begin to talk with one another about those issues and questions that matter most to us in life; about what creates our pain and what gives us joy; about what holds us down and what enlivens us and sets our creative juices flowing.

The structure of dialogue is meant to help us create and sustain such conversations. By focusing and refocusing our attention on four mainstays—suspension of judgment, identification of assumptions, deep listening, and inquiry and reflection—we expand the range of thoughts and feelings and diversity we are able to explore and contain without damaging one another. Whatever context you are in, whatever strategy you may be experimenting with, if you keep reminding yourself to return to these four foundations, they will serve you well.

And now, two last thoughts and a thank you.

Dare to remember what you know about the power of conversation to open new doors and heal old wounds. You will not be disappointed.

Remember these three essentials of Zen practice. They apply to dialogue as well.

- ○ *Continue under all circumstances.* (If you persist relentlessly, then even on the worst of days the practice will sustain you; it will kick in automatically when you need it most.)
- ○ *Don't be tossed away* (by adversity from outside or inside).
- ○ *Make positive effort for the good each day* (even if it is only to practice suspension of judgment or listen one minute longer to one person whose perspective you don't understand or agree with).

And last, but far from least, I cannot close without personally thanking you from my heart and from a deep belief in this work, which is of such importance to me. I thank you for reading these pages and for whatever efforts you make every day for the good of your work group, your organization, your family, your community, and our world.

Out beyond ideas of wrongdoing and rightdoing
There is a field.
I will meet you there.

—Rumi

Glenna Gerard

The morning sun is pouring in through the windows in my breakfast nook, and it is time I draw together last thoughts for this book. I notice both sadness and delight that the book is now complete. It has been a challenging learning experience in witnessing it come together between the combined efforts of our editors at Wiley, Glenna, and me. Though it is *not* the book I would or could have written by myself, I am glad that the ideas expressed here will be more available in the world through our work together.

My sadness comes from knowing that there is so much more to say about dialogue than what we were able to include here. Much that was written will have to be saved for future works such as how dialogue can work in our personal lives, our communities, schools, and in an array of other social arenas. We also were not able to include material that concerns the specific interests of organizational practitioners. Since the inception of the The Dialogue Group, Glenna and I have tried to provide learning spaces for these practitioners to integrate and experience dialogue firsthand. Such topics as the role of the facilitator and how to weave dialogue into conventional organizational development activities such as building teams, visioning, and large-group processes are areas to be addressed in the future.

Because we needed to focus on the organizational reader, we were not able to share much about dialogue as a way of life. My own life has been touched, changed, and blessed by personal practice of dialogic principles. When I first encountered dialogue, I never imagined how it would work its way into what feels like every cell of my body. I never could have known how it would slow me down from my peripatetic lifestyle, help me take more conscious note of what was important in life, and make choices accordingly. I never could have known how it would alter the very locus from which I now live my life. All of this, too, must be left for other writings.

The delight I am feeling is how this book can serve as foundational material for those in organizational settings. It contains seed ideas that can lead to more interest in dialogue in the workplace.

I have always known that if an individual or a whole organization has a strong intention to change, it is completely possible. I would say to you that if you and your work group or organization strongly want to move in the direction of partnership and collaboration, the ideas we have presented here will help you. But, you must now take the next step and breathe life into them. You must see how they can work for you in ways we never could have anticipated.

About four months ago I had the pleasure of meeting a new friend who had never heard of dialogue. As I explained what it was, I noticed that he nodded as though he had always known these principles were important. He said plainly that everyone working in his organization should learn about dialogue and how to use it. He talked about all the wasted time in meetings he experienced and how it was clear that very few people had much skill in simple conversation for getting work done.

As I have come to know my friend better, I have also found that he personally incorporates many of the principles of dialogue naturally. I have asked him how he learned to "hold such a marvelous space for listening," for instance. He told me that he learned the hard way from experience. He participated in an artists' community for years after college and came to understand how damaging judgments were to relationships and to the creative process. He learned about the importance of listening with no evaluations being imposed.

I think much of what we have presented here is really about learning what it means to care about our lives and those around us. Perhaps this is what wisdom and maturity are all about on a collective level. Perhaps the interest in dialogue is indicative of our society moving out of adolescence towards adulthood. Through the sharing of life's experiences that is possible in dialogue, we learn what works and what doesn't. We watch and become aware. We rise above the cultural norms and ways of behaving that, at least in the western world, can cause our relationships irreparable harm. Perhaps we also remember the wisdom that we have inside ourselves. These principles are not new. They have been around since the dawn of humankind.

It seems to me that we have an opportunity in our world right now. It is to more consciously evolve. Adapting and altering the culture we share may be the most strategic long-term lever of planetary evolution we have. Up until now, few of us have stopped to consider how essential culture is in the human condition. Few of us reflect on what it might be like to live in the world that reflects a relational reality that the new sciences tell us is the core life pattern. Finally, few of us have considered how to consciously create the kind of culture that might lead to a whole new world order and certainly to different ways of living and working together in our personal lives.

I have learned this about how dialogue works: Practicing it is everything. My eight-year-old son hears me say the following like a broken record: "Colin, if you want to get better at *anything* whether it is your reading, taekwondo, or roller hockey, all you have to do is *practice*." It is the same with developing skills in relationship. If you have made your way through these pages and find yourself strongly motivated to improve your relationships and interact with more awareness, dialogue will help you. Find others who would like to practice with you. Experiment in small ways. Build confidence through taking small steps and noticing the changes that come about.

The other day, I observed how I was sitting with my new friend for quite some time in complete silence. It felt wonderful. Neither one of us had the need to break in and fill the space with words that didn't lead anywhere. I could not have experienced the quality of this kind of comfortable relationship before coming to know dialogue. I can only hint at the powerful way dialogue has changed me and how I now enter conversation and hold relationship.

I hope this book has inspired you. I hope that some of what you have read will take hold in your life and you will be moved and changed as have I and others who have woven dialogue into the fabric of day-to-day living. I honor our connection here that bridges the writing and the reading. Like the "noiseless patient spider" in Whitman's poem who "flings its gossamer threads in hope that it catches somewhere," it is your active participation as reader that makes the writing time well spent.

A Noiseless Patient Spider

"A noiseless patient spider,
I mark'd where on a little promontory it stood isolated,
Mark'd how to explore the vacant vast surrounding,
It launched forth filament, filament, filament, out of itself,
Ever unreeling them, ever tirelessly speeding them.

"And you O my soul where you stand,
Surrounded, detached, in measureless oceans of space,
Ceaselessly musing, venturing, throwing, seeking the spheres to connect them,
Till the bridge you will need be form'd, till the ductile anchor hold,
Till the gossamer thread you fling catch somewhere, O my soul."

Walt Whitman

If you have been touched by the "filament" we have spun, together let us create a web that can change the world.

With love and in the spirit of dialogue,

Linda

Linda Ellinor

APPENDIX

These pages are meant to be of service to two groups of readers: 1) facilitators and coaches helping leaders who are committed to bringing dialogue into their work environments, and 2) leaders who feel comfortable with and even enjoy bringing activities to their colleagues and work groups for exploration. We've divided the activities[1] roughly according to focus of attention, that is, listening, assumptions, etc.

All the activities are ones we have found useful in our work. Their primary purpose is to help heighten your awareness in specific areas without relying on complicated techniques. They are designed to aid you in remembering what it is like: to listen in ways that are co-creative and synergistic; to ask questions from a place of curiosity; to allow yourself time to reflect on what you are hearing; to begin to hear the assumptions behind your thinking; to discern threads of collective meaning within a group.

We have tried to make the instructions as simple as possible. The process steps speak to you as if you are the leader or host for the activity. As you experiment it will help if you keep in mind that it is the intention behind the activity that is most important, rather than the exact execution of it. Here, technique is meant to be in service of the primary impulse to be in dialogue. If you put technique before intention, you may become an accomplished technician and still miss the essence of dialogue itself. But if you keep your intention for open and honest inquiry and listening foremost in your mind, even the most fumbling of efforts will reward you with a sense of your own innate knowing about what it is to engage in meaningful and powerful dialogue.

We hope that you will explore these activities with a spirit of play and reverence and be rewarded accordingly.

✳ Focus: Discovering a Starting Place ✳

The start of a dialogue can often be uncomfortable for groups new to the practice. What will the group talk about? Who will begin? If your group has a particular topic or issue on the table for consideration and the purpose of the dialogue is its exploration, then you are all set. If not, here is one way to find a starting place.

The Two-Step

We were introduced to a version of this very useful tool at a weekend seminar on Process Work, lead by Arlene and Jean-Claude Audergon.[2]

Purpose

The Two-Step is one of many processes you can use to help a group "feel out" a starting point. (*Note:* It is important to emphasize that in this process the goal is not to come to a group decision on which idea is best, it is simply to notice where there seems to be a significant amount of interest and energy and begin there. The group may then take the dialogue anywhere, but at least a leaping off place has been found.) Here's how it works.

Process

1. Everyone stands up.
2. There is a moment of silence when you all reflect and listen within for what you have some energy and interest in exploring.
3. If you identify something of interest to you, step forward into the circle and make a statement of what you would like to explore with the group.
4. Anyone who is interested comes and stands with you.
5. Then the next person makes an offering and people who find that of interest move to stand with him/her. (*Note:* If you put forth the first idea but one of the subsequent ones sounds more interesting, just move over to stand with that group. You might even want to

add a twist and say "This conversation would interest me even more if we could include 'x' in it."

6. Allow yourselves to move and shift with the ideas put forth until a strong focus of energy becomes apparent. This becomes the starting point. (*Note:* The group is using physical movement to actually listen for the flow of energy. They are combining verbal and nonverbal forms.)
7. Once the starting point has been created, you take your seats and begin the dialogue with a moment of silence.

Focus: Listening
Good Listener/Poor Listener

This activity is an adaptation of an activity we were introduced to by Carl Zaiss in a workshop based on the work of Tom Gordon. We extend our thanks to both of them for the inspiration.

Purpose

To elevate awareness of the impact that poor listening has on both speaker and listener.

Materials

A bell or chime to use for signaling starts and stops, so you don't have to shout over people.

Process

1. Explain the purpose of the activity. Emphasize awareness building.
2. Ask participants to quickly call out the characteristics of a good listener. They will mention things like eye contact, attentive body language, verbal acknowledgments, or whatever signals are appropriate to their culture.
3. Next ask for a list of the characteristics of a poor listener. Examples are looking at your watch, interrupting, poor or no eye contact, and so forth.

4. Explain that they will need a partner. Ask them to pair up and decide which person will go first.

5. Ask everyone to think of something they can tell their partner about, something that they have a lot of energy about. It might be something they are angry or frustrated about or happy and excited about, as long as it's important to them.

6. Explain that when you say "start," whichever partner has decided to go first will begin to tell the other person his/her story about whatever is so important to them. The listening partner will demonstrate as many characteristics of a poor listener as he/she can, short of getting up and leaving the room. Let them know that you won't let it go on very long, but they need to really go for it. Remind them: "Speaker, see if you can get your point across. Listener, be a poor listener."

7. After about 30 seconds, tell them to stop. Then instruct them to immediately reverse roles. The listener now becomes the speaker, and the first speaker becomes the poor listener. Say "start" and go for another 30 seconds.

8. When they have completed the second round, debrief the activity by asking:

   ○ What was the experience like? What was it like to not be listened to? Specifically ask them what it *felt* like. Take several responses. Explain that although this is just a put on, a fake even so, we have a negative emotional and physical response to not being listened to. Imagine the impact it has in real life. What impact do they think this feeling would have on a relationship?

   ○ What impact did the poor listening have on the speaker's ability to express himself/herself? People will often observe that when they are not being listened to, it is hard to maintain a focus, to be concise, to continue speaking. The key here is that the quality of our listening directly influences the quality of the speaker's expression, so one way we can help a speaker be clear and concise is to listen attentively.

9. Complete the activity by asking participants to bring their heightened awareness of the impact of their listening into the next dialogue.

Co-Creating Conversation

The basic form of this activity has been around so long, we don't even know where to attribute credit. We have adapted it to help people gain an appreciation for what it is like to co-create conversation with a minimum of attachment to outcome.

Purpose

To give participants an experience of co-creating conversation that has many parallels with how we build collective conversation in dialogue.

Materials

A bell or chime to signal handoffs.

Process

1. Explain the purpose of the activity.

2. Ask participants to pair up with a partner and sit facing each other close enough for easy conversation. (If you have an odd number, a trio will work fine. Just have them adjust for the extra person.) Ask the groupings to decide who will go first.

3. Explain that when we begin, the person who goes first will start to tell a story. The story is make-believe, but it is not a known make-believe story like "Little Red Riding Hood." It is one they will make up as they go along. Here is an example: "Early this morning I went for a walk. I was passing a stand of trees when a huge kangaroo jumped out from behind it and stopped right in front of me. I jumped. He (I think it was a he) said "Has anyone warned you? This a very strange road you are on and if you continue there is no telling what adventures you may find yourself in the middle of. . . ." Tell the pairs that when you clap your hands (or ring a bell, which is easier to hear), the other partner will pick up the story and continue. The only rule here is: There must be continuity at the point of transfer.

So, if John stops and we are flying above the Atlantic at 30,000 feet, Mary cannot pick us up in a submarine on the ocean floor. After the transfer, the new storyteller can take the story anywhere he/she wants. Every time you hear a clap (or the bell), transfer the story.

4. Allow each person to "get into the flow" before a transfer. Initially this takes about 30 seconds to 1 minute. As time passes, the transfers will become more fluid and you can decrease the time between transfers. You'll get a feel for it. Allow about four to six transfers.

5. Debrief the exercise by asking people to comment on what they observed about their listening. Sometimes this is the only prompt needed. Sometimes you will have to ask more questions, such as: "What was it like to listen for the transfer? What did it feel like to have the other person pick up the story and take it somewhere else? Describe the way you were listening." Draw as many parallels with dialogue as you can. Some of the key ones are: "I listened without thinking about what I was going to say next, because I didn't know. I had to just listen for where my partner was going, so that I could pick up the thread at the transfer." "It was fun to see where the other person would take the story. I felt like we were on an adventure together." "There was no right or wrong way to go. We could create anything."

6. Conclude the exercise by asking the participants to see if they can listen in the same way to the contributions of everyone in the dialogue. Listen for the essential offering to the story. Listen without attachment to what the other person says. Listen as if they were jointly building a collective conversation.

The Talking Stick

The talking stick comes to us from indigenous peoples who use it to call for respectful listening. The person who holds the stick speaks the wisdom, or "medicine," that they have to offer the circle. Each speaker will, in turn, pick up the stick, speak, and then either place the stick again in the center of the circle or pass it to the next speaker. Often a rattle is used as a talking stick. Speakers may punctuate the beginning and conclusion of their words by shaking the rattle, an additional call for attention and a signal of completion.

A talking stick is always a request for listening, to the words spoken and the silences in between. There are times when one may pick up the talking stick and simply sit in silence with the group; another form of speaking has occurred. The talking stick calls forth the listening and focus of the speaker as well. It is a reminder to listen within and speak directly from the heart, the simple truth of one's perceptions and/or questions.

Groups may choose to use talking sticks in different ways. Initially, the stick can help a group to focus on listening and speaking about what really matters. It can help to slow down the pace of the conversation and provide more opportunity for silence and reflection, to notice how the conversation ebbs and floods. Some groups use talking sticks for entire dialogues; others when a member wishes to call for a slowing of the pace; and still others simply place the stick in the center of the circle to be picked up by anyone, at any time, as a call for listening and attention.

A very powerful ceremony for any group is to collectively create a talking stick for their use. Each member brings something that symbolizes deep listening and heartfelt, authentic speaking that can be attached to the stick either with glue or yarn or some other material. Examples might include: a bead or crystal, braided thread, feathers, or a ring. Whatever has been chosen as the stick is then passed and each person speaks to the symbol they have brought and attaches it to the stick. When the stick is complete, it is passed and each person speaks words of honor and respect for the symbol that will help to hold a space of deep listening and heartfelt speaking for the group.

✳ Focus: Inquiry and Reflection ✳
Inquiry and Reflection Circles

We have designed a number of versions of this activity. It is structured to help groups focus on combining inquiry and reflection and developing a trust in their intuitive faculties. We recommend rereading chapter 4, Inquiry and Reflection, in Part II before beginning.

Purpose

To help individuals develop the ability to generate open-ended questions that take an inquiry to deeper levels through a combination of silence, listening, and trust in their intuitive faculty. To hone the capacity to listen without the need to reply.

Materials

A talking stick for each group/circle. A chart and markers for recording beginning questions generated by the whole group.

Process

1. Groups of between six and ten are best for this activity. Fewer numbers result in insufficient diversity of input. Greater numbers create an attention problem and take too much time. Create the groups accordingly and have them sit in circles. Each group will need to have one person willing to begin the process and have some object that can be used as a talking stick. You will need to explain that whoever holds the talking stick in this exercise is the only person who speaks. The rest listen. (This activity is purposely structured so that there is no response to or questioning of any speaker during the exercise.)

2. The starting question is based on: 1) preprogram surveys, 2) your knowledge of key issues for the group to consider, or 3) a list of questions generated by the group that are of interest to them. If you do the latter, you'll need about ten minutes more in which to chart the questions; between three and six questions will be sufficient. There is no need to vote on which question to use. This is simply a way to get ideas out.

3. The starters for each group will either take the question you have created or choose one that is of interest to them from the list the group generated. They pick up the talking stick and repeat the question aloud. Then they silently reflect on the question until a

response comes to them. (We suggest that people experiment with allowing a response to show up, versus analytically thinking about it. Remember, we are not looking for correct, authoritative answers. We are not out to show what we know. Our attitude is more one of curiosity about what the questions evoke in each of us.) Once the starter has responded, he/she will once more become quiet and reflect, asking within for the next question that wants to be asked into the group. At this point, we always laugh and let them know that "And what do you think, Rob?" *is not* the next question. We ask that they allow time for a question to arise. It does not necessarily have to be related to the question they started with. It is whatever comes to them.

4. When they have the next question, they speak it to the person on their right and pass the talking stick to that person.

5. The person with the talking stick now reflects in silence on his/her response to the new question. (*Note:* People sometimes ask if there is a time frame, a need to limit time/person. The answer is no: most groups will initially move very quickly with very little reflection. If they finish the round in short order, suggest that on the next one they pause a little longer for each reflection step.) After reflecting, they respond and return to silence to reflect on the next question. When they have it, they speak it to the person on their right and hand them the talking stick.

6. Step 5 repeats until the talking stick has gone around the circle and everyone has participated. Each person will have responded to a question, generated a new one, and passed the talking stick on. Allow about 20 to 30 minutes to complete the round.

7. If one group finishes before the others, tell them to continue another round until all the groups are complete. If the circles are in different rooms, one person from each group, or you as the leader/host will have to coordinate stopping times.

8. Debrief the exercise by asking people what their experiences were. There will be many responses, including some people who were uncomfortable with the structure. Accept all the responses. You

may need to explain that this is not dialogue. Rather, this is a structured activity to help us focus on inquiry and reflection. We do it this way because most often we do not pause and reflect before we answer, nor do we often take the time to reflect and generate new questions that deepen our inquiry.

9. Conclude by asking the participants to take their heightened awareness around inquiry and reflection into the next dialogue. This can also be a wonderful way to bridge into a dialogue immediately following the exercise. One way to accomplish this is to ask that when people finish the circle they take a few minutes to journal (write) their reflections. You can move into the dialogue directly or ask each person to read a short selection from their journaling. When the round is complete and all voices have been heard (even if to say "I pass"), then continue into dialogue.

Focus: Assumptions
Left-Hand Column Work[3]

There are many different versions of left-hand column work, all of which owe their foundation to the work of Chris Argyris and Donald Schön. We and many others are indebted to them for the models they have created to help people make the links more visible between values, beliefs, actions, and results.

Purpose

To increase people's awareness of the nature of what remains unspoken in their interactions with others. Because much of what is unspoken and the reasons why it remains so are related to assumptions, this activity helps create a visceral experience of the importance and impact of assumptions on relationships and results.

Materials

A sheet of paper and pen or pencil for each person.

Process

1. Ask each person to perform the following reflection: Think of an interaction with someone that you were involved with recently that was less than satisfactory. This could have been because it ended in argument, you felt misunderstood or discounted, or the task was going in a direction you didn't like. Recommend that they choose something that is important but that they will also feel comfortable sharing with a partner. (*Note:* You will need about 15 minutes for these first 3 steps.)

2. On a blank sheet of paper, draw a line down the middle. On the right side, write down the conversation that took place between you and the other person(s). Write the conversation exactly as you remember or imagine it. (*Note:* Don't worry about being technically correct. Just jot down the gist of what you remember being said.)

WHAT WAS NOT SAID	WHAT WAS SAID
_____	She said . . .
_____	I said . . .
_____	She said . . .

3. Go back and in the left-hand column write what you were thinking and feeling but did not communicate during the conversation.

4. Once both columns have been completed, ask each person to find a partner to work with. Together, consider the following questions. By acting as coaches for each other, you can help discover hidden assumptions, disconnections between intentions and results, and much more.

   ○ What is the nature of the material in the left-hand column? How would you describe it?

   ○ Why do you withhold the information in the left-hand column?

   ○ What might be some possible impacts of withholding the information on results? On the relationship?

○ What do you think might have been in the left-hand column of the other person(s)?

○ If you could replay the interaction, how might you bring more of the left-hand column into the conversation? Consider the following model for helping to bring "challenging" material over to the right-hand column. What you will be doing is disclosing your own ladder of inference. One essential key to success here is to "own" your left-hand column as yours. It is not the responsibility of the other person. Using "I" statements and distinguishing between observations (something you can tape-record or take a picture of) and interpretations (your inferences and assumptions) will go a long way towards speaking in a way that the other person can hear. What follows is a simple structure that can help you think through how you might present any left-hand column material you decide it might be useful to share. Consult with your coach to explore how this might work in your actual case. Role playing the revised conversation can be extremely useful.

A simple feedback model

"When I heard . . ."

"I think/interpret it to mean/assume/wonder . . ."

"And I feel . . ."

"I'd like to check in with you and see what you were thinking and assuming . . ."

"I would appreciate . . ." (optional request for some action)

○ From this exercise, what have you learned about your assumptions?

NOTES

Foreword

1. Dr. William Isaacs is president of *dia logos* and director for The Dialogue Project of MIT's 21st Century Project.

Part 1

1. David Bohm was born in Wilkes-Barre, Pennsylvania on December 20, 1917 and died in England in 1992. A contemporary of Albert Einstein and a student of Oppenheimer, his work in quantum physics led him to philosophical speculation about the nature of the universe as implied by quantum phenomena. Dialogue was an outgrowth of his search for ways to bring about cultural transformation that would bring society more in alignment with the quantum worldview he saw.

2. We will be referring to the new worldview coming out of the new sciences of chaos theory, self-organizing systems, and quantum physics later in Part I.

3. We use the term communication here as the broader category in which conversation is a form. Communication encompasses written, verbal, and nonverbal forms. We normally talk about dialogue being a conversational form of communication, but dialogue can also bring in the nonverbal as well. (See Part II, page 128 for more on the nonverbal forms of dialogue.)

4. The exact amount of dollars would be impossible to estimate. Perhaps it is billions of dollars.

5. Generativity is the capacity of a person(s) or process to originate, to participate in the unfolding of emergent forms and futures.

6. Dr. Isaacs is completing a book titled *The Art of Thinking Together* which will be published by Doubleday (NY) in 1998. The book develops a theory of dialogue as well as a set of principles for its practice and will contain examples from large system change efforts within institutions and corporations conducted over several years.

7. We will use the term dialogic communication when we are being inclusive of qualities of conversation that are typically found in the practice of dialogue. While there are many forms of dialogic communication, we might say that the "practice of dialogue," as was inspired by the work of David Bohm, is a specific kind of dialogic communication.

8. David Bohm, *On Dialogue*.

9. See Appendix for more information on how you can incorporate a talking stick within dialogue.

10. Patrick de Mare, *Koinonia*. More about de Mare's work and its influence on Bohm's proposal of dialogue is in the next chapter.

11. This does not mean that many do not find opportunities for personal healing and growth in dialogue. They do. It is just not the main objective or focus of attention.

12. Metacognition refers to becoming aware of our thinking process. We discuss this in more detail later in Part I and again in Part II.

13. Other important writings by Bohm on the subject of dialogue include *On Dialogue*; *Wholeness and the Implicate Order*; and *Science, Order, and Creativity* (co-authored by David Peat).

14. An incoherence is a discrepency between what we say we want and the results we actually get.

15. Metacognition is becoming aware of our thinking or thought process. It is "thinking about our thinking," or reflecting on our thinking.

16. Born in India, Jiddu Krishnamurti lived betwen 1895 and 1986. He wrote extensively on the topic of consciousness and spirituality. Bohm came across Krishnamurti's book "The Last Freedom" in 1959 and two years later began a series of dialogues and talks on the intersection between quantum mechanics and consciousness.

17. In Part II we delve into assumption identification and suspension of judgment and expand on what we mean by learning how to witness thoughts and the unfolding meaning that occurs in dialogue. The idea of witness is essential in current-day practice of dialogue.

18. In de Mare's book *Koinonia*, he calls the communication process he uses dialogue. We refer to it here as dialogic communication so as not to confuse it with the practice of dialogue we refer to in this book.

19. At a quantum particle level, matter and energy waves are the same thing. In other words, everything that appears solid to us as we look through our eyes, turns out to be nothing but energy waves at the quantum level. Energy waves interconnect and interweave with each other to form a continuous whole universe.

20. We will refer to the new worldview that is emerging from the new sciences as the quantum worldview. We could just as correctly refer to it by other names such as an evolving ecological or new sciences worldview. There are many ways of referring to the new worldview.

21. "Permanent whitewater" is a term coined by Peter Vail in his book *Managing as a Performing Art*, 1989.

22. This was before quantum physics demonstrated that at very small levels matter acts more like energy waves than anything solid.

Part II

1. The depiction of conversations here is based on interpretation of events and the results of investigations conducted at the time. We do not claim it to be the truth, rather one possible description that illustrates the importance of conversational dynamics in how decisions are made.

2. "Mental models are deeply ingrained assumptions, generalizations, or even pictures or images that influence how we understand the world and how we take action." Peter Senge, *The Fifth Discipline* (New York: Currency/ Doubleday, 1990).

3. Charles T. Tart, *Living the Mindful Life* (Boston, London: Shambala Press, 1994), p. 67.

4. Argyris, Chris. *Organizational Defensive Routines*.

5. Marcel Proust.

6. David Bohm, *On Dialogue* (London: Routledge, 1996).

7. Coleman Barks, *The Essential Rumi*, Coleman Books (New York: HarperCollins, 1995).

8. Sarita Chawla, "Dialogue: The Language of Community," *Vision Action*, Volume 13 (Winter, 1994).

9. Margery Williams, *The Velveteen Rabbit* (NY: Doubleday, 1971).

10. Offered with the permission of Sarita Chawla, MetaLens Consulting, Inc., copyright 1996.

11. Statistically, according to Myers Briggs Type Indicator (personality style assessment instrument) data, approximately 75 percent of our society in the United States is extroverted.

12. Paul Simon and Art Garfunkel, "The 59th Street Bridge Song."

13. Such times represent one context in which nonverbal forms such as art, music, and movement may be useful in bringing in new information. Refer to the Appendix for descriptions of such activities. Attention to synchronous events may also be useful. In Part IV, there is a chapter on synchronicity that may be of interest.

14. An example of such a reflection period can be found in Part V, which is a transcript from a dialogue followed by comments collected during the reflection period.

15. Gabrielle Roth and The Mirrors: *Bones*, 1989 Gabrielle Roth, Raven Recording, P.O. Box 2034, Dred Band, NJ 07701; *Ritual*, 1990 Gabrielle Roth.

16. Judith Cornell, *Mandala* (Wheaton IL: The Theosophical Publishing House, 1994).

17. For more information on the models included here see the following publications: Bruce Tuckman, "Development Sequence in Small Groups," *Psychological Bulletin*, (1965); Will Schutz, *The Human Element*, (San Francisco: Jossey-Bass, 1994); M. Scott Peck, *The Different Drum* (New York: Simon & Schuster, 1987).

18. William N. Isaacs, "Taking Flight: Dialogue, Collective Thinking and Organizational Learning," *Organizational Dynamics*, Volume 22.2 (Autumn 1993) pp. 24–39.

Part III

1. Funk and Wagnall (n.p.: J. G. Ferguson Publishing Company, 1982).

2. Carl Zaiss, "Sales Effectiveness Training," a workshop based on the communication skills work of Tom Gordon.

3. Margaret Wheatley, *Leadership and the New Sciences*, (San Francisco: Barrett-Koehler, 1992).

4. Some other profiles. Barbara "BJ" Hateley and Warren Schmidt, *Exploring*

Differences in the Workplace: Assessing Management Practices and Diversity Acceptance in Your Organization, Penguin Index, Xicom. Tuxedo, NY, 1995).

5. Books have been written on various ways to involve people in the decision-making process. Some of the best and simplest material can be found in Interaction Associates programs and the book *How to Make Meetings Work* by Michael Doyle and David Straus, (New York: Berkley Publishing Group, 1982).

6. Edgard H. Schein, "On Dialogue, Culture and Organizational Learning," *Organizational Dynamics*, Vol. 22, (Autumn 1993).

7. William N. Isaacs, "Taking Flight: Dialogue, Collective Thinking and Organizational Learning," *Organizational Dynamics*, Vol. 22, (Autumn 1993).

8. It is also unfortunately true that many groups of people do not have the resources to hold programs in such locations. If you can, do it. If you can't, then ask yourself "What can we do to introduce as many elements into the environment as we can that will help us slow down, listen, and create a spirit of inquiry and desire to learn?" Consider music, quotes posted on the walls, simple art supplies, a selection of percussion instruments (even spoons). Be creative.

9. Books that contain native American stories, fairy tales, or fables are all rich resource material.

10. A description of the work can be found in Peter Senge's *The Fifth Discipline Fieldbook* (New York: Doubleday, 1994).

Part IV

1. David Whyte, *Songs for Coming Home* (Langley, WA: Many Rivers Press, 1989).

2. If you'd like more information on each of these, see *Synchronicity: Science, Math and the Trickster* by Allan Combs and Mark Holland (New York: Marlowe and Company, 1996).

3. Duane Elgin, A working paper. "Collective Consciousness & Cultural Healing," May 1997.

4. Jeremiah Abrams, *The Shadow in America* (Novato, CA: Nataraj Publishing, 1994) p. 22.

5. Chris Argyris's term for actions (theories in use)

6. Chris Argyris's term for talk (espoused theories)

7. In "Identification and Suspension of Assumptions" in Part II we spoke about sets of assumptions and the usefulness of investigating them.

8. Fred Kofman and Peter Senge, "Communities of Commitment," *Organizational Dynamics*, Vol. 22.2 (Autumn, 1993) pp. 5–23.

9. An image borrowed from the philosopher Hieddeger, via Sarita Chawla.

10. This refers to an on-line organization out of England and coordinated by a man named Huevel. Those who participate have a primary interest in the practice of dialogue as set forth by David Bohm.

11. Greg Kramer and Terri O'Fallon are the developers of this form. They have done significant work with developing guidelines that have the intention of bringing the power of meditative practices to focus attention on dialogue.

12. We are indebted to Peter and Trudy Johnson-Lenz of Awakening Technology for a brief history from which they gave us permission to borrow.

13. Earlier we spoke of how a focus on something we value can also bring forth its opposite. This is encouraged by our desire to deny the shadow side in favor of pursuing what we value so highly.

14. Eastern meditative practices, including yoga, breath work, and working with silence, all help. Any practice that helps you personally become quiet and open to listening will be useful.

15. We believe these questions are directly related to the importance of exploring the nonverbal medium we wrote of in Part II.

16. J. Gage, "Traversing the topical landscape: Reading and writing as ways of knowing." Paper presented to the American Educational Research Association, San Francisco, 1986.

17. In Part III we described a way of thinking through learning edges. The same basic principles will serve you in dealing with the group learning edges we consider in this chapter.

18. Lao Tzu, The Complete Works of Lao Tzu, translated by NI, HUA-CHING (Malibu, CA: The Shrine of the Eternal Breath, 1989).

19. Juanita Brown and David Isaacs, "Conversation as a Core Business Process," *The Systems Thinker*, Vol. 7, No. 10, (Dec. 1996/Jan. 1997).

20. Although this poem is widely circulated within the AA community, we are unaware of a written reference. If anyone can so refer to one, we will be glad to provide a reference in a future edition.

Part V

1. *Universalism* is where everyone is like everyone else. *Particularism* is where everyone is distinct.

Appendix

1. Many of the exercises are our original design (the inquiry and reflection circle), some are adaptations from the work of others (left-hand column work, Chris Argyris), others have been around so long that they seem part of our collective knowledge pool. We attempt to give credit in all cases where we are knowledgeable enough to do so. Other sources for activities useful in building awareness and skills may be found in Peter Senge's The Fifth Discipline Fieldbook (New York: Doubleday, 1994).

2. From the work of Arnold Mindell.

3. This is an adaptation design based on our understanding of the work of Chris Argyris and Donald Schön. The research method was first presented in their book *Theory in Practice* (San Francisco: Jossey-Bass, 1974).

BIBLIOGRAPHY

Aikido

Crum, Thomas F. *The Magic of Conflict: Turning a Life of Work into a Work of Art*. New York: Touchstone, 1987.

Anthropological

Eisler, Riane. *The Chalice and the Blade: Our History, Our Future*. San Francisco: HarperSanFrancisco, 1990.

Bohm Publications

Bohm, David. *On Dialogue*. Ed. Lee Nichol. New York: Routledge, 1996.

————. *Unfolding Meaning: A Weekend of Dialogue with David Bohm*. London: Ark Paperbacks, 1985.

————. *Wholeness and the Implicate Order*. London: Ark Paperbacks, 1980.

————. *Thought as a System*. Ojai, Calif: David Bohm Seminars, n.d.

Bohm, David, and Mark Edwards. *Changing Consciousness, Exploring the Hidden Source of the Social, Political, and Environmental Crises Facing our World*. New York: n.p., 1991.

Peat, F. David. *Infinite Potential: The Life and Times of David Bohm*. Menlo Park, Calif.: Addison Wesley, 1997.

Brain Consciousness

Gazzaniza, Michael S. *The Social Brain: Discovering the Networks of the Mind*. New York: Basic Books, 1985.

Grof, Stanislav, and Hal Zina Bennet. *The Holotropic Mind: The Three Levels of Human Consciousness and How They Shape Our Lives*. San Francisco: HarperSanFrancisco, 1990.

Ornstein, Robert. *The Evolution of Consciousness*. New York: Prentice Hall, 1991.

————. *The Roots of the Self: Unraveling the Mystery of Who We Are*. San Francisco: HarperSanFrancisco, 1993.

Buddhist

Beck, Charlotte Joko. *Nothing Special: Living Zen*. San Francisco: HarperSanFrancisco, 1993.

Chodron, Pema. *The Wisdom of No Escape and the Path of Loving Kindness*. Boston: Shambhala Publications, 1991.

Espstein, Mark, M.D. *Thoughts Without a Thinker*. New York: Basic Books, 1995.

Goldstein, Joseph. *Insight Meditation: The Practice of Freedom*. Boston: Shambhala Publications, 1993.

Kabat-Zinn, Jon. *Full Catastrophy Living: Using the Wisdom of the Body and Mind to Face Stress, Pain, and Illness*. New York: Dell Publishing, 1990.

————. *Wherever You Go, There You Are: Mindfulness Meditation in Everyday Life*. New York: Hyperion, 1994.

Kornfield, Jack. *A Path with Heart: A Guide Through the Perils and Promises of Spiritual Life*. New York: Bantam Books, 1993.

Tart, Charles. *Living the Mindful Life in the Present Moment*. Boston: Shambhala Publications, 1994.

Communication

Bolton, Robert. *People Skills, How to Assert Yourself, Listen to Others, and Resolve Conflicts*. New York: Simon & Schuster, 1979.

Gordon, Thomas. *Leader Effectiveness Training: The Foundation for Participative Management and Employee Involvement.* New York: G.P. Putnam's Sons, 1977.

Hills, Christopher. *Creative Conflict: The Secret of Heart-to-Heart Communion.* Boulder Creek, Calif.: University of the Trees Press, 1980.

Miller, Sherod. *Connecting with Self and Others.* Littleton, Colo.: Interpersonal Communication Programs, 1988.

Community and Community Building

Berry, Wendell. *What Are People For? Essays.* San Francisco: North Point Press, 1990.

————. *Sex, Economy, Freedom, and Community: Eight Essays.* New York: Pantheon Books, 1993.

Peck, M. Scott. *The Different Drum: Community Making and Peace: A Spiritual Journey Toward Self-Acceptance, True Belonging, and New Hope for the World.* New York: Touchstone, 1987.

————. *A World Waiting to Be Born: Civility Rediscovered.* New York: Bantam Books, 1993.

Rumi. *The Essential Rumi.* Trans. Coleman Banks and John Moyne. New York: Harper Collins, 1995.

Schultz, Will. *The Human Element.* San Francisco: Jossey-Bass, 1994.

Whitmyer, Claude. *In the Company of Others: Making Community in the Modern World.* New York: Jeremy P. Tarcher, 1993.

Conflict Resolution

Mindell, Arnold. *The Leader as Martial Artist: Techniques and Strategies for Resolving Conflict and Creating Community.* San Francisco: HarperSanFrancisco, 1994.

Creativity and the Arts

Cameron, Julia, and Mark Bryan. *The Artist's Way: A Spiritual Path to Higher Creativity.* New York: Jeremy P. Tarcher, 1992.

Chase, Mildred Portney. *Just Being at the Piano.* Berkeley, Calif.: Creative Arts Books, 1985.

Cornell, Judith. *Mandala: Luminous Symbols for Healing.* Wheaton, Ill: Quest Books, 1994.

Edwards, Betty. *Drawing on the Right Side of the Brain: A Course in Enhancing Creativity and Artistic Confidence.* New York: Jeremy P. Tarcher, 1988.

Nachmanovitch, Stephen. *Free: The Power of Improvisation in Life and the Arts.* New York: G.P. Putnam's Sons, 1990.

Rogers, Natalie. *The Creative Connection: Expressive Arts as Healing.* Palo Alto, Calif.: Science and Behavior Books, 1993.

Shlain, Leonard. *Art and Physics: Parallel Visions in Space, Time, and Light.* New York: Quill William Morrow, 1991.

Critical Thinking

Brookfield, Stephen D. *Developing Critical Thinkers: Challenging Adults to Explore Alternative Ways of Thinking and Acting.* San Francisco: Jossey-Bass, 1987.

Dialogue—General/Miscellaneous

de Mare, Patrick, Robin Piper and Sheila Thompson. *Koinonia: From Hate, through Dialogue, to Culture in the Large Group.* London: Karnac Books, 1991.

Dixon, Nancy. *Perspectives on Dialogue: Making Talk Developmental for Individuals and Organizations.* Greensboro, N.C.: Center for Creative Leadership, 1996.

Howe, Reuel L. *The Miracle of Dialogue.* New York: The Seabury Press, 1963.

Diversity

Morrison, Ann M. *The New Leaders: Guidelines on Leadership Diversity in America.* San Francisco: Jossey-Bass, 1992.

Economy/Business

Hawken, Paul. *The Ecology of Commerce: A Declaration of Sustainability.* New York: HarperBusiness, 1993.

Education

Freire, Paulo. *Education for Critical Consciousness.* New York: Continuum Publishing, 1992.

Jarvis, Peter. *Paradoxes of Learning: On Becoming an Individual in Society.* San Francisco: Jossey-Bass, 1992.

Postman, Neil, and Charles Weingartner. *Teaching as a Subversive Activity.* New York: Dell Books, 1969.

Indigenous

Arrien, Angeles. *The Four-Fold Way, Walking the Paths of the Warrior, Teacher, Healer and Visionary.* San Francisco: HarperSanFrancisco, 1993.

Cahill, Sedonia, and Joshua Halpern. *The Ceremonial Circle: Practice, Ritual, and Renewal for Personal and Community Healing.* San Francisco: HarperSanFrancisco, 1992.

Johansen, Bruce E. *Forgotten Founders: How the American Indian Helped Shape Democracy.* Boston: Harvard Common Press, 1982.

Journaling Process

Progoff, Ira. *At a Journal Workshop: The Basic Text and Guide for Using the Intensive Journal Process.* New York: Dialogue House Library, 1975.

Krishnamurti

Holroyd, Stuart. *Krishnamurti: The Man, the Mystery, and the Message.* Rockport, Mass.: Element, 1991.

Leadership

Autry, A. James. *Love and Profit: The Art of Caring Leadership.* New York: William Morrow, 1991.

Block, Peter. *Stewardship: Choosing Service over Self-interest.* San Francisco: Berrett-Koehler, 1993.

Bolman, Lee G., and Terrence E. Deal. *Leading with Soul: An Uncommon Journey of Spirit.* San Francisco: Jossey-Bass, Inc., 1995.

Conger, Jay A. *Learning to Lead: The Art of Transforming Managers into Leaders.* San Francisco: Jossey-Bass, 1992.

Covey, Stephen R. *The Seven Habits of Highly Effective People: Powerful Lessons in Personal Change.* New York: Fireside, 1989.

DePree, Max. *Leadership Is an Art.* New York: Bantam Doubleday, 1989.

Greenleaf, Robert K. *Servant Leadership: A Journey into the Nature of Legitimate Power and Greatness.* Mahwah, N.J.: Paulist Press, 1991.

Hawley, Jack. *Reawakening the Spirit in Work: The Power of Dharmic Management.* San Francisco: Berrett-Koehler, 1993.

Heider, John. *Tao of Leadership: Leadership Strategies for a New Age.* New York: Bantam Books, 1986.

Heifetz, Ronald A. *Leadership Without Easy Answers.* Cambridge, Mass.: Belknap Press of Harvard University Press, 1994.

Nair, Keshavan. *A Higher Standard of Leadership: Lessons from the Life of Gandhi.* San Francisco: Berrett-Koehler, 1994.

Nanus, Burt. *The Leader's Edge: The Seven Keys to Leadership in a Turbulent World.* Chicago: Contemporary Books, 1989.

Spears, Larry, ed. *Reflections on Leadership: How Robert K. Greenleaf's Theory of Servant-Leadership Influenced Today's Top Management Thinkers.* New York: John Wiley & Sons, 1995.

Mediation

Baruch Bush, Robert A., and Joseph P. Folger. *The Promise of Mediation: Responding to Conflict through Empowerment and Recognition.* San Francisco: Jossey-Bass, 1994.

Miscellaneous

Csikszentmihalyi, Mihaly. *The Evolving Self: A Psychology for the Third Millennium.* New York: HarperCollins, 1993.

Eck, Diana L. *Encountering God: A Spiritual Journey from Bozeman to Banaras.* Boston: Beacon Press, 1993.

Gelb, Michael J., and Tony Buzan. *Lessons From the Art of Juggling: How to Achieve Your Full Potential in Business, Learning, and Life.* New York: Harmony Books, 1994.

Handy, Charles. *The Age of Paradox.* Boston: Harvard Business School Press, 1994.

Maynard, Herman Bryant Jr., and Susan E. Mehrtens. *The Fourth Wave: Business in the 21st Century.* San Francisco: Berrett-Koehler, 1993.

Quinn, Daniel. *Ismael.* New York: Bantam Books, 1992.

Semler, Ricardo. *Maverick: The Success Story Behind the World's Most Unusual Workplace.* New York: Warner Books, 1993.

Swimme, Brian. *The Universe Is a Green Dragon.* Santa Fe, N.Mex.: Bear, 1984.

Whyte, David. *The Heart Aroused: Poetry and the Preservation of the Soul in Corporate America.* New York: Doubleday, 1994.

Zukav, Gary. *The Seat of the Soul.* New York: Simon & Schuster, 1990.

New Sciences

Briggs, John. *Fractals: The Patterns of Chaos.* New York: Simon & Schuster, 1992.

Combs, Allan, and Mark Holland. *Synchronicity: Science, Myth, and the Trickster.* New York: Marlowe, 1996.

Darling, David. *Equations of Eternity. Speculations on Consciousness, Meaning, and the Mathematical Rules that Orchestrate the Cosmos.* New York: Hyperion, 1993.

Goerner, Sally J. *Chaos and the Evolving Ecological Universe.* Amsterdam B. V.: Gordon and Breach Publishers (Overseas Publishers Association), 1994.

Goldstein, Jeffrey. *The Unshackled Organization: Facing the Challenge of Unpredictability through Spontaneous Reorganization.* Portland, Ore.: Productivity Press, 1994.

Hiley, B.J., and F. David Peat, ed. *Quantum Implications: Essays in Honour of David Bohm.* London: Routledge & Kegan Paul, 1988.

Kelly, Kevin. *Out of Control.* New York: Addison-Wesley, 1994.

Talbot, Michael. *The Holographic Universe.* New York: HarperCollins, 1992.

Weber, Renee. *Dialogues with Scientists and Sages: The Search for Unity.* London: Routledge & Kegan Paul, 1986.

Wheatley, Margaret J. *Leadership and the New Science: Learning about Organization from an Orderly Universe.* San Francisco: Berrett-Koehler, 1992.

Wheatley, Margaret J., and Myron Kellner-Rogers. *A Simpler Way.* San Francisco: Berrett-Koehler, 1996.

Zohar, Danah, and Ian Marshall. *The Quantum Society.* New York: William Marrow, 1994.

Organizational Learning

Argyris, Chris. *Overcoming Organizational Defenses.* New York: Prentice Hall, 1990.

Argyris, Chris, and Donald Schon. *Organizational Learning.* New York: Addison-Wesley, 1978.

Oshry, Barry. *Seeing Systems: Unlocking the Mysteries of Organizational Life.* San Francisco: Berrett-Koehler, 1995.

Senge, Peter M., Art Kleiner, Charlotte Roberts, Richard Ross, and Bryan Smith. *The Fifth*

Discipline: The Art and Practice of the Learning Organization. New York: Doubleday/Currency, 1990.

Senge, Peter M., et al. *The Fifth Discipline Fieldbook.* New York: Doubleday, 1994.

Organizational Transformation

Chappell, Tom. *The Soul of a Business: Managing for Profit and the Common Good.* New York: Bantam Books, 1993.

McWhinney, Will. *Paths of Change: Strategic Choices for Organizations and Society.* Newbury Park, Calif: Sage Publications, 1992.

Philosophy

Buber, Martin. *I and Thou.* New York: Macmillan, 1958.

———. *The Way of Man, According to the Teaching of Hasidism.* New York: Carol Publishing Group, 1990.

Heidegger, Martin. *Discourse on Thinking.* New York: Harper and Row, 1966.

Poetry

Eliot, T.S. *Four Quartets, East Coker V,* New York: Harvest Books, 1971.

Oliver, Mary. *New and Selected Poems.* Boston: Beacon Press, 1992.

Rilke, Rainer. *Book of Hours. Love Poems to God.* Trans. Anita Barrows and Joanna Macy. New York: Riverhead Books, 1996.

Whitman, Walt. *Leaves of Grass and Selected Prose.* Rutland, Vt.: Everyman, 1993.

Whyte, David. *Fire in the Earth.* Langley, Wash.: Many Rivers Press, 1992.

———. *Songs for Coming Home.* Langley, Wash.: Many Rivers Press, 1989.

———. *The House of Belonging.* Langley, Wash.: Many Rivers Press, 1997.

Political

Abrams, Jeremiah. *The Shadow in America: Reclaiming the Soul of a Nation.* Novato, Calif.: Nataraj Publishing, 1994.

Grieder, William. *Who Will Tell the People? The Betrayal of American Democracy.* New York: Simon & Schuster, 1992.

Schmookler, Andrew Bard. *The Illusion of Choice: How the Market Economy Shapes Our Destiny.* Albany: State University of New York Press, 1993.

———. *Out of Weakness: Healing the Wounds that Drive Us to War.* New York: Bantam Books, 1988.

Psychology

Blanton, Brad. *Radical Honesty: How to Transform Your Life by Telling the Truth.* Stanley, Va.: Sparrowhawk Publications, 1994.

Friedman, Maurice. *Dialogue and the Human Image: Beyond Humanistic Psychology.* Newbury Park, Calif.: Sage Publications, 1992.

Rogers, Carl R. *A Way of Being.* Boston: Houghton Mifflin, 1980.

Schaef, Anne Wilson. *Beyond Therapy, Beyond Science: A New Model for Healing the Whole Person.* San Francisco: HarperSanFrancisco, 1992.

Stone, Hal, and Sidra Winkelman. *Embracing Each Other: Relationship as Teacher, Healer, and Guide.* San Rafael, Calif.: New World Library, 1989.

———. *Embracing Ourselves: Voice Dialogue Manual.* Marina del Rey, Calif.: Devorss, 1985.

———. *Embracing Your Inner Critic: Turning Self-Criticism into a Creative Asset.* San Francisco: HarperSanFrancisco, 1991.

Quaker

Brinton, Howard H. *Friends for 300 Years.* Wallingford, Pa.: Pendle Hill Publications, 1991.

Sheeran, Michael. *Beyond Majority Rule: Voteless Decisions in the Religious Society of Friends.* Philadelphia Yearly Meeting of the Religious Society of Friends Fourth Impression, 1991.

Priestman, Rosalind. *Listening to One Another: Some Ideas about Creative Listening Groups and Other Ways of Getting to Know One Another.* Birmingham, UK: Woodbrooke College, 1989.

Social Psychology

Anderston, Walter Truett. *Reality Isn't What It Used to Be: Theatrical Politics, Ready-to-Wear Religion, Global Myths, Primitive Chic, and Other Wonders of the Postmodern World.* San Francisco: HarperSanFrancisco, 1990.

Freiere, Paulo. *Pedagogy of the Oppressed.* New York: Continuum, n.d.

Gergen, Kenneth J. *The Saturated Self: Dilemmas of Identity in Contemporary Life.* New York: HarperCollins, 1991.

Gibb, Jack. *Trust: A New Vision of Human Relationships for Business, Education, Family, and Personal Living.* North Hollywood, Calif.: Newcastle Publishing, 1991.

Goleman, Daniel. *Vital Lies, Simple Truths: The Psychology of Self-deception.* New York: Simon & Schuster, 1985.

Handy, Charles. *The Age of Unreason.* London: Arrow Books, 1995.

Johnston, Charles M. *Necessary Wisdom: Meeting the Challenge of a New Cultural Maturity.* Seattle, Wash.: ICD Press, 1991.

Spirituality

Moss, Richard. *The Second Miracle: Intimacy, Spirituality, and Conscious Relationship.* Berkeley, Calif.: Celestial Arts, 1995.

Story Telling

Simpkinson, Anne and Charles. *Sacred Stories: A Celebration of the Power of Stories to Transform and Heal.* San Francisco: HarperSanFrancisco, 1993.

Teams and Team Building

Schrage, Michael. *Shared Minds: The New Technologies of Collabroation.* New York: Random House, 1990.

Katzenback, Jon R., and Douglas K. Smith. *The Wisdom of Teams: Creating the High-Performance Organization.* Boston: Harvard Business School Press, 1993.

Periodic Literature

Argyris, Chris. "Good Communication that Blocks Learning." *Harvard Business Review* (July–August 1994).

Brown, Juanita, and David Isaacs. "Conversations as a Core Business Process." *The Systems Thinker* (December 1996/January 1997).

Collins, James C. and Jerry I. Porras. "Building Your Company's Vision." *Harvard Business Review* (September/October 1996).

Cook, Scott D.N., and Dvora Yanow. "Culture and Organizational Learning." *Journal of Management Inquiry* (December 1993).

Evered, Roger and Bob Tannenbaum. "A Dialog on Dialog." *Journal of Management Inquiry* 1, no. 1 (March 1992): 43–55.

Isaacs, William N. "Taking Flight: Dialogue, Collective Thinking, and Organizational Learning." *Organizational Dynamics* (1993).

Tuckman, Bruce. "Development Sequence in Small Groups," *Psychological Bulletin*, n.d.

INDEX